LANFORD WILSON

Fig. 1. Lanford Wilson, Ozark, Missouri, 1955; photographer unknown; Lanford Wilson Collection, Special Collections and Rare Books, University of Missouri Libraries, Lanford Wilson Estate.

LANFORD WILSON
EARLY STORIES, SKETCHES, AND POEMS

Edited by David A. Crespy

With an Afterword by Marshall W. Mason

UNIVERSITY OF MISSOURI PRESS
COLUMBIA

Copyright © 2017 Lanford Wilson Estate
All rights reserved.

University of Missouri Press edition 2017
The Curators of the University of Missouri
University of Missouri Press, Columbia, Missouri 65211
Printed and bound in the United States of America
First printing, 2017

ISBN: 978-0-8262-2133-9
Library of Congress Control Number: 2017942350

∞™ This paper meets the requirements of the
American National Standard for Permanence of Paper
for Printed Library Materials, Z39.48, 1984.

Typefaces: Minion Pro, Wagner Modern

This work was supported by the University of Missouri Research Board.

CONTENTS

List of Illustrations / ix

Acknowledgments / xi

Introduction by David A. Crespy / 3

SECTION 1: Six Stories

A Section of Orange / 29

Goodbye Sparta / 35

Miss Misty / 43

The Beautiful Children / 51

The Polar Bear / 59

The Canary (A Fairy Tale) / 79

SECTION 2: Travels to and from the City

The Train to Washington / 87

The Water Commissioner / 95

Fish Kite / 107

SECTION 3: Sketches of Town Life

The Rimers of Eldritch / 149

Green Grow the Rushes / 153

Chalk Eye / 163

Drift / 169

SECTION 4: Sketches of City Life

Mama / 173

Fuzz on Orion's Sword / 177

Uptown in Snow / 193

Dear Mr. Goldberg / 197

Doors / 201

SECTION 5: Poems

Outside Tulsa / 207

Mountains / 208

Orange Grove / 210

Flower Box / 211

Marigold / 212

Oakwood Gothic / 214

[Well, there she is, after all] / 215

Cathedral of St. Paul / 216

The Street Artist / 217

Village Walking Rhyme / 218

On a Day of Crisis / 219

[Fifth Avenue was quiet] / 220

Winter / 222

So the Sky / 223

Lullaby / 224

Lullaby (2) / 225

[If yours cannot be] / 226

I Saw All the Workers in the Field at Noon / 227

Why When I Love You / 229

Notes on a Poem for Bill / 233

Noel / 235

[The great-hearted dean] / 237

A Love Story about the Next Best Thing / 238

Afterword by Marshall W. Mason / 241

Editorial Note / 245

ILLUSTRATIONS

Fig. 1. Lanford Wilson, Ozark, Missouri, 1955; photographer unknown; Lanford Wilson Collection, Special Collections and Rare Books, University of Missouri Libraries, Lanford Wilson Estate.

Fig. 2. First page, "A Section of Orange" manuscript, undated; Lanford Wilson Collection, Special Collections and Rare Books, University of Missouri Libraries, Lanford Wilson Estate.

Fig. 3. First page, "Fish Kite" manuscript, undated; Lanford Wilson Collection, Special Collections and Rare Books, University of Missouri Libraries, Lanford Wilson Estate.

Fig. 4. Lanford Wilson, Ozark, Missouri, 1955; photographer unknown; Lanford Wilson Collection, Special Collections and Rare Books, University of Missouri Libraries, Lanford Wilson Estate.

Fig. 5. Lanford Wilson, Sixth Avenue, across the street from the Waverly Theater, New York City, February 19, 1966; photographer, James D. Gossage.

Fig. 6. Lanford Wilson, Ozark, Missouri, 1952; photographer unknown; Lanford Wilson Collection, Special Collections and Rare Books, University of Missouri Libraries, Lanford Wilson Estate.

Fig. 7. Lanford Wilson and Marshall Mason, Circle Repertory, Broadway and 83rd Street, New York City, November 3, 1973; photographer, James D. Gossage.

ACKNOWLEDGMENTS

THE COMPILATION AND editing of a volume such as this requires many hands, many eyes, and many resources; I would be remiss if I didn't take a moment to acknowledge the assistance of the numerous persons who made this book a reality. I would first like to thank the University of Missouri Research Board for its generous support. The volume would not exist without the patient guidance and support of Tanya Berezin, the executor of the Lanford Wilson Estate, who provided insight and thoughtful stewardship, preserving the integrity and spirit of Lanford Wilson himself as contained in these writings. Based on a forty-year relationship as a director and, in fact, dramaturg of Wilson's plays, the distinguished director Marshall W. Mason helped me find a chronology for the various stories, affording me an understanding of how the geography of Wilson's career progression provided a means to assign a timeline to the otherwise undated stories and poetry—to Marshall I owe deep, resounding thanks. The stories and poetry here would not have been discovered at all without the tireless archival organizing skills of Michael Holland, Head of the Special Collections, Archives, and Rare Books Division at the University of Missouri's Ellis Library, and Anselm Huelsbergen, Technical Services Archivist, who created the Lanford Wilson Collection from the massive bequest of the Lanford Wilson Estate, which had been quickly boxed and sent to the University of Missouri with little or no time to organize the files. Additionally, special thanks to Kelli Hansen, Print Collections Librarian at Special Collections and Rare Books, who provided ongoing support and access to the resources of the Wilson Collection, retrieving a seemingly endless array of boxes, files, and folders as we worked our way through many different manuscript iterations. Special mention should also go to my associate editor, Dr. Shawna Mefferd

Kelty, who unwearyingly worked her way through all the stories and poetry to copyedit the typed copy against the originals in the collection, checking version against version to determine the final version of the story in the archive, and get at the clearest, cleanest edit for each of these stories and poems.

Thanks also go to Elaine Dunn, Lanford Wilson's stepsister; Ronald Tindle, Lanford's best friend in high school; and a small army of friends from Lanford's high school years in Ozark, Missouri, who were willing to share stories and anecdotes about Lanford's life there as a young man, when he first started writing. These include Byrne Blackwood, Joe Berbereia, Elise M. Crain, Betty Forrester, Glenna Frazier, Shirley Gott-Stoecker, Annabelle Jackson, Ron Melton, Dale and Rachel Robertson, Kay Simpson, and Novella Whittington. An acknowledgment, too, for Jolene Michelle VanHoose, who led us to this small cadre of Lanford's friends and family.

A special thank you to Jackson Bryer, who served as a consultant on the volume and provided perceptive guidance on how to frame these stories and poetry for general readership in addition to those interested in Lanford's achievements as a playwright. Jackson's own volume of edited essays on Lanford Wilson provided special insight into how these stories generally corresponded with Wilson's work as a writer and dramatist.

This volume would not have come together as a cohesive whole without the advice and direction of Gary Kass, acquisitions editor, Clair Willcox, former Editor in Chief and Associate Director, and Andrew Davidson, the current Editor in Chief of the University of Missouri Press. After several attempts to make sense of the sheer volume of material available from the Lanford Wilson Collection, it was Gary who finally helped me find a clear vision for what we wanted to try to do in publishing a volume of work that was both unlike Wilson's later plays, and yet the seeds for what was to come. Finally, a special thank you to Meg Phillips Crespy, my wife, who helped to type and edit some of the early stories as they were discovered in the collection, much to the delight and excitement of the editors. Uncovering this work and the worlds and landscapes of Lanford Wilson's earliest writings was akin to discovering the artifacts and treasures Wilson dramatizes in his play *The Mound Builders*. I was so lucky and grateful to have an incredible team to help me bring this volume to fruition, and to share in the magic of this discovery.

LANFORD WILSON

INTRODUCTION
BY DAVID A. CRESPY

This selection of early short stories and poetry by Lanford Wilson, never before published, chronicles the exceptional development of a young writer discovering his language, the tales and characters he would come back to again and again, and perhaps most importantly, the progression of his craft as a storyteller and lyric dramatist. The writings here reveal Wilson's ability to find the universal in the particular, the lyric quality of human speech, and the haunting American landscape of lives led nearly invisibly at the edge of societal acceptance. This volume of his early fiction and poetry has merit in its own right beside Wilson's voluminous output as a playwright, as it represents just the tip of the iceberg of his entire manuscript collection, and provides a leaping off place for research and exploration into the life of one of America's great writers.

In spring of 2012 the University of Missouri–Columbia, where I teach playwriting, was informed that Lanford Wilson had donated all his papers—forty-seven boxes of manuscripts, photographs, letters, poetry, fiction, theatre artifacts—to the Special Collections and Rare Books department of the campus's Ellis Library. It is in this collection that the stories and poetry of Lanford Wilson may be found. It was a historic bequest, and one that will permit Missouri faculty, students, and scholars from around the world to explore the work of the state's own Pulitzer Prize–winning playwright in extraordinary detail.

Wilson had visited Mizzou at my request back in October 2006, and we had a delightful time with him—he had managed to fit us in between his teaching work at the University of Houston and his busy writing life in Sag Harbor, New York. I directed a concert reading of Wilson's play *The Mound Builders* with his guidance in our Rhynsburger Theatre, and later he and I had a wonderful onstage discussion about his life and work. It was an amazing experience; Wilson deeply connected with our Missouri theatre students. During his life Lanford Wilson mentored countless playwrights, directors, and actors, and his plays inspired a generation of theatre artists, including his own mentor and close friend, Edward Albee. And this important legacy, his manuscript collection, will continue that work, providing opportunity for theatre research into his writing, his process, and his life.

For those who don't know Lanford Wilson, his major calling was as a playwright, and it was with his work as a dramatist that he reached his zenith as a writer. As one of the founding members of the Circle Repertory Company in New York City, Wilson was resident playwright of the single most important Off-Broadway theatre of its time, and it is there that he created many of his greatest plays, including *The Hot l Baltimore*, *The Mound Builders*, *Serenading Louie*, *Fifth of July*, *Talley's Folly*, *Talley & Son*, *Angels Fall*, *Burn This*, and *Redwood Curtain*. Many of Wilson's plays moved from either the Circle Repertory Company or regional theater companies to Broadway. His plays were nominated for the Tony Award three times, and in 1980 he received the Pulitzer Prize for *Talley's Folly*. Wilson was elected to the Theater Hall of Fame in 2001 and to the American Academy of Arts and Letters in 2004. He lived in Sag Harbor, New York, but was a native of Ozark, Missouri, and was born in Lebanon, not far away, where his mother had grown up. And it was there that he began his work as an author, beginning to write short stories in high school.

These stories and poems provide an important glimpse into Wilson's life as a young writer in the 1950s and 1960s, which is when most of this work was created, before he decided to become a playwright. Though Wilson was not primarily an autobiographical writer—he wrote only one play that was unabashedly so (his beautiful coming-of-age play, *Lemon Sky*)—here you will find his imagination at work in the world of his childhood, his early life in Lebanon and Ozark, and the wonders he found when he traveled to San Diego, Chicago, and finally, New York, where he became one of America's most respected contemporary dramatists.

Intriguingly and ironically, what becomes evident in the stories and in his poetry are Wilson's distinctive talents as a dramatist: a keen eye for description which perhaps grew out of his early work as a visual artist and served him well as he wrote for the physical reality of the stage, a gift for dialogue which led to his switch to writing plays that were essentially tone poems of human conversation, and an eye for "wrighting" behavior rather than simply writing words—the rare ability to "show, not tell," to check the urge to reveal everything, and let the reader discover for her or himself what is going on in the minds of the characters. In these early stories and poems, Wilson demonstrates a dramatist's restraint, allowing the reader to supply the subtext that slips mysteriously beneath the language and directly into the heart.

Wilson was not the first playwright to write short stories, of course. One of the playwrights whom he most admired, and whose work he adapted for the contemporary stage, was Anton Chekhov, whose own career began with the writing of short stories. Chekhov not only mastered the form, but became one of its innovators, ending stories without a discernible "wrapping up," catching the stubborn idiosyncracies of his characters, and building his short fiction on an internal "structure of love."[1] Wilson's stories share a fundamentally wry, comic spirit with those of Chekhov's, as well as a love for characters who fall between the cracks in their quotidian lives. Wilson's "short short stories," as he describes them in notes on some of the manuscripts in the Collection, are very similar to Chekhov's innovative flash fictions like "At the Barber's" or "Fat and Thin," or even his classic "Gooseberries," in that they push minimalism to the limit, revealing all through almost invisible, tender moments of the human heart. Also present in Wilson's stories is Chekhov's disinterested narrator, who seems to be "writing about nothing," all the while letting the readers connect the dots for themselves.[2] Both writers walk the knife edge of comedy and drama in each moment of their stories and plays, and they share a complexity and compassion revealed in the depth of their comic exploration of characters who exist in society's forgotten corners.

Tennessee Williams is a useful comparison as well, as he moved effortlessly between writing short fiction and plays, and his stories provided material for his drama. Wilson was an admirer of Williams, and, like Williams's, the stories in this volume were the basis for some of their author's plays. Williams began his plays as short fictional sketches; stories like "Portrait of a Girl in Glass" and "The Angel in the Alcove" became *The Glass Menagerie* and *Vieux Carré*, respectively. Though, as Gore Vidal notes in his introduction to Williams's stories, Williams didn't write stories simply for this purpose:

> It has been suggested that many of the stories are simply preliminary sketches for plays. The truth is more complicated. Like most natural writers, Tennessee could not possess his own life until he had written about it. This is common. But what is not common was the way that he went about not only recapturing lost time but then regaining it in a way that far surpassed the original experience.[3]

Williams framed his experience into a story, reexplored it as a play, and then went back and revised the original story, in an almost obsessive cycle (as no story or play, even when published, was ever entirely finished for Williams). In this collection, for the first time, we can discern the similarities between Williams's and Wilson's process. Both were driven, hard-working writers who constantly revised their work. Wilson was enamored of Williams's plays, later writing the libretto for the opera version of Williams's *Summer and Smoke*. Williams, as Vidal notes, never wrote an adequate autobiography, and instead biographical details may be found in his short stories. This is also true of Lanford Wilson, as the stories in this volume chronicle Wilson's early life in ways that have never previously been seen in print. Many of the stories delve into the quiet, unexamined life of a young gay artist, struggling to come to terms with his talent while facing the harsh puritan reality of midwest America in the 1950s.

One other dramatist who also wrote fiction comes to mind, and this is Thornton Wilder, who famously won the Pulitzer Prize in both fiction and drama, and who began his career as a student at Yale writing short fiction even as he was finding his voice as a playwright. Both Wilder and Wilson gave up writing short fiction early in their lives, and Wilder went on not only to write plays, but novels as well. One discerns in Wilder's early stories like "Spiritus Valet" and "The Marriage of Zabett" the same pioneering theatricality, experimentation with form, unique and mysterious characters, and seemingly inconsequential lives that are lived in a subdued frenzy of "quiet desperation" that we find in Wilson's stories. Though these early works were not the culmination of their efforts as writers, it is clear from archival evidence that even in this youthful period Wilson and Wilder wanted their work to be heard, to be published, and to be read by audiences willing to dive deeper into their fragile world of everyday eccentrics. Knowing the accomplished dramatists these writers would become, even as they discovered their early voices as storytellers, makes the reading of their early works all the more fascinating.

Wilson was a native Missourian; one could hear it in his voice and see it in his gentle, frank, ironic, effervescent, and down-to-earth Midwestern manner. He was born in 1937 in Lebanon, Missouri, to Ralph and Violetta Tate Wilson. In 1942, his father left his mother for another woman and moved to California, leaving his wife and yet another woman pregnant in the wake. Lanford and his mother moved to Springfield, Missouri, where she found work in a garment factory. His mother had been left in a precarious financial state, and they shared a roll-out bed in whatever living arrangements they could find. When Wilson was eleven his mother married Walter Lenhard, a farmer from Ozark, Missouri, who later worked as a field inspector for the local cheese plant, the Major Cheese Company. Wilson lived in Ozark, went to Pitkin Junior High School, and graduated from Ozark High School in 1955.

During his senior year he was taken to a production of *Brigadoon* at what was then Southwest Missouri State University (now Missouri State University in Springfield), and recalled being "mesmerized" by the production. During his single year as a student at SMSU, he saw a production of *Death of a Salesman* that struck him visually as "the most magical thing" he'd ever seen. He was specifically struck by one moment "when, in the middle of the man's remembrance, the clothesline from the old buildings all around the house gradually faded into big, huge beech trees. I nearly collapsed! I'd never seen anything like that in my life." Wilson confessed that from that moment on he was "hooked on theatre," and thereafter, he was desperately trying "to recreate some of that magic" from that production.[4] Despite his eventual decision to focus on playwriting, Wilson began his literary career by writing stories in high school, and he wrote fiction occasionally throughout his life, though the material in this volume dates mostly from 1955 through 1964. In 1955, after graduating from high school, he completed summer and fall semesters at SMSU before moving the following year to San Diego, California, to live with his biological father—a disastrous reunion (detailed in *Lemon Sky*) that ended in his moving to Chicago.

Wilson's years in Ozark stayed with him throughout his writing life, and despite growing up poor, he had a happy childhood. The town itself is just outside of Springfield, and rises in a picturesque group of small homes and businesses around the Finley River, with the cheese plant by the river, and a garment factory that once provided work for locals, including Wilson's mother. There was a Hill Cafe up by the highway that is a feature of Wilson's *The Rimers of Eldritch*; and Harpers Hill, where there had once been a mansion, became the location for the Talley farmhouse featured in his Talley trilogy of plays—*Talley's Folly*, *Talley & Son*, and *Fifth of July*.[5] The fictional Lebanon, Missouri, of the trilogy was a depiction of Ozark (there is no river flowing through the actual Lebanon, Missouri), with its intriguing local characters including Sheriff "Buff" Lamb, famous for riding bulls and broncos and, as a motorcycle daredevil, jumping burning buildings and rows of cars, and Buttermilk Johnson, a wino who was thought to have been intimate with sheep, who became the model for Skelly in *The Rimers of Eldritch*. And of course, Ozark, Missouri, is at the heart of many of the stories in this collection.

Lanford grew up with two stepsisters, Judy and Elaine, and he remained in contact with them his entire life, though he was closer to Judy, as his many letters to her reveal. Elaine married young and moved in different circles, but she remembers Lanford shutting himself away in his room, furiously writing stories, and often painting or drawing as well. He was close to his mother,

Violetta, and sent her clippings, which she meticulously kept in scrapbooks. She was a tireless worker in her home, at the 4-H club, and at the garment factory in Ozark; and he acquired his writerly work ethic from her. He was not close to his stepfather, who was a dairy inspector and was also involved with breeding cattle and 4-H activities. They were two very different men, and neither was able to relate to the other. Wilson was haunted by his desire to connect with a father figure, leading to his disastrous reconnection with his real father in San Diego. He was close to several classmates at Ozark High School, and Ron Tindle, one of his boyhood friends, remembered his artistic talent; Wilson had always assumed he would work as a graphic designer and artist. Both he and Tindle were gay, and suffered at the hands of their classmates; both left Ozark as soon as they were old enough. It was clear they would never be accepted there; both were taunted and bullied, and the pain of rejection and isolation is reflected in these stories.

Despite the challenges of growing up gay in a small Missouri town, his Ozark classmates remember Wilson as a fun-loving boy who was prone to spinning cartwheels, who designed decorations for school events, and who was always involved with theatre—he loved to act, and performed in several productions. He was greatly influenced by his high school English teacher, Rex Bower, who directed him as Tom in *The Glass Menagerie*. It was Bower's "merciless" cutting of the play into a one-act for school competition purposes that profoundly affected Wilson's desire to tightly edit his own work; he even wrote a high school essay on the subject, "Cutting a New York Play for Small Town Use," which is in his manuscript collection.

In San Diego, Wilson worked at an airplane manufacturing plant and enrolled in San Diego State College (now San Diego State University), where he took courses in fiction, art, and art history. He studied creative writing with professor John Theobald, a distinguished poet, and became friends with several other students: Miles Payne, who later became the editor of *The Light Year*, a beat literary journal in San Francisco; Tanya Newton Rose, who later became well known as a folk singer in San Diego; and Tony Brown, another young writer who had worked with Theobald and whose mother, the poet LoVerne Brown, opened her home to Wilson and became a kind of literary matriarch to him. The fictionalized details of the Browns' literary salon may be found in Wilson's play *The Sand Castle*, and it was during this time that Wilson began to think of himself as a writer. He became known among his writerly friends as "Oz" (as he came from Ozark); in later years, in his correspondence with Payne, Rose, and Brown, they always referred to him as Oz, and he signed his letters with this pseudonym. Even after he left San Diego, he often wrote to his

San Diego writer friends, sharing his new stories with them, asking for critiques, and reading their work in return. Payne, one of the more literary of his San Diego friends, was quite moved by Wilson's writing, and touched upon a signature quality in Wilson's early technique that became even more apparent later in his plays:

> All in all, your writing, your fiction, poems, and letters, I am moved by your evident impulse of combined strength and sweetness, liveliness, but with sadness never far away. Moved by what I can only think to say as being the power of tenderness, the faculty which above all others is most lacking today in human beings and which is most needed.[6]

Wilson also maintained an extensive correspondence with Rose, who recognized Wilson's ability to create complex, idiosyncratic characters with just a few words, writing to him about his story "Green Grow the Rushes":

> I enjoyed the story very much, in fact, you captured a mood I can't quite put my finger on, it was so weird and yet so real. You balanced the flow of the story very well, I was taken with it a lot. I must say you're developing year by year your talents for making real people. There's a believability and credence to the people yet they and their surroundings go beyond just the mundane and touch on symbolism which make them universal. I'm proud to know you and I hope some day everyone will know what I do . . . that you are damned talented and deserve to be famous.[7]

Rose was often critical in her responses to Wilson's work, although she was also the most supportive early voice in praise of his writing talent—this despite the fact that Wilson still thought of himself primarily as a graphic designer. In one letter she instructed Wilson to stick to his guns about writing honestly and not for profit:

> I was glad to see your comment about trying to write good stuff and not just try to make money. The minute you change your attitude I'll personally kick your ass. You know I've always believed in you . . . and I'd be disappointed if you sold out.[8]

Wilson clearly took Rose's advice to heart; in his stories and plays he was far more interested in the lonely outsiders, the dispossessed, the shunned, than the lives of the rich and famous. "Selling out" was a key social concern for youth in the early 1960s, and Wilson's art was shaped by this social consciousness. Some of the earliest stories, including "A Section of Orange," "Cling to the Valley" (which became "Green Grow the Rushes"), and "The Beautiful Children," were written during this period, and sensitively depict the aged, the lost, and the forgotten living just below the radar of society.

In 1957, Wilson moved to Chicago and worked as a graphic artist for an advertising agency. From 1957 to 1962 he lived at 5316 Spaulding Street, not far from Northeastern Illinois University in the Lincoln Square neighborhood, where he most likely wrote "Mama," "Green Grow the Rushes," "Miss Misty," and "Goodbye Sparta." Just before he left for New York, in 1962, he lived at 9 Walnut Road in Glen Ellyn, Illinois, further west in the Chicago suburbs, near Wheaton College, where the stories "Dear Mr. Goldberg," "Fish Kite," "The Polar Bear," and "The Rimers of Eldritch" were composed. It was in Chicago that Wilson recognized that the short stories he had been writing for years actually worked better in play form, and though he continued to write fiction and try to publish it, he decided to learn more about the craft of dramatic writing and enrolled in an extension class in playwriting at the University of Chicago. Due to a lack of live theatre opportunities in Chicago at that time, Wilson relocated to New York City in July 1962. Even in New York, however, he continued writing short stories and unsuccessfully tried to sell them to popular and literary magazines.

Wilson often discussed his transition from fiction to drama, which occurred sometime in 1961, and in a 1987 interview, he pointed out that his prose was fine, but when dialogue stood alone, "it was something that I had under control and had always been attracted to—juxtaposed sounds and rhythms of characters—and so it was really natural."[9] In a later interview, he identified the actual moment this switch from fiction to drama occurred, in Chicago about a year after having left San Diego. Wilson had found a job as an illustrator with an advertising agency, and during his lunch hour, wrote stories and sent them out to magazines, boasting that he had "rejections from the best magazines in the country." But just after starting another story to send out, he had a revelation:

> One day I had an idea and I thought, "That's not a story, that's a play." So I started writing it as a play and within two pages I said, "Oh, I'm a playwright." It was just as easy as that.[10]

While in New York, working odd jobs to support himself, Wilson discovered the Caffe Cino, a coffeehouse run by Joe Cino that later became a pioneering

Off-Off-Broadway theater producing plays by many young and, later, famous playwrights. In the early 1960s, his one-act play *So Long at the Fair* was produced at the Caffe Cino and became a success. He soon became one of the star playwrights of the Cino, writing many one-act plays for performance there. Using his graphic arts talents, he also created sets, props, and posters for Caffe Cino productions.

The Caffe Cino premiered Wilson's short play *The Madness of Lady Bright* in 1964 and it became one of the playhouse's major, long-running hits. He also produced longer works for another playhouse, La MaMa Experimental Theatre Club, in 1965, including *The Rimers of Eldritch*, which was later produced by Edward Albee and his partners, becoming one of the first major professional productions of the new generation of Off-Off-Broadway playwrights. It was while having his play *Home Free!* performed at the Caffe Cino for a second time that Wilson met a young director named Marshall Mason. Mason directed Wilson's first full-length play at La MaMa, *Balm in Gilead*, in January 1965, followed by *The Sand Castle* that summer. Thereafter, Mason and Wilson formed a professional collaboration and friendship that would continue throughout their careers. They were among the cofounders of the Circle Repertory Company, and Mason would go on to direct nearly every professional premiere of Wilson's plays throughout his life. Their collaboration became one of the longest-lasting playwright/director relationships in the American theatre. In 2016 Mason was honored with a Special Tony Award for Lifetime Achievement for his Broadway productions of Wilson's and many other playwrights' plays, which were first developed at Circle Repertory Company.

During these early years in New York City, from 1963 to 1964, when Wilson was living at 320 West 76th Street, he continued to write short stories. He and Michael Warren Powell briefly lived together at the Ansonia, where Wilson observed the life nearby in 72nd Street's Verdi Square, then known as Needle Park, populated by drug pushers and junkies, who would be crafted into his play *Balm in Gilead*. Powell was a friend from Chicago who came with Wilson to New York in 1962 and became the leading man in many of Wilson's plays, and later the director of Circle Repertory Company's Lab. The two discovered the Caffe Cino together and built their careers in the downtown Off-Off-Broadway theatre of that time, with Wilson most likely having stopped writing short stories by 1964. The stories from this early time in New York City include "Doors," which he first wrote in Glen Ellyn and later revised in New York; "The Train to Washington," a longer story, written in a period style from the 1940s; "Uptown in Snow," a haunting depiction of a woman who loses touch with reality; "I'll Be Honest with You" (not included in this collection), a piece about the antique trade in Greenwich Village and perhaps an early precursor to his short play *Brontosaurus*; "Chalk Eye," which appears to have been written after the assassination of John F. Kennedy; "The Water Commissioner," which looks at the underground lives of the gay community of St. Louis in the 1950s; "Why When I Love You" (a short story version of the poem published here); "Drift," an early exploration of Cora Groves and Walter, two outsider characters in *The Rimers of Eldritch*; and "Fuzz on Orion's Sword," which Wilson later transformed into his play *The Great Nebula in Orion*.

During this period of flux, moving from Ozark to San Diego to Chicago to New York from 1955 through 1964, Wilson wrote over twenty-seven short stories and about forty-four poems. Many of the stories are highly autobiographical and explore, in detail and with great sensitivity, growing up gay in Missouri in the 1950s. The dialogue is powerful, gripping, capturing the rhythms and idiosyncrasies of natural speech, and while Wilson's narrative style is rich, genuine, and a match for his dialogue, the authenticity of these voices makes it clear why he made the shift to dramatic writing. The stories also reflect an uncanny restraint for a young author, as Wilson is more interested in having his readers uncover the characters' hidden desires than in spelling them out himself. It was in these stories that Wilson began to hone his ability to write dialogue, craft dramatic situations, and experiment rather wildly in style and form. Some of the stories are quite short—almost prose poems—while others are long and detailed, following complex plot lines.

Wilson's short stories and poetry have the honest simplicity and rough-hewn quality that he loved in the outsider art he collected. Wilson once attended a retrospective exhibition of the brightly colored works of self-taught artist Clementine Hunter in Natchitoches, Louisiana, and was instantly struck by a personal connection to her art: "I thought I knew [what art was], was pretty cocky about it in fact, and it slapped me (as mother would say) into next Sunday." Wilson's short stories and poetry have a similar quality to Hunter's art (he purchased one of her floral still lifes), which he called "honest, shockingly sincere, and unfettered."[11]

It is important to note that like these artists, Wilson invented himself as a dramatist—he took only one playwriting course, at the University of Chicago. These short stories, and the poetry in the fifth section of this book, were the training ground for his experiments with language. It was a natural transition from short stories into the short plays that began Wilson's career, like *Home Free!* and *Ludlow Fair*, and Wilson remained obsessed with the short play form, publishing a volume of twenty-one short plays that resonate beautifully with the short stories here. Through this same kind of artistic investigation,

Wilson learned his craft of playwriting in the fire of production at the Caffe Cino, playing at times to no audience but the walls of the storefront theatre itself—and it was enough to take him a step further to become the resident playwright of Circle Repertory Company, which was, in its innovative artistic inquiry and openness to emerging theatre artists, a direct descendant of the Cino. And perhaps this is the best way to think of these early works, as the first brilliant splashes of color by an outsider artist who evolved and raised himself by his own bootstraps to become one of the most celebrated and emulated dramatists of his time.

The stories are grouped based upon commonality of theme and style. The first section, titled "Six Stories," is a suite of unique, tightly crafted stories that create a portrait of Wilson's early imagination. These include "A Section of Orange," which grew out of Wilson's deep attachment to his birthplace of Lebanon, Missouri, home to his grandmother and the town he spoke of as his "childhood-fantasy place." Though he left Lebanon at an early age and grew up mostly in Ozark, "A Section of Orange" grows out of his remembrance of a time when small things had a significance of immense proportions. The story follows a traumatic experience in the life of a little boy, Kirk, who is visiting his grandmother one afternoon. Wilson recalled: "I still remember those magic summers of my childhood. Lebanon is still where I dream."[12] But what gives this story particular impact is the gift of Wilson's description, and how he captures characters in an instant, noting the moment when Kirk's grandmother's neighbor, Mr. Farthing, notices Kirk's interest in a yellow bush by his grandmother's house, "staring at Kirk as a chicken might stare at a passing snake." Or a description of the bush itself, "that spread its thin brown arms bowed by the weight of a thousand yellow stars across the steps to her front porch."[13]

Moving into Wilson's years living and working in Chicago, and written in the voice of a young Arkansas sojourner in the Windy City, "Goodbye Sparta" relates the tale of a North Shore apartment house of oddballs and sad prostitutes, with the culminating moment of a naked fifty-year-old woman named Mrs. Prude who is locked out of her apartment by a "hillbilly" she has picked up for the night. Written with a sense of gentle irony and filled with Mrs. Prude's misadventures in the buff, the story is perhaps an initial sketch for the characters later explored in Wilson's play *The Hot l Baltimore*. One moment that captures Wilson's comic gifts and brilliant touches of character in dialogue and description is when Mrs. Prude tries to lay down the law with her hillbilly lover:

> Mrs. Prude's friend was as bare as she was. She went running into the room as I came to her with the towel. "You get out of here. Out. Out. Out. Out. Out." And

stood shaking her finger at the door, which, of course, made her whole body shake like red aspic.[14]

"Goodbye to Sparta," with its blend of comedy and pathos and written from the point of view of a young graphic artist from Arkansas trying to make his mark in Chicago, is filled with the kind of eccentrics that would later people many of Wilson's plays: Ronnie the genius; Minnie, who believes in ghosts; enormous Marilyn and her little daughter; Marie McViekre, the beautiful prostitute seemingly untouched by her profession (who would later be replicated as The Girl in *Hot l*); and Billy, the beautiful boy and "a bit of a roamer" who is murdered in the park.

Featuring the full impact of Wilson's gift with dialogue, in "Miss Misty," a young man and his girlfriend attempt to "straighten out" a flamboyant drag queen so that her homophobic father will pay for her to go to college. The hilarious attempt at converting Miss Misty into a "real" man is both disastrous and successful, though by the surprise end of the story, it is clear that Misty will succeed in her own way. The description of Miss Misty's initial appearance on the beach sets the stage for the 1930s screwball comedy of the story: "Then we saw her; pressing through the crowd with ceremonious smiles and nods, trailing an entourage of perhaps seven 'young things' who carried a folding beach chair, thermos, towels, a radio, an enormous candy striped umbrella (unfolded) and clattering collections of various tanning lotions."[15] Her "pink pedal pushers and aqua thong sandals" will evoke for fans of Wilson's play *The Madness of Lady Bright* hints of Leslie Bright, signaling Wilson's interest in writing candidly, with affection and compassion, about LGBTQ issues while documenting the reality of those lives in the 1950s and 1960s.

One of the most moving of the stories in this section is the autobiographical "The Beautiful Children," which again takes place in Wilson's birthplace, Lebanon, Missouri. It is the story of a brilliant young woman from a poor, white outcast family of vaguely threatening, somewhat inbred "beautiful children" with "pure white . . . hair" and is a mixture of rural comedy and Southern gothic horror, with an oddly hopeful ending. Again, Wilson's ability to define character instantaneously is apparent in their brief description.

> Every one looked like the other; more than any family I've seen. They all had saucer blue eyes, pure white or tow-yellow hair; on the girls it fell straight to their shoulders, the boys brushed it from their eyes and behind their ears. I never remember seeing a fresh haircut among them.[16]

These are the same "white-haired children" discussed with a certain amount of dread by the character of June in Wilson's play *Fifth of July*, and the story perhaps reveals June's own prejudices and misconceptions about this somewhat creepy, otherworldly family, who turn out to have uncanny business acumen in their various odd jobs, splitting wood, harvesting blackberries, and serving as "Good Cheap Labor" in Wilson's mythical Lebanon.

"The Polar Bear" is one of the longer and more heartfelt stories, about the friendship between Joel, a little boy living on New York's Upper West Side, and Emile, a hobo who lives in Central Park. The story follows the day-to-day adventures of the two as they enjoy a summer in the park, visit the Central Park Zoo, and share their admiration for the polar bear that lives there. A year later, after the winter passes and with no sign of Emile, Joel makes a journey to a cemetery in Queens to place Emile's gift of a polar bear carved out of a bar of soap on the grave of Joel's now-dead friend. The remarkable restraint Wilson demonstrates in capturing the little boy's inner life through his revealing behavior can be seen in this final moment:

> "Emile?" Joel said. He looked at the neighboring graves and considered bringing their flowers to his friend's stone. "I brought your bear." He unwrapped the soap polar bear from the tissue paper and sat it above his friend's name on the red stone. "See? I saved it." Joel looked around the graveyard again. "I'm going now. I'm leaving," he whispered. "Why didn't you tell me, Emile?"[17]

The power of the story is its simplicity; nothing is explained that can be shown. Intriguingly, a bar of soap in the shape of a bear figures strongly in the first notebook draft of *Fifth of July*, becoming a symbol of the Eskimo story that is at the heart of that particular play.[18]

The last story in this section is "The Canary (A Fairy Tale)." This bit of whimsy takes place in Blue Willow, a mythical rural town, and focuses on an old woman, her pet canary, and Sean McCaffery, who is in charge of Blue Willow's weather. The story, perhaps one of Wilson's earliest, contrasts the thorny disposition of its natives with the natural oddity and magic of the Ozarks themselves. What makes the story magical is Wilson's ability to explore style at such an early point in his career. His eye for visual detail can be found in "a soft gray-blue smoke arose straight up from the many chimneys and lingered high over Blue Willow in one long amethyst cloud," or the description of the canary's special ability: "for although canaries are very small, some people believe that their insides are nothing except lungs and music box for they can sometimes sing very loud indeed."[19] "The Canary" has the comedy and Victorian "gingerbread" sensibility of Wilson's short plays *Days Ahead* and *Victory on Mrs. Dandywine's Island* and reveals the writer's interest in exploring period styles within the context of a fractured valentine that was to be his signature style in *Talley's Folly*.

The second section, "Travels to and from the City," comprises ambitious, extended, and perhaps mostly autobiographical stories reflecting both Wilson's own experiences in Missouri in the late 1950s and the New York City of his mother's memories from the 1930s and 1940s. These stories offer a rare glimpse into the lives of the lonely outsiders, outcasts, and the disenfranchised who became the focus of Wilson's later dramas, and are a kind of roman à clef of the world that Wilson inhabited in his youth. The first of these extended stories is "The Train to Washington." A sly, sideways New York City period piece, taking place not long after World War II, it is about a street-smart prostitute, Irene, who hails from a small town, Willard, Maryland, and her clever young son, Eddie, who linger in the Oyster Bar near Times Square. Irene is discovered by her brother, John, who has come up by train, and finds his sister plying her trade. John's brutal response permanently ends Irene's ruse about working as a secretary, cutting off any chance of Eddie going back to the small town he loves. In this story, Wilson's ability to capture his characters' inner life is particularly haunting as Eddie says nothing but quietly turns a matchbook over and over in his hands:

> I could see that Eddie was looking past her shoulder to the door, which was covered with a kind of bright decal to make the panes of the windows look almost like the stained glass windows of a church. But he was not looking at them or at anything definite, but just past her, as she held him tightly.[20]

"The Train To Washington" captures a small boy's fiction about a home he'll never see again, and perhaps more importantly, reveals Wilson's own sense of homesickness and longing for a place that he rejected and that had rejected him.

Another of these longer, parabolic stories is "The Water Commissioner," a troubling and mysterious memory tale. In it, a young man comes to St. Louis from Springfield in his neighbor's dairy truck (a reminder of Wilson's stepfather's work as a dairy inspector for Major Cheese Company in Ozark), in order to find a job and make an independent life for himself. The story is built on the young man's sympathy for an older man's loneliness and his ironic view of the man's pathetic attempt to take advantage of him, and is a poignant portrayal of LGBTQ lives in the 1950s. The desperately regal façade of the shabby water commissioner provides subtle insight into the man's sense of himself:

> Not trampish exactly, but just a touch seedy. There was a delicate little ring of neck that bulged out of the collar of his shirt. He had loosened his maroon knit tie to where the broad knot hung like a lopsided medallion over his chest, the tie trailing across his lap.[21]

The youthful narrator—knowing, kind, sometimes sardonic, always a step ahead of the other characters and their foibles, but persisting, nevertheless, for the sheer adventure of it—is emblematic of later characters in Wilson's dramas who turn to the audience in a moment of metadrama and reveal their hearts to us, with a sudden shock of intimacy that forces us to engage.

One of the strongest, strangest, and most melancholy of these stories, "Fish Kite," explores the misadventures of two young men as they make their way in Tulsa, having driven from Springfield, Missouri, by siphoning gas from other people's cars. Shelton, the more innocent of the two, finds a job, awful as it is, in a small diner. Otis spends his time drinking and gambling away their money. The two are an odd couple, and the sad lessons they learn involve loan sharks, prostitutes, and the working poor. What they share is a lack of connection with parents who seem to have forgotten them. Again here, Wilson's dialogue, quietly poetic, simple, honest, and real, sums up the reality of these two boys' lives:

> Otis was nearly asleep, but he managed a grunted laugh. "Mom? Why would Mom give a damn where I am? Mom knows I can take care of myself. She'd probably be satisfied not to see me again for about five years anyway."
> "My folks sure couldn't care less where I've gone," Shelton said hollowly.
> "That stepfather of yours won't. If I had a stepdad like Carl I would have left when I was about ten years old."
> "Yeah." Shelton blinked at the milky window that distorted the streetlight into halos and dreamed for an instant of having never met his stepfather.[22]

The autobiographical aspect of the story, especially in the yearning for a real father figure, resonates powerfully. The story, like many in the collection, seems to have its roots in the exuberance and longing that Wilson, a popular young man in Ozark High School, may have felt living just outside of Springfield, Missouri, which was not yet the sprawling metropolis that it later became, and far from the larger and somehow exotic city Tulsa was in the late 1950s.

The details of the hard-scrabble times, the back-breaking jobs, the rough and tumble of the long road trip have the somewhat unreal beat quality of Kerouac and Burroughs, while deeply entrenched in the all too real, inescapable reality that Wilson was so deft at creating in his plays.

The next two sections, titled "Sketches of Town Life" and "Sketches of City Life," are a mix of shorter stories and what today might be considered flash fiction, and touch upon Lanford Wilson's evolution from a small town Missouri raconteur to the sophisticated, nuanced chronicler of urban ambiguity. The first story in the "Town Life" section is "The Rimers of Eldritch," the only short story that Wilson adapted directly for the stage, for his later play of the same title. It was his first full-length play to be commercially produced in New York City. The story features much of the same material as the play, but it begins with the death of Eve Johnson, a crippled girl who dies giving birth. The themes of small town corruption and malevolence haunt both the story and the play, and it is intriguing to see how Wilson fleshed out this small story into a full-length drama told in the manner of Dylan Thomas's *Under Milk Wood* by creating an entirely new world of characters who don't exist in the story other than as shadows and the murmurs of a disapproving small town crowd.

"Green Grow the Rushes" is a revised version of an earlier story, "Cling to the Valley," which was written as an assignment for John Theobald in Wilson's creative writing course at San Diego State College. Theobold harshly criticized the story, and Wilson subsequently undertook a massive revision, crafting one of the most affecting love stories of the collection. In the story, a reclusive farm boy, Lon, who loves to linger by the river, meets Carol, a beautiful troubled girl from St. Louis whose parents are going through a divorce, and she longs to stay with Lon by the river. Especially vivid is Carol's description of 1950s St. Louis as an "awfully filthy place" where "buildings are just black from coal smoke" and people are "dirty." Sad, haunting, filled with wonderful imagery, and clearly affected by Tennessee Williams's descriptions of St. Louis, the story centers on the mill pond and the Finley River, which flows by a local park and a stretch of small farms where Wilson's stepfather owned land.

"Chalk Eye" is the disturbing story of a young boy who, hiding in a broken-down shack in his backyard, witnesses the rape and murder of a young girl by a back-alley bully. It prefigures the sudden, unexplainable bursts of senseless violence and death that explode in such Wilson plays as *Serenading Louie*, *The Mound Builders*, and *Book of Days* and that are later covered up, lied about, and serve to corrupt the innocence of small town life. But what is riveting here is Wilson's extraordinary gift of description, particularly of the most horrific moment of the story:

> I pressed myself hard against the stack of papers. I saw only his arm and hand. The beaded lamp raised high, singing excitedly in the voice of Chinese wind chimes. He brought it down in a wide arc, swift as lightning with a crash of thunder behind the chairs. Again it raised, throwing off a shower of beads that flashed in the sun like multicolored fireworks and made hail-sounds, rattling through the shack.[23]

We don't need to see the the actual violence; instead we get the boy's awful experience of it, and its aftermath, as he contemplates how that same bully, now grown, neatly groomed, with a genteel façade, is quietly taking control over a new terrain, the fiend within a photo-op blur to those who long to be a part of his political campaign.

In "Drift," a flash fiction piece, we encounter another bit of plot from the play *The Rimers of Eldritch*, describing in about five hundred words the relationship between middle-aged Roslyn, the owner of a truck stop, The Hilltop Cafe, and Buddy, an eighteen-year-old drifter. Here Wilson, rather than telling us what is going on between the two, describes the transformation that occurs to Roslyn and Buddy after she takes in the young drifter: "People did talk of the change in Roslyn. She began somehow to look younger, gaining a vitality in her walk; she was gayer than anyone remembered, even attractive and always laughing." Rosyln loses weight and looks "healthier" and "Buddy didn't look at all like the kid who had drifted in that fall."[24] Wilson backs away from the sentimentality of romance and simply describes its aftereffect, evoking Buddy's later disappearance in discomfiting tremors of evocative Midwestern silence. While the story provides profound insight into the development of the roles of Cora and Walter (who is Buddy in the story) in *The Rimers of Eldritch*, more importantly it reveals the subtle brush with which Wilson renders characterization.

In the "Sketches of City Life" section, a young Lanford Wilson is obsessively absorbing the language and behaviors of a new urban jungle that both enthralls and terrifies him, looking into its dark corners and finding bits and pieces of humanity that he can tease out—both the tenderness of private miniature worlds and the brutal anonymity of the crowd. Like "Miss Misty," the flash fiction piece "Mama" brings to mind *The Madness of Lady Bright*, Wilson's play about a fading drag queen. In the spirit of Alfred Hitchcock's *Rear Window*, however, the narrator in "Mama" is a voyeur, who becomes fascinated with an eccentric figure who coos and fusses over an infant and whose apartment abuts his own. What is particularly touching is the delicate depiction of how the neighbor looks after the baby:

> Some evenings very softly he sang a slow mournful lullaby, high and sweet as a choir. At first I thought of a puppy, as my mother would have treated a newborn pup or kitten.[25]

The narrator finally manages to sneak into the apartment—and the surprise found there transforms the voyeuristic journey into something far more profound, a detective story about the malleable resilience of the human heart. The story throbs with a gentle kindness, peering quietly into the mystery of a secret transgendered bohemian universe, and lends insight into the fragile gossamer reality of *Lady Bright*.

In "Fuzz on Orion's Sword," a sister, Yvonne, comes from Boston to visit her brother, Leonard, in New York City, and in the midst of cab rides, museum visits, drinks, and dinner, she gradually relates her romancing of an "interesting" young man, Anthony, a poet and astronomer, who becomes obsessed with the inevitable end of our sun. While it is fascinating to see how the characters in "Fuzz on Orion's Sword" morph, evolve, and change gender to become the two old college friends—Carrie and Louise—in Wilson's later short play *The Great Nebula in Orion*, what is more important here is Wilson's ability to dramatize through fiction the behaviors of someone wrestling with unrequited love. The story sizzles with Wilson's intimate, crackling dialogue between brother and sister, and the heart of the story is Yvonne's description of the aftermath of a supernova:

> "Well, then pay attention, it's very interesting. You see, the Great Nebula is a lot of hydrogen or some kind of gas that's lit up by a couple of stars behind it somewhere. But see, this gas is condensing, getting compact, and after a few hundred years it's going to be so compact it'll start burning of its own accord, and then it'll be a star. And we could see that: it's sorta a big fuzzy spot at the center of the sword. A kind of pale green. And Anthony said there would be a star there someday."[26]

As Yvonne and Leonard journey through a wintry New York, the action really a long unending conversation, we learn of the profound unhappiness of Yvonne's marriage, the disjointed quality of her life and motherhood, and the attachment of brother and sister, as Leonard carefully unpacks the melancholy reality of Yvonne's life. But in her description of the Great Nebula of Orion is the shockingly sad reality of both the beauty and fragility of Yvonne's predicament, and Wilson's genius can be found in the brother's contemplation and understanding of how his sister's constant babble of banalities hides terrible pain and longing.

"Uptown in Snow" is a tightly written marvel of simplicity and expressionism. An older woman, Miss Matthews, suffers a stroke at her office, and, as she becomes more and more confused, decides to leave work for a quick cab ride home through the snowy world of New York City in winter. We hear only snippets of Miss Matthew's barked orders, and Wilson's skill here lies in his quicksilver description of her increasingly fracturing reality in the office, "the rapid staccato snapping of a dozen typewriters keyed in various stiff-pitched monotones," and as she moves outside and observes the blizzard covering the city: "It was the kind of snow that seemed to move sideways instead of downward; though the wind that directed it was hardly perceptible." Even as Miss Matthews is secure in the world of her apartment, the crystal clear hyperreality of it becomes oppressive: "Only the very faint *ssss* of cars outside and the refrigerator's low, very low murmur; the soft continuous mechanical sound of the clock in the next room." As we enter Miss Matthews's inner sanctum we gain a sense of her character, the extravagance of her Louis Quinze writing desk, and on it, "a green blotter to protect the rose and myrtle marqueterie of roses." The fascination Wilson had with older female characters such as Sally Talley in *Fifth of July*, D. K. Eriksen in *The Mound Builders*, and Marion Clay in *Angels Fall* can be seen in this sketch of Miss Matthews, fiercely independent, tough, quirky, and, at the same time, astonishingly human and utterly vulnerable. We discover the essence of Miss Matthews in the things she owns, the stationery in her drawer: "In the fibers of the paper, against the green, the watermark Carter Ta-na-ak was visible upside down on the sheet."[27]

"Dear Mr. Goldberg"—a flash fiction piece that reveals Wilson's sensitivity to anti-Semitism—deals with a copywriter interviewing for a position in an ad agency. Subtle, brief, it shows the same sensitivity toward Jewish culture that Wilson would later draw on for the character of Matt Friedman in *Talley's Folley*. So much in this story lies in what is not said, however, as Wilson relies instead upon the collegial grace of the bigoted interviewer; we hear it in his silky professionalism:

> "You see, we have to have a man, as well as someone that fits well into our group; we have to have a man who can create new approaches; a creative fellow. Now I am familiar with your work at Standard and I think you've been doing very well there."[28]

Nothing is said here that belies the interviewer's intentions, and what speaks far louder is Wilson's ability to unmask the behavior hidden just below the surface of dialogue: "You've had success—a good deal of success, Mr. Goldberg, with one kind of campaign. I've seen all of your samples on it and, of course, they are good. But I have strong reservations about your ability to adapt to our way of thinking." Again, the interviewer takes extraordinary pains to compliment, to warmly praise, to cleverly repackage his neatly worded dismissal. This can't be discrimination, can it? And even the interview's outcome is dealt with summarily, with a secretary taking a subtle cue from the interviewer, hardly noticeable. But Wilson trusts the reader to understand, to read beneath the language, to find the dog whistles and quiet innuendo that makes "Dear Mr. Goldberg" such a profound statement, and it is in that private covenant, between himself and his reader, that Wilson's virtuosity lies.

The final story is "Doors," a perfect place to end the fiction portion of the book, as it brings us full circle to a young Lanford Wilson hunting for an apartment in New York City, and the secrets that may be found there. The sad accommodation to life's necessities made by the characters in the story is revealed with simplicity, dignity, and a gentle candor that does nothing to take the sting out of what must be a heartbreaking reality. Again, the resilience of the major character—Cora Bloom, the proud, outspoken landlady, as she takes the young apartment hunter on an expedition into the clean but dismal interior of a single-room-occupancy building—implies an entire landscape of life's compromises. Cora reacts sharply to the narrator's own smalltown beginnings:

> "I don't think I know a soul that wasn't born and grew up in some jerkwater town." Mrs. Bloom lit a fresh cigarette from the old one, puffing vigorously: "Grow up in a small town, move to the city to make it rich and move back out to a small town–suburb. Never could see living like that." Her cigarette wagged when she spoke like a scolding finger. "Well, not in a long time have I thought about small towns. Used to think that would be the kind of life I'd have. I wouldn't have liked it much."[29]

When we encounter her own apartment, where Cora's young, seemingly disabled husband lies in wait, the description becomes cinematic: "The door at the end of the hall was ajar and light striped out across the floor." And Mrs. Bloom, for all her bluster, suddenly deflates before the reader, as the reality of her arrangement becomes clear. We are left, like the young room-hunter in the story, with a kind of admiration as the landlady disappears into the gloom of what becomes, in his mind and ours, a haunted tomb.

The final section of this book includes twenty-three poems, selected from the approximately forty poems that may be found in the Lanford Wilson Collection. The arrangement is based upon Wilson's journey as a writer, moving from small towns and the country, beginning with "Outside Tulsa," and culminating with his move to New York City, beginning with "Well, there she is, after all." The poems provide another kind of biography, one structured by the music of Wilson's language. Here, too, are a treasure trove of suggestions for interpreting Wilson's dramas. A poem like "Oakwood Gothic" could easily be a description of the Talley mansion on Harper Hill in Ozark, Missouri, towering over the Finley River, which is where Wilson imagined it to be in *Talley's Folly*, *Fifth of July*, and *Talley & Son*. Several of the poems hint at Wilson's private world of relationships, family, and friends, inviting us into his emerging consciousness as a writer. This final section ends on an evocative note with his last poem, "A Love Story about the Next Best Thing." It begins with the line "Write about us, Lance," which describes exactly what would be Lanford Wilson's life work.

Lanford Wilson was one of the top dramatists in New York from his beginnings Off-Off-Broadway in the 1960s at the Caffe Cino to his Broadway successes of the 1970s, 1980s, and 1990s through the beginning of the new millennium. He was a playwright's playwright and a self-taught craftsman of lyric dialogue, complex characters, and wildly inventive theatricality. His early plays like *The Rimers of Eldritch*, *Balm in Gilead*, *Serenading Louie*, and *The Hot l Baltimore* were delicately structured waves of language, overlapping, crashing into each other. He was fascinated by, among many other subjects, history, anthropology, astronomy, finance, and the mysterious and sometimes dark heart of rural America. Like the outsider artists he championed (he owned over three hundred pieces of outsider art), he was an autodidact, and prized his ability to teach himself the nuances of science, literature, visual art, and dance. He developed a dramaturgy that ranged in technique from choral collage to expressionism, metatheatricality to political theatre, hyperrealism to comic farce, finally fusing these many modes in a unique lyric realism and deep exploration of complex, yet utterly accessible characters that was his signature style and that of the writers he mentored at Circle Repertory Company.

He was a theatre artist coming of age in the tumult of the 1960s, with its mix of happenings, pop and camp, rock 'n' roll, and wild experimentation, but he transformed himself and his writing in each successive decade. Like Tennessee Williams, at the heart of his technique was revision—a relentless, rigorous, painstaking, and restless rewriting that revealed a playwright who was never satisfied, never quite ready to put down his pen, and deeply connected to the actors and, more importantly, the character voices for whom he was writing, like a jazz musician in an ongoing improvisation. Dialogue, the dissonant harmonies of human voices interacting, and the music and cadence of the desire that surged beneath it, was Wilson's métier—built on structure, revision, restructuring, experimentation, and the serious, meticulous investigation into the seething, surging underworld of his characters' inner lives.

As you explore these short stories and poems, you may find yourself thinking of the kaleidoscope of characters created by Wilson over the extent of his career: the yearnings of wandering Midwesterners; brittle, smart, and cryptic New Yorkers; languid and ironic West Coast types; earnest and soul-searching youth; the unblinking eyes of middle-aged wage slaves; and the sober comedy of honest people chasing tiny and tremendous dreams as they travel through the pratfalls and disasters of daily life. What follows, then, is the gorgeous canvas of Lanford Wilson's crucial youthful journey to find his own voice as a writer, an outsider dramatist whose plays delved into undiscovered country. Prepare to be quietly dazzled by this young adventurous writer and the world in which he lived not so many years ago.

NOTES

1. Virginia Woolf and John Cheever qtd., respectively, in Anne Frydman, "Chekhov in English," *The Threepenny Review* 43 (Autumn 1990): 31–32.
2. Carol Flath, "Writing about Nothing: Chekhov's 'Ariadna' and the Narcissistic Narrator," *The Slavonic and East European Review* 77, no. 2 (April 1999): 223–239.
3. Gore Vidal, introduction to Tennessee Williams, *Collected Stories* (New York: New Directions, 1985), xxi.
4. Gene A. Barnett, "Recreating the Magic: An Interview with Lanford Wilson," *Ball State University Forum* 25 (1984): 58.
5. Mel Gussow, "Lanford Wilson on Broadway," *Horizon* 23 (May 1980): 30–36.
6. Miles Payne, letter to Lanford Wilson, July 20, 1959, Series I Box 3—Correspondence, Lanford Wilson Collection. Special Collections and Rare Books, University of Missouri Libraries.
7. Tanya Rose, letter to Lanford Wilson, March 3, 1965, FF105, Series I Box 3—Correspondence, Lanford Wilson Collection. Special Collections and Rare Books, University of Missouri Libraries.
8. Tanya Rose, letter to Lanford Wilson, January 14, 1967, FF105, Series I Box 3—Correspondence, Lanford Wilson Collection. Special Collections and Rare Books, University of Missouri Libraries.
9. Gene Barnett, *Lanford Wilson* (Boston: Twayne, 1987), 3.

Introduction / 25

10. David Savran, *In Their Own Words: Contemporary American Playwrights* (New York: Theatre Communications Group, 1993), 308.

11. William Keyse Rudolph, "The Lanford Wilson Collection of Self-Taught Art," *Antiques* 179, no. 6 (November–December 2012): 102–104.

12. Ross Wetzsteon, "The Most Populist Playwright," *New York Magazine* 15, no. 44 (November 8, 1982): 40–45.

13. Lanford Wilson, "A Section of Orange," manuscript, undated, FF 44, Series III—Works, Subseries I—Prose & Poetry, Box 9, Lanford Wilson Collection, Special Collections and Rare Books, University of Missouri Libraries.

14. Lanford Wilson, "Goodbye Sparta," manuscript, undated, FF 30, Series III—Works, Subseries I—Prose & Poetry, Box 9, Lanford Wilson Collection, Special Collections and Rare Books, University of Missouri Libraries.

15. Lanford Wilson, "Miss Misty," manuscript, undated, FF 36, Series III—Works, Subseries I—Prose & Poetry, Box 9, Lanford Wilson Collection, Special Collections and Rare Books, University of Missouri Libraries.

16. Lanford Wilson, "The Beautiful Children," manuscript, undated, FF 39, Series III—Works, Subseries I—Prose & Poetry, Box 9, Lanford Wilson Collection, Special Collections and Rare Books, University of Missouri Libraries.

17. Lanford Wilson, "The Polar Bear," manuscript, undated, FF 36, Series III—Works, Subseries I—Prose & Poetry, Box 9, Lanford Wilson Collection, Special Collections and Rare Books, University of Missouri Libraries.

18. Lanford Wilson, notebook, January 31, 1977, "5th of July" and "The Eskimo Story," Series III—Works and Manuscripts, Sub-Series III—Notebooks, Box 21, Folder 19, Lanford Wilson Collection. Special Collections and Rare Books, University of Missouri Libraries.

19. Lanford Wilson, "The Canary," manuscript, undated, FF 20, Series III—Works, Subseries I—Prose & Poetry, Box 9, Lanford Wilson Collection, Special Collections and Rare Books, University of Missouri Libraries.

20. Lanford Wilson, "The Train to Washington," manuscript, undated, FF 46, Series III—Works, Subseries I—Prose & Poetry, Box 9, Lanford Wilson Collection, Special Collections and Rare Books, University of Missouri Libraries.

21. Lanford Wilson, "The Water Commissioner," manuscript, undated, FF 53, Series III—Works, Subseries I—Prose & Poetry, Box 9, Lanford Wilson Collection, Special Collections and Rare Books, University of Missouri Libraries.

22. Lanford Wilson, "Fish Kite," manuscript, undated, FF 28, Series III—Works, Subseries I—Prose & Poetry, Box 9, Lanford Wilson Collection, Special Collections and Rare Books, University of Missouri Libraries.

23. Lanford Wilson, "Chalk Eye," manuscript, undated, FF 22, Series III—Works, Subseries I—Prose & Poetry, Box 9, Lanford Wilson Collection, Special Collections and Rare Books, University of Missouri Libraries.

24. Lanford Wilson, "Drift," manuscript, undated, FF 27, Series III—Works, Subseries I—Prose & Poetry, Box 9, Lanford Wilson Collection, Special Collections and Rare Books, University of Missouri Libraries.

25. Lanford Wilson, "Mama," manuscript, undated, FF 35, Series III—Works, Subseries I—Prose & Poetry, Box 9, Lanford Wilson Collection, Special Collections and Rare Books, University of Missouri Libraries.

26. Lanford Wilson, "Fuzz on Orion's Belt," manuscript, undated, FF 29, Series III—Works, Subseries I—Prose & Poetry, Box 9, Lanford Wilson Collection, Special Collections and Rare Books, University of Missouri Libraries.

27. Lanford Wilson, "Uptown in Snow," manuscript, undated, FF 51, Series III—Works, Subseries I—Prose & Poetry, Box 9, Lanford Wilson Collection, Special Collections and Rare Books, University of Missouri Libraries.

28. Lanford Wilson, "Dear Mr. Goldberg," manuscript, undated, FF 25, Series III—Works, Subseries I—Prose & Poetry, Box 9, Lanford Wilson Collection, Special Collections and Rare Books, University of Missouri Libraries.

29. Lanford Wilson, "Doors," manuscript, undated, FF 26, Series III—Works, Subseries I—Prose & Poetry, Box 9, Lanford Wilson Collection, Special Collections and Rare Books, University of Missouri Libraries.

SECTION I
SIX STORIES

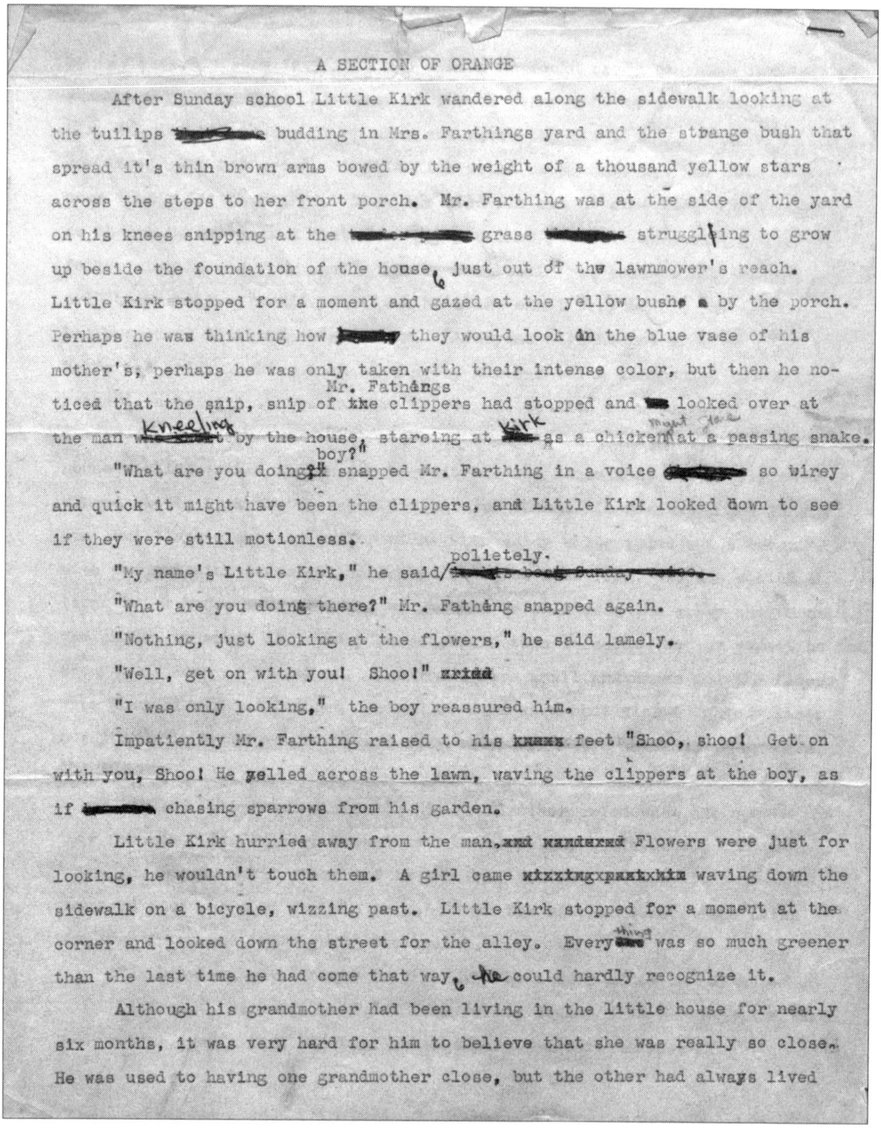

A SECTION OF ORANGE

After Sunday school Little Kirk wandered along the sidewalk looking at the tulips budding in Mrs. Farthings yard and the strange bush that spread it's thin brown arms bowed by the weight of a thousand yellow stars across the steps to her front porch. Mr. Farthing was at the side of the yard on his knees snipping at the grass struggling to grow up beside the foundation of the house, just out of the lawnmower's reach. Little Kirk stopped for a moment and gazed at the yellow bushe by the porch. Perhaps he was thinking how they would look in the blue vase of his mother's; perhaps he was only taken with their intense color, but then he noticed that the snip, snip of the clippers had stopped and Mr. Fathång looked over at the man kneeling by the house, stareing at Kirk as a chicken at a passing snake.

"What are you doing, boy?" snapped Mr. Farthing in a voice so wirey and quick it might have been the clippers, and Little Kirk looked down to see if they were still motionless.

"My name's Little Kirk," he said politely.

"What are you doing there?" Mr. Fathång snapped again.

"Nothing, just looking at the flowers," he said lamely.

"Well, get on with you! Shoo!"

"I was only looking," the boy reassured him.

Impatiently Mr. Farthing raised to his feet "Shoo, shoo! Get on with you, Shoo! He yelled across the lawn, waving the clippers at the boy, as if chasing sparrows from his garden.

Little Kirk hurried away from the man. Flowers were just for looking, he wouldn't touch them. A girl came waving down the sidewalk on a bicycle, wizzing past. Little Kirk stopped for a moment at the corner and looked down the street for the alley. Everything was so much greener than the last time he had come that way, he could hardly recognize it.

Although his grandmother had been living in the little house for nearly six months, it was very hard for him to believe that she was really so close. He was used to having one grandmother close, but the other had always lived

Fig. 2. First page, "A Section of Orange" manuscript, undated; Lanford Wilson Collection, Special Collections and Rare Books, University of Missouri Libraries, Lanford Wilson Estate.

A Section of Orange

After sunday school Little Kirk wandered along the sidewalk looking at the tulips budding in Mrs. Farthing's yard and the strange bush that spread its thin brown arms bowed by the weight of a thousand yellow stars across the steps to her front porch. Mr. Farthing was at the side of the yard on his knees snipping at the grass struggling to grow up beside the foundation of the house just out of the lawnmower's reach. Little Kirk stopped for a moment and gazed at the yellow bush by the porch. Perhaps he was thinking how they would look in the blue vase of his mother's, perhaps he was only taken with their intense color, but then he noticed that the snip, snip of Mr. Farthing's clippers had stopped and looked over at the man kneeling by the house, staring at Kirk as a chicken might stare at a passing snake.

"What are you doing, boy?" snapped Mr. Farthing in a voice so wiry and quick it might have been the clippers, and Little Kirk looked down to see if they were still motionless.

"My name's Little Kirk," he said politely.

"What are you doing there?" Mr. Farthing snapped again.

"Nothing, just looking at the flowers," he said lamely.

"Well, get on with you! Shoo!"

"I was only looking," the boy reassured him.

Impatiently, Mr. Farthing raised to his feet. "Shoo, shoo! Get on with you, shoo!" he yelled across the lawn, waving the clippers at the boy, as if chasing sparrows from his garden.

Little Kirk hurried away from the man. Flowers were just for looking, he wouldn't touch them. A girl came weaving down the sidewalk on a bicycle, whizzing past. Little Kirk stopped for a moment at the corner and looked down the street for the alley. Everything was so much greener than the last time he had come that way, he could hardly recognize it.

Although his grandmother had been living in the little house for nearly six months, it was very hard for him to believe that she was really so close. He was used to having one grandmother close, but the other had always lived so far away, in some town whose name he could never remember. At first it seemed strange to have a woman smothering him, hugging him in her plump arms and squeezing him to her. "Oh, you little darling!" she had cried. Little Kirk would never have let her know he was more than a little scared. Then she held him out at arm's length admiringly, as though he were a statue. "Do you know you look exactly like your father when he was your age?" He could not believe his father had ever been small. "Don't you think he's the exact copy of his father?" she had beamed at Little Kirk's mother. "Everyone says he has my eyes," Mrs. Wolfe had said, looking down at the boy who was being surrounded by his grandmother's arms again. Grandmother Wolfe. It sounded so strange to him. Here was one with his own name.

It had not taken her long to get settled in the house her son had chosen for her—it was the house that had really convinced Little Kirk that he should visit her often. It was not huge like his own, but tiny—almost as a plaything—with shiny white sides and surrounded with red, pink roses and asparagus let grow into fern. It sat behind a large brick house so it was necessary to walk down the alley and through the garden to enter it. Every house should turn its back on the street, he had thought as soon as he saw it. The rooms were small and the floors were covered with a blue rug instead of dark varnished wood that glared in your face; everything in the house was small and cozy.

"Hello! Who have we here?" his grandmother cried when she opened the door for him. Little Kirk looked down at his shiny Sunday shoes and smiled. "Come in, sweetheart, don't stand out in the sun, you'll fade away it's so strong." She held the screen door open for him to step into the little house. "You haven't run away from home, have you?" She smiled.

The boy laughed, "Mother said I could come over after Sunday school."

"I know," the woman said. "I know my boy wouldn't do a thing like that. Your mother just called and told me to expect a little invader after the services."

"You weren't surprised?" he asked almost sadly.

Grandmother Wolfe looked at him a moment. "Wasn't surprised? What do you mean? I couldn't imagine who she was talking about." He didn't quite believe that, but it made him feel better anyway.

"Would you like some milk?"

"We had milk and cookies at Sunday school."

"Little Kirk!" the woman said so suddenly that he almost jumped. "Is that a new jacket? How handsome it looks."

"Mother said I was growing out of my other one. It's the first time I've worn it," he said, standing erect so his grandmother could admire him.

"Like a weed. Just like a little weed. You keep growing like that and you'll be as big as Big Kirk in another year. We'll have to call *you* Big Kirk and your dad Little Kirk."

The boy beamed.

The old lady's hands shook slightly. Everything she touched trembled gently as she held it. Little Kirk had never been able to understand. His mother had said it was because she was getting old. He didn't mind, but still when she sat with her hands in her lap, folded together, he always saw her thumb moving, almost jerking, and he looked away. He looked at the picture of the lake on the wall over the little love seat, at the gold Christ on the cross or just down at his shoes; when he looked back, the thumb was always still trembling. "Well, honey, your grandmother has to finish her dinner, or she'll not have it ready in time," the old woman said at last. "She's having Mrs. Winrod over for lunch and she's got to get busy. Do you want to set on the divan and look at a magazine? I'll talk to you from the kitchen, would that be alright?"

Little Kirk nodded that it would and his grandmother selected a magazine that would be suitable for him to turn through. She went slowly into the kitchen separated from the living room by a half wall to the sink where she had left her pan of potatoes. "Did you notice the roses, Little Kirk?" she called.

"They were pretty," he said, not remembering if he had taken special notice of them or not.

"There were nine this morning—I was wondering if any more had opened. Several were just ready to."

"I didn't think to count." The boy put down the magazine. There were practically no pictures at all. He looked around the bright sun-filled room again. On a table across the room a large bowl, that he hadn't seen at first, was filled with oranges. He jumped off the divan and walked over to it. They were so shiny he had to stick his thumbnail into the skin of one to be sure that they weren't wax. He had hardly sat down again when he began to wish he had asked for one when his grandmother asked him if he wanted milk. He got up again, but this time went into the kitchen. "May I help you?" he asked.

His grandmother looked at him. "Did you get tired of the magazine?" She smiled. "Well, you can watch, if you like, I'm going to cover the pie before long."

Little Kirk tried to approach the subject as discreetly as possible. "When did you get the oranges?" he asked.

"Just this morning. They're for the salad, some of them. OH! My gracious! I never even thought, would you like one, Little Kirk?"

The boy nodded.

"Do you know I never even tasted an orange until I was fourteen. I forgot little children ate them, I guess. Do you want to squeeze it, or should I peel it for you? Would you rather have it in little individual pieces?"

Little Kirk always delighted in the way that oranges' parts fit together under the skin; like a group of children hiding. "Would you peel it?"

"I suppose I sure could—would you like to get one for me?"

Little Kirk ran into the living room, and selected the orange he had dug his thumbnail into and took it back to the kitchen, handing it to his grandmother with punctured side down.

"It won't take but just a minute," she said. "You'd better go wash your hands, though. I don't know how you get them dirty doing nothing."

He went into the bath and washed his hands, standing on tip-toe to reach the basin. He didn't bother to see if the soap was the kind that floated.

When he went back into the kitchen the orange was still sitting on the drain board. His grandmother saw that he was looking at it, and smiled. "I'll be just a minute, why don't you sit down in the living room?"

Little Kirk went back to the divan and opened the magazine. It seemed that he had sat there an awfully long time. He stretched his neck up to see over the half wall, but the woman was at the sink with her back turned and he could not see what she was doing. He had always liked oranges better than any fruit, better than grapes, or bananas, which were dry tasting. He liked to line up the sections in a row, as though they were boats at a harbor, and eat them one by one as though he was renting them from the owner. Finally, he could stand it no longer. "Do you about have the orange peeled, Grandmother?"

"Just about, impatient. It doesn't want to work right."

He couldn't though he tried to remember the last time he had eaten an orange. His mother would like it that he had enjoyed himself at his grandmother's house.

"Here it is," his grandmother said at last, "do you want to come eat it over the sink?"

He walked into the kitchen very casually and his grandmother put a chair up to the sink for him to stand on. "It didn't want to do right, the skin was too thin," she said.

Little Kirk looked down at the torn bits of orange in the saucer.

"It pulled apart in all the wrong places," she laughed.

He looked at the mess of fruit in the saucer and then at her again. Anyone could peel an orange right; they just worked that way.

The woman took a saucepan from the stove and sat it on the table. It shook gently in her hands. Was that why? Couldn't she hold it still?

He took one piece of the orange and put it in his mouth. The juice from it squeezed out on his hand. Were some more torn apart than others? It splattered, and his eyes were watering.

"You should have just squeezed the juice," his grandmother said. "That wouldn't have made such a mess. I guess they're juice oranges." She was busy at the stove again.

Little Kirk got off the chair and stood looking at her as she slowly prepared dinner. He felt his throat tighten, and he didn't know why, but he knew he was going to cry if he didn't leave. He started walking toward the front door.

"Where're you going, honey?" His grandmother looked up.

"I better go home, now," he said reaching the door.

"Oh, you could stay awhile. I'm gonna cover the pie shortly."

"Mother'll wonder where I am," he said, holding the screen door and looking back at her.

"My, such a big boy to worry about his mother."

He looked back at her standing at the door and bit his lip, but he put his hand up as if he was scratching his face.

"Bye," he said.

Little Kirk shut the screen softly and walked carefully around the house, through the garden and to the alley before he began to run. He ran to the corner and down the sidewalk, then slowed; breathing in heaves, he walked the rest of the way home. His eyes were so blurred he didn't notice Mrs. Farthing snipping long straight stems of the yellow bush for the centerpiece of her table.

Goodbye Sparta

This story is made up. There's not a word of it the real truth, but it's written like it happened to me. I was eighteen, that much is true, but the rest is made up.

I couldn't wait to get out of high school and get out of town. I was living in a place called Sparta, Arkansas, so I guess I won't have to explain that. One thing I will say and say truthfully, I've never been sorry that I left. I guess I could have come to some place a little bit nicer than Chicago, but I've never been sorry because I left Sparta. Just the name of the town made me think of wrestling youths and naked boys practicing discus and that sorta thing so I was glad to leave it.

In school I'd always had a particular talent for drawing; I guess I neglected some of my other studies because I was so interested in that one thing. But I wanted to go into advertising, which I thought was a very wise thing to do. Just looking at all the magazines and newspapers that they have to print because of all the people that want to advertise made me realize that it must be a big thing. So I came to Chicago. About the hardest thing in the world to do is break into something when you're new in town and just out of school. I'll bet I swore that I had no intention of ever going back to my hometown or of ever going to college at least a thousand times. Probably more than that. So finally I took a job in an office, just so I could live. I moved into an apartment house on the far north side. In Chicago they have a Nearnorth and a Farnorth. The far north is where almost everyone in Chicago lives, except the important ones that live in the Nearnorth or way to hell and gone in the suburbs which are some of them over forty miles away. If that's easy living they can have it. The house I moved into was alright; it was filled with the weirdest characters in the world but they were wonderful too and I was made to feel right at home. You can imagine that being from Arkansas I didn't sound exactly like they did and I always had just a bit of feeling that they were not really laughing at me but smiling at me when I talked to them. Back home we say "Yes, ma'am," and "I beg your pardon, sir," and in Chicago they don't talk like that at all. No one ever calls anyone else ma'am or sir, and it's hard to break yourself of something like that.

I wish I could say all the things that I thought when I first came in here. Sometimes I was afraid that I had done the wrong thing, and that my folks had been right when they said I'd be back before the year was out, but I made up my mind to stick it out at least a year just to prove that they were wrong. Then sometimes I got to thinking of the thousands of kids just out of school that must be pouring into Chicago and cities like Chicago all over the world. Not just this country, but all over the world, and they all had the same dream and goals as I did. They all wanted to make their mark somehow and be something good. Everyone was sure that they would make it. Not be the mayor of the town, but just to make a living at something they really liked, and find someone and settle down and live happily. But I knew in my heart that not every one of those kids would get his dream. A lot of them would but a lot of them wouldn't at all.

I don't mind saying that I tried to do something to change my thoughts whenever I got to thinking something like that. It seems that there are two kinds of people. There are the ones that are happy with their circumstances and those that aren't. You can spot them a mile away. If it hadn't been for school I would have been lost from the beginning. I had saved some money before I came here. I wouldn't want anyone to think that I had just struck out extemporaneously without a cent. It didn't take me long to learn that I was going to at least take a course in layout and probably design before an advertising agency or studio would ever look at me even. So I started nights at the Academy. It was an interesting school, and I learned a lot, but that's not what you want to know about, and not what I want to tell you either. The people I met there are important; but I'll only tell you about Ronnie.

Ronnie lived in the same building I did. We're weren't really close friends either, but he was nice, probably the nicest boy I'd ever met, but very quiet and sometimes he seemed to be wanting to get away from me. I can't say I blame him. He was one of the most talented people I'd ever met. Just go to art school if you think you're the world's new Da Vinci; you'll see ten people better than you are before you have time to set up an easel. It's not the most comforting feeling in the world. Ronnie lived on the floor just above me, but like I said, he didn't seem too anxious to be outgoing. Right at first he did. When we met at school the first day (we'd seen each other in the house before) he came over and spoke. We ate in the school cafeteria together and he talked through the whole meal a blue streak, jabbering like a magpie. He had a way of talking and pronouncing his words so very, very distinctly that it was a pleasure to listen to him. And he was very funny. But as I said later he never seemed to be so outgoing.

Just for instance, I remember one evening I came home about 8:30. I heard music from upstairs, and he has a wonderful record player with two speakers that I enjoyed listening to, so I went up. I could hear that there was someone else in the room, there was another boy's voice, and they were laughing, and someone was dancing, you could tell by the scrape, scrape on the floor. So I knocked, in the party mood, as loud as I could; and suddenly everything was quiet except the music. I knocked again and even the music stopped, or rather the record ended, but I could hear the *ssss, ssss* scraping of the needle at the end of the record as the disc kept turning on the machine. His machine was manual, and doesn't reject like most. Then the noise stopped and I knew someone had lifted the needle off the record, but still there wasn't a sound. I knocked it once more, I guess I can't take a hint, but no one came to the door, so I went away.

That's what he's like. My own thoughts are that maybe the girl he was dancing with, or the other fellow was dancing with, didn't want it to be any bigger a party. But he could have come to the door and told me that, see? That's what he's like. Minnie lived across the floor from Ron. Minnie was a very thin woman who believed in ghosts. Not really ghosts, but spirits from the dead, reincarnation and that sort of thing. She always had at least two traveling companions, a departed uncle or a distant cousin; some of the more lonely souls in the building were terribly jealous of Minnie's assumed popularity. And she was a brilliant person to talk to. It was a little embarrassing, for being mostly concerned with the soul, she tended to be a bit sloppy with the body. Like walking around the building with her dress unbuttoned down the middle to her waist, and it's hard to talk to someone when you have to look at the ceiling, or the floor, or stare them straight in the eye.

But the whole thing, the important thing began with going to the Academy. There was a different kind of crowd than I'd ever associated with before. Not that they were more worldly, although they were, but they were more interested. And more interesting. I'd never before been able to carry on a conversation with anyone about art. That's not all they talked about, but it's a good example. And music, and all the fine arts; drama, and so forth. And then, I'll admit that when I came to Chicago I was a bit more naïve than I'd like to believe. I won't go into a lot of embarrassing examples, on just how naïve I really was, but I'll just say at random that I thought a cumdrum was some sort of South African musical instrument, and let it go at that.

So I learned a great deal about art, and a great deal more. And a great deal more. I've wandered on and on and not really said anything, which is one of my greatest shortcomings. I guess I should have really started when I first met Samantha. Samantha was the name of Delilah's older sister, the one that Samson married; I knew that much about the Bible, not much more. Samantha was twenty-six, and a little older than the rest of the crowd. We (the whole gang) used to go to parties, usually uninvited, and it was Samantha's car that took us. She wasn't always along but we took her car. I never really knew her, she was just another one of the gang until one Christmas party. And that's really where I should have begun.

Living in an apartment was a new experience to me, furnished sheets and maid service and so on. I make it sound great, but if you've ever lived in an apartment on the far north side (one of the one room, 75 dollars a week variety) then you know it's a long way from luxury. One of my friends in the apartment was Marilyn, an enormous girl with a little daughter a year old; her husband worked nights, so Marilyn and I often spent the wee hours together talking of things in general, you know how people talk. Occasionally one of her friends from the second floor (there were three prostitutes, and very attractive ones at that, that we knew) would join us, but unlike all my writing friends, I find prostitutes very saddening people and I won't trouble you with them. They are wonderful symbols of independence and freedom, but they're sad.

Marie McViekre was more free, and not sad. Marie was really free, without attachments psychological or emotional to anything in this world. And she might not have been happy, but she wasn't sad. Engrossed in the world, would best describe her. The real world, not the cinema and five-day clerk world. Not the crass commercialism that rules so many people, she was completely untouched by it. You can say that that's the real world, the five-till-nine and cinema routine, but it isn't, and actually everyone knows that it isn't. But Marie McViekre comes along later and she's out of place here.

As I said, Marilyn was large. She was jolly and funny and had a beautiful face. One evening, I remember she was telling me about the other people in the house; not that I like gossip, but it was fun, considering the collection that had congregated in the building. There was the woman in 207, who lived with her son who was seventeen, Billy was his name, and he was what I don't think it's improper to say, a beautiful boy—happy and gay and cheerful, a bit of a roamer, or something; what I mean is he was no angel, but very nice just the same. I have never seen anyone quite so attractive, and apparently he wasn't aware of it. So his hair was combed up and down into his eyes, like all the teens and pre-teens then, and now even, and he had eyes that always made you feel like you were gazing into the sky, the palest blue morning eyes, with heavy brown lashes, and a strong face, supple body, and all youth, and absurd slangy speech. I've seen him putting out a cigarette at the front door of the building and hiding the package in his inside coat pocket before he went up to his apartment; so I know he wasn't much different than I or anyone else was at that age.

But one evening when his mother worked late he brought a girl up to the apartment, a sweet moonlight girl, with taffy hair, very much the type he deserved, and they were together for several hours alone. The next evening Billy was stabbed to death in a park several blocks away. He died alone in the park, hours before anyone found him. The police in their blundering way blamed it on teenage gangs, questioned a number of hoods, and apparently lost interest in the case when nothing much turned up. I have no idea what happened that night in the apartment, but I like to think that Billy discovered the innocent and sweet pleasure of being loved that tender night before he died. Across the hall from where Billy and his mother lived at that time was Mrs. Prude, who was the most inaptly named woman in the world. Mrs. Prude was perhaps fifty-five, and lived by herself. Everyone in the building knew that her husband was in prison, but then, she didn't mind that, and I believe that she had probably told them herself; although he was dragged away one night from the building and it didn't take much imagination to know where he was going. Mrs. Prude was promiscuous. We didn't know it exactly at the time. Marilyn and I were talking about it but we found out suddenly that night. She had a rather good reason for what she did, I guess; Mrs. Prude was lonely. I remember that we were talking about the only ordinary couple on the floor when we first heard the commotion out in the hall. I know that a couple of people stuck their heads out of the door and yelled, "Shuddap" before we went out, but it had only just started. After the first "shuddap," most of the people on the floor shut themselves in their room, and what happened after was not their business even if the house burned down.

The first commotion was just a moaned and exasperated "Oh," and a few timid knocks on a door, then an almost frantic "Oh, my god, let me in," but still soft and quiet. Not being from the shuddap group, I walked out in the hall to see what the trouble was. There stood Mrs. Prude, naked as a jaybird, dimpled and just a little plump, beating on her door. On hearing us she turned straight forward and looked at us, put both her hands rather modestly over her breasts and said, "Oh." Then she turned and pounded violently on the door screaming, "Goddamnit, let me in, you tramp!" Billy, whose room was across the hall from her, stuck his head out the door, and it was a narrow hall. Mrs. Prude looked him square in the eye and exclaimed, "Tramp right off the street. Hillbilly," and went scurrying to the back staircase and disappeared into the door. Of course by this time Marilyn was roaring with laughter. Any very serious predicament always causes Marilyn to break forth with gales of laughter. Billy stuck his head out of his door and yelled down to us: "Wow, did you see that? Isn't this the crummiest house?" We walked down to Billy's door. "What's going on, who's she got in there?" Marilyn said. "Some hillbilly, she said, off the street." Mrs. Prude stuck her head from behind the hall door and said, "You mind your own business, go on, get away from there, now." This startled us, and we all hurried into Billy's room and shut the door. But no longer had we got it closed than there was a soft tap at the door. Mrs. Prude, looking the part of a salvation army worker in distress, her hands crossed over her bare bosom, said meekly, "Help me. Help me get that lug outta my apartment," and she stepped inside. I've never been that close to an undressed fifty-five-year-old woman before, and I'm sure Billy hadn't, and I'm sure that from the burning, my face was as red as ham. Our compound embarrassment, and Mrs. Prude's plight dawned on Marilyn again and she started off on uncontrollable laughter. I had gone to the bathroom to fetch the poor woman a towel. And to get out of sight for a minute and try to control myself, for I was very nearly at the stage Marilyn had reached.

But before I could return with the towel, Mrs. Prude's hillbilly friend opened the door across the hall, yelled, "Alright, alright, wake up the whole goddamned house." And he left the door standing open, returned to the sofa bed, which was folded out, and rumpled up, and laid down. Mrs. Prude's friend was as bare as she was. She went running into the room as I came to her with the towel. "You get out of here. Out. Out. Out. Out. Out." And stood shaking her finger at the door, which, of course, made her whole body shake like red aspic. The fellow picked up a magazine and started flipping through the pages.

"Out!"

"Why the hell'd you drag me up here?"

"Out, you horrible hillbilly, you tramp. Chasing people out of their own apartments into the halls—brute!"

"What'd you drag me up here for?"

"Out!"

"Why don't you shut up and shut the door?" He put down the magazine and Mrs. Prude reached out and shut the door.

Billy and Marilyn and I went back to her apartment, after the storm. Only as could be expected, we had just shut the door when uproarious commotion was raised up and down the hall. We all ran out into the hall, and Mrs. Prude, still nude, was pounding violently on her door. "Good lord," said Billy. "This is nothing but a goddamned flop house."

"That's what it is," moaned Mrs. Prude, pounding on her door. "It's nothing but a goddamned flop house."

That was about nine o'clock that evening and Mr. Williams came reluctantly out of his door and went to the telephone to call the police. Mr. Williams worked days and tried to sleep nights and once or twice a week he came sadly into the hall to call the police on a disturbance of the peace charge. About midnight the police came and things quieted down a little—until nearly twelve thirty.

Miss Misty

You don't know Miss Misty; you think you do, but you don't. Picture the loveliest face, the most luscious tan and perfect figure you've ever seen. Picture it on a boy six feet tall with artificially platinum hair. Picture the wildest, most constant and satirical characterization of the female; the animation and charm of four starlets rolled into one startling queen: Miss Misty is almost internationally famous. I didn't know her myself until one day last summer. Sitting one Sunday on Oak Street Beach (Chicago) I met him, but you can't say him, you must say *her*—it's the only natural pronoun. Sex, or at least gender, to Miss Misty, was an attitude.

As I said, I was on the beach with the girl I know; taking in the sun and water and the sweeping sight of the city's skyline from this most perfect vantage when another sense crept into our consciousness. Hearing. A ripple of commotion that started near the Dearborn Street entrance and spread, like on water, in circles began to reach us. A generally curious titter of questions and comments: Where? Over there. You don't say. I don't believe you. Good God. And: Get a load of that hat. Then we saw her; pressing through the crowd with ceremonious smiles and nods, trailing an entourage of perhaps seven "young things" who carried a folding beach chair, thermos, towels, a radio, an enormous candy-striped umbrella (unfolded) and clattering collections of various tanning lotions. Miss Misty stood out. She (he) wore pink pedal pushers and aqua thong sandals, a white silk shirt open down the front and tied above the waist to expose six inches of tanned midriff. Over her taffy hair was a mammoth straw picture hat, set back on the head, brim flapping. With a large straw basket she moved as the crowd bowed automatically in front of her, allowing a wide aisle as she breathed "thank you, thank you" to either side. Everyone stared as the caravan moved along the beach. They wound on until the striped umbrella was only a tiny pink balloon bobbing daintily in the distance, and Miss Misty's hat finally disappeared altogether.

My real acquaintance with Miss Misty came a few months later. Diane and I were living then on the Near North side in a small coach house. Our little house was set behind the main three-story mansion, which was now divided into apartments. Miss Misty lived in the mansion in a smallish (said Diane) room near the top. Between the main house and ours was a paved courtyard where Miss Misty would sometimes sunbathe, spreading blanket and lotions and music in front of our living room window. She would sometimes pluck a rose from one of three bushes Diane nurtured at the side of the house, but of course, at our consent. It became natural to have Miss Misty in for coffee or a "tall cooling one" on warm afternoons that she spread out just beyond our open door.

It started one day all at once and quite suddenly. At about ten that morning Miss Misty came flying across the courtyard, losing her sandals, singing excitedly: "My dears, my dears, are you home?" Miss Misty always called everyone *my dear*. "My dear," she burst fluttering into the room and throwing herself across the sofa, "I've just received the most incredibly fabulous letter from my father."

"I thought he never wrote you."

"Oh, now and again, but only the most awfully depressing sort of *merde* about having a girl who's really a boy or a son who's really a daughter, that sort of vague nonsense, but at last he seems decided to do something about me."

"What, Misty?" I asked tentatively.

She looked at Diane and then to me. "Darlings, you really mustn't laugh or I'll cast some awful spell on you; but I've always desperately wanted to go to school." We both nodded. "Only he wouldn't send me and as a proper lady can hardly be expected to make her own way . . ."

"Well, what is he going to do?" Diane interrupted. When Miss Misty starts going like that she can forget altogether about something important for days.

"He's offering to send me to college. Scot-free, my dears. Everything paid."

"That's wonderful."

"At Northwestern College. I wouldn't even have to leave Chicago!" Diane winced a bit at that, imagining Miss Misty among the ivy and sedate stone of that Evanston campus, but it only lasted a moment. "That's really wonderful, Misty."

"I'll study education and become a teacher. Roger Craig—you probably know her by the name of Ms. Gladys, and she's the biggest queen on the West side—teaches drawing in Oak Park." Here she leaned forward with a malicious squint: "and if that teased-out bitch can teach school so can I." She had stood up, but now sat down again sadly. "There's only one catch."

"I knew there was something," Diane said.

"And it's impossibly dreadful. Or dreadfully impossible."

"What?"

"I have to straighten out for the rest of the summer. You know, get a job and all that crap."

"Misty, you're not afraid of work are you?"

She looked up, almost irritated. "Of course I'm not afraid of work. I'll have you know when my nails are filed down I can type ninety words a minute. You see the problem isn't working, it's getting the job in the first place." She looked down a moment, then scattered through the straw bag for a cigarette; fitting it into an ivory holder, she lit it with a tiny jeweled lighter and blew a long plume of smoke across her nails.

"I see what you mean," said Diane.

"It is going to be a problem," I agreed.

Miss Misty looked up with a smile and almost pleading eyes. "Do you think you could possibly make me look like a man?" She paused. "In, say, three days?"

I spent the summer once working on the docks in San Diego, and for a month in Gary, Indiana, I was employed building brick blast furnaces for iron smelting in temperatures over a hundred and five. A friend of mine worked his way through college by cleaning the monkey cages at the Bronx Zoo, but I can't think of any occupation that, from sheer unrewarding fatigue, I would not accept sooner than relive those three days following the letter from Miss Misty's father.

The project was later summarized by Diane as taking the natural grace of a swan or flamingo and attempting to make it act like, say, a Dalmatian.

The problem, as with all mammoth problems, was where to begin. We decided to begin with how to walk. "That seems to be where you originally went astray. And probably where it all started," Diane commented.

"My dear, what's wrong with the way I walk?"

"Well," I attempted, "the only thing it has in common with a man's gait is that it gets you where you're going." She walked across the room for us.

"Now show me how you do it," she asked. One of the most difficult things in the world to do is walk across a room in your natural manner when someone is watching how you do it. Misty was the only one of us who could at first. "It's very easy," she explained, "pretend you're on a runway." We decided the image would lead nowhere but disaster. When we got the rotation of her hips controlled, it required her to lift her feet like a cat crossing snow. With each step her head turned to the side and then back front as automatic as a swimming stroke. When she tried dragging her feet the hips came back into swing. Our estimate was, had the walking done that first afternoon been applied to a straight course, Miss Misty could have traveled from Chicago to San Francisco. Trailing havoc, of course, in her wake. She could not relax her arms but kept them extended, as above a flowing skirt or displaying a chiffon stole. When we had her pull her arms in she doubled them over her breast. When we dropped them at her sides her shoulders pivoted in counterpoint to her step, and caused her to wrinkle up her nose as if she were going to say: "You're cute!"

I've always stated with pride once I started something I never finished until the thing was done. It was long after midnight before Miss Misty walked like a man. It was a kind of vivid characterization of a man, but it would do. It would do, but we were all much too tired to celebrate, and we were only beginning to realize how far we had to go. Miss Misty said, "My dears, could we please rest for a while before we start on anything else?" walked (like a man, nearly) to the sofa, sat down, arched her foot, crossed her legs, sighed and reached for a cigarette.

"Well, that might as well be next," Diane said weakly.

"What?"

"The way you hold your cigarette."

"Is it really ghastly?"

"It really is." We tried several times, but the thing done wrong was some subtle gesture we never quite captured and we ended by asking her not to smoke during her job interview. When Miss Misty bent at the waist to sit, she bent at the knee to cross her legs; either kicking her leg high out in front of her and crossing it over her other knee, or doubling both legs up into the chair.

"Can't you just sit down and spread your legs apart?" She couldn't.

"I've always been so damn proud of my posture I just can't seem to slouch."

"It isn't slouching exactly, Misty, it's a kind of relaxing." When she sat down relaxed, it cause her to arch her neck, throw back her head and open her mouth. Either that or collapse like a rag doll.

"My dear, I'm very high strung. I've always been very nervous; I've never relaxed a moment in my life."

"Well, you're going to have to," said Diane. "Butch men seem to have nothing to be nervous about." Had Miss Misty entered old Mrs. Judith Loftus's house dressed like a girl that night instead of Huck Finn, the disguise would have worn beautifully. She would probably have suspected her disguised visitor to be a queen. And she'd have been right in assuming it.

We decided to put her in the right mood for her change, we must call her by her proper name instead of Miss Misty.

"Must I tell you? Couldn't you just call me buddy?"

"Misty, you may be walking pretty good, but it's more than I could possibly muster to call you buddy," said Diane.

"I suppose. Well, my dear, my real name is Oliver. You must promise never to tell a living soul."

"That's not so bad. Oliver is a perfectly good name," I said encouragingly.

"Oliver Dillard," breathed Miss Misty, sadly.

"But that's perfect," Diane said.

"I'm afraid my parents were terribly unimaginative and unromantic."

"Oliver Dillard is a perfectly good name," I said.

"I don't suppose you could call me Ollie?"

"Certainly not, we'd be right back where we were."

On the following day, after warning Oliver that he must drop the *my dears* and the *darlings* from his vocabulary, we decided to concentrate on his appearance. Diane had left early that morning to purchase the proper dyes to get his hair back to something like a natural color. Preferably his natural color, but almost any would do.

"Oh, you don't mean it," he announced when he saw the bottle. "I'll have you to know I spent seven-fifty last Wednesday for a touchup. That damn little queen at Carl's charges me a fortune every other week." When Diane insisted it was of the utmost importance, he relented. "But I'll have you know, my dears, that that damn stuff stings like fire."

"Stop saying 'my dears,'" said Diane.

"Well, I'm trying to but my—I—dea—goddamnit, it's half my vocabulary. Try cutting your vocabulary in half and see if you can express yourself." While he sat with a pile of chocolate suds on his head, he practiced speaking without gestures, which rendered him without anything to say. When he spoke, his hand came up to whiff the words on their way or snap a thought aside. Nearly every sentence found his hands higher than his shoulders, in some pontiff blessing. Diane commented that if he sat like that on the beach he'd get his palms sunburned. "But isn't it natural to gesture reasonably in conversation?" he asked, throwing both hands over his head and getting the brown suds on his sleeves. "Now look what I've done; I've got it all over me. Isn't it enough that it smarts like hell and smells like formaldehyde? My dears—oh,

I'm sorry—damn. Do you think it's flammable? Would you hand me a cigarette?" We decided the best practice would be for him to sit on his hands and try as best he could to keep them from going to sleep.

When his hair was rinsed and dried and combed as neatly as we could—for it was no easy chore; his hair had been teased so high it fluffed up and resisted any parts for masculine style with a mind of its own—Oliver stared into Diane's hand mirror and proclaimed: "Mouse! I knew it. It looks exactly like it had never been touched. Though I suppose that's what we're driving at, isn't it?"

"Of course it is, Oliver, and once we get your hair to lay down you're not going to look bad at all. What do you intend to do with your fingernails?"

"No, I really must insist that I keep my fingernails. I used to bite them to the quick and it's taken me years to shape them properly."

"Come on," Diane said, "no boy has nails like that."

"Couldn't I just look a bit eccentric?"

Diane said, "Don't forget you're only doing this so you can work during the summer and prove to your father you can straighten out. After you're enrolled in school I suppose you could be eccentric enough to let your nails grow out, but not for the employment agency." Logic won, but painfully, and we agreed to let him keep his nails until the following morning when he had to leave for the interview.

Miss Misty's proudest achievement was her artistry and cosmetics. To keep her nose from shining she would whip a pocket compact into action and give the shiny offender a quick and professional dusting. This she managed to do most usually at a counter in a coffee shop as the waitress came for her order, or just before dashing to the men's room. She had cooperated with painful dedication, if complaint, to all our demands and had tried most ardently to please us. But when Diane told Oliver quite casually that he would have to wash off his makeup, he stared at us with probably the same expression a flamingo would have assumed on hearing he was expected to paint on Dalmatian spots. "You can't be serious," he said finally.

"Well, of course she's serious, Oliver. You said you wanted to look like a man."

"Well, yes, but I never dreamed for a minute that I couldn't fix my face."

"Well, you don't suppose men wear makeup, do you?"

"But I couldn't go out into the street like that. I simply can't face the lights, darlings. It's very important to one's sense of well being." With utmost reluctance he went into the bathroom to wash his face. Much later he opened the door and stood against the wall beside the door. He looked like someone dead. Dead and without eyes.

"I tried to tell you it's just no good," he said.

"That's ridiculous," Diane said. I was speechless. "You look great." On closer inspection we discovered he had no eyebrows at all.

"I shaved them off. They were quite in the wrong place anyway."

"Never mind, maybe Diane can draw them on to look real. You have anything to wear? A suit?"

At this he cheered some. "Oh, yes! I have a divine suit. I only got it last month. It's the newest thing."

"I'm sure," Diane said mournfully. The suit was brought and rejected. It was a pale-green linen without lapel of any kind, five slanted pockets on the front of the jacket and at least a dozen velvet buttons down the front. We shaped him up as nearly as we could in my navy blue suit.

The following morning we were both quite proud. Oliver had cut his nails reasonably shorter and voluntarily removed his jewelry. He had practiced taking the Bette Davis inflection from his voice and almost succeeded. He was only short on nerve as we all trod out into the sun, and insisted that I accompany him to the employment agency. I agreed readily enough. He looked great. Even he sensed it and couldn't suppress a wink when one of his own "young things" looked up at us without recognizing Miss Misty.

The subway ride was a triumph. He stubbed his toe at the door just for effect and seemed to be enjoying himself; but as we neared the agency he became more nervous.

"Really, darling, I'll remember everything, but I do think I should smoke. It looks so mannish to smoke and I'm frightfully nervous."

"Just don't think about it, Oliver. Worry about what you're going to say."

We entered the agency and Oliver filled out the employment card. While we were waiting he opened a copy of *Field & Stream* just for the hell of it and winked at me.

I believe I had a premonition that we had failed. And thought vaguely that perhaps Miss Misty wouldn't be too sad, not going to Northwestern.

The interviewer sat directly across from me, and I could see into his office. He sat in the hot office occasionally mopping his perspiring brow delicately with a lavender handkerchief. He sat at his desk, legs crossed, speaking vaguely to the ceiling and flourishing his handkerchief softly. When his applicant had left, he stood up and walked around the desk and into the outer room. "Mr. Dillard," he said vacantly and turned back to his room without seeing who responded. Miss Misty walked to the door, stomped almost, like a lumberjack, and stood before the interviewer. The man looked up, sucked in his cheeks as he read Miss Misty's application. Finally he purred in a sweetly sarcastic tone, gazing up again. "And what do you do?" He tossed Miss Misty's application onto his desk.

    A change came over my protégé as if some electric button had been touched. Miss Misty raised one shoulder and dropped the other, one knee bent and the opposite hip swayed out. She stared down onto the interviewer as a queen examining the newest and lowest of her entourage. In her own way, I suppose, she triumphed after all. Her voice was acid: "You name it, sweetie, and I can do it!" she said.

The Beautiful Children

My grandmother takes a good deal of pride in keeping up a fairly lively correspondence with each of her nine grandchildren. At least once, more often twice, a month her letter, penned in a labored steady hand, chronicles the local scene. Old Mrs. Goldie Winrod, I've learned, is fading fast. She has been in the hospital for seven weeks; the congregation prays for her each Sunday. The First Baptist Church downtown has a new pastor. Grandmother hasn't been there for six years but still she keeps abreast of its functions (The congregation that prays for Miss Winrod is the colored Baptist Church across the street). Alma King has begun work on her master's degree; she was on television last week, participating in the College Quiz Bowl. Most of her family, the ones still at home, gathered at grandmother's house to see the program. She seldom watches the television set Uncle Lewis gave her last Christmas but her neighbors often come in for favorite programs. The pear tree behind the house promises to outdo itself, barring a late frost; the Indian Cling at the southwest corner of the kitchen, barren for the last few years, has decided to produce again this season. I remember it as the darkest red and most unusually delicious peach I've eaten; I have never seen another like it anyplace.

These letters remain my only association with the hometown or what I call my hometown, in fact I only lived there during summer vacations from school. The town I recall from years ago and though I've been back (hardly recognizing anything) I envisage it as it was; as grandmother somehow still sees it and relates it to me. Of course Old Town, the area where she lives is much unchanged. In summer stray trucks jolt along rocky, holey Poplar Street, lifting a pale-yellow, screen-like pollen that sometimes is thinly visible half an hour later. People walk at the edge of the road or along wandering hard-packed lanes.

There were not many white families in the neighborhood when I stayed my summer vacations there; I suppose there are even fewer now. From the front yard you can see the Johnson's house two blocks west at the far edge of town. Beyond there the road gives over to open field and pasture. There is a couple named Caffey who keep to themselves. Old Man Caffey works, or did, as I remember, at the cheese plant in town. The Winrods are a block to the east. Grandmother's house is one of the oldest in the county; square-nailed and strong, its chimney is built of brick from a Southern fort that once stood on the property and apparently fell down of its own accord during a rather crucial siege in 1862; her east doorstep is a millstone from the Williamson Granary that preceded the fort a few decades.

The remainder of the community is principally colored. It is a beautiful and mellow neighborhood. The houses, mostly tall and straight, are of oak gone white with age and hard as flint; gardens of vegetable and melon are at their sides and back. Sweet pea and morning glory devour fences everywhere and encroach on roads; everywhere is open range for fat orange hens and blue-black prinking roosters.

When I was very young the tribe that used to congregate in grandmother's yard was a strange one: Maxie and Patsy Johnson, twins my age; Ewell Atkinson, the colored preacher's son and his younger sister Catherine. Dozens of others visited from time to time but we were the ones who owned the yard and inhabited its enormous oak tree fortresses. One of the four was always there, especially Patsy, who was my girlfriend at the time. We used to walk into town for the Saturday afternoon movies at the Lyric Theater, which were a dime and composed of twelve cartoons; but we walked in an honest terror there and back, for to get to town we had to pass the Kings.

The King family was the most frightening element of the neighborhood. At least to us. Their green tarpaper house crouched on concrete blocks like fat uneven stilts. The yard was worn bare and scattered with junk machinery gone the rusted tin of the house's roof. When a chick was missing, the Kings had stolen it. When a dog or pet died, even canaries, the Kings had surely poisoned it; we were certain. Sometimes the tales we whispered about them were so terrifying they caused us to avoid the Saturday movies for two weeks running. We walked the mile to town in apprehension of fifty feet that stretched endlessly before their house. Always there seemed to be an army of them around the house; I never knew the yard to be deserted. They stood totally still as we passed, moving only their eyes to follow us.

Looking back now I have no idea what we imagined was frightening about them. They were, if they had been scrubbed, beautiful children. There were twelve or thirteen of them, speculations varied. Every one looked like the other; more than any family I've seen. They all had saucer blue eyes, pure white or tow-yellow hair; on the girls it fell straight to their shoulders, the boys brushed it from their eyes and behind their ears. I never remember seeing a fresh haircut among them. They dressed in sadly plain and faded hand-me-downs of shapeless print and flour sack shirts; the boys wore washed-out, almost white jeans.

On occasion we saw their mother; sometimes the grandmother, stirring a large black-iron vessel over an open fire in the backyard; rendering lard for making lye soap that we swore was never used. The grandmother glancing up through the steam of her caldron with a gaping, toothless grin appeared for all the world a witch. We bolted into a wild and terrified run on sight of her.

Probably it was the gregariousness of the King clan that alarmed us most. They never traveled alone; they came upon us at times in twos or threes, walking barefoot from the store, on their way to town or the cannery. We gave them single-file room and they sneered as they passed. The girls as well as boys could swear a vicious oath that I don't remember today and didn't understand at the time. I remember though it sounded fully as self-confident as Uncle Lewis, who had been a sailor. I suppose the King children knew we were frightened of them but I only remember once coming into direct contact. Only two days earlier Patsy had undergone the childhood ordeal of a smallpox shot: her left arm was swollen and irritated, she wore a Band-Aid across it. As we walked toward town suddenly there were three of them sauntering back along the path. Lead by Lela, the eldest, probably fourteen or fifteen and beginning to look like an awkward young woman; much too tall, she towered over us. We saw them approach and would have given them full run of the path but along that stretch it parallels a wide gully on one side, too wide to jump across, and on the other a tall thorny hedge, and allowed us no detour short of retreat. We crowded into the hedge to let them pass by but they stopped, drawing a semicircle around us. Patsy bent closer into the hedge and looked up, *way* up to Lela King's scowl: "You let us pass, now." She demanded unevenly to the giant.

"What do you want?" I echoed with as much manly bravery as I could muster.

"Hit 'em!" encouraged the second King girl to Lela. With Lela was a girl ranking somewhere in the middle of the litter and Ezekiel, a silent boy our age who stood between his two sisters looking very brave. I never knew the second girl's name but she was probably the most hateful of all the Kings. She was several years older than we were and heads taller. She stood looking us over and announced again: "Hit her on her sore arm!" She was an impressionable little brat but huddled in the hedge Patsy and I must have made a pathetically defenseless picture for Lela didn't advance.

"You been tellin' dirt on us?" Lela demanded.

"No!" I shook my head.

Patsy stuck out her chin: "My ma says your pa's the biggest drunk in Laclede County and oughta be taken out and hanged." I had a horrible sick feeling in my stomach that Patsy didn't understand our situation but the trio seemed not offended. I believe Lela even looked pleased.

"You been tellin' dirt on Ezekiel!" The middle girl accused.

"I ain't either," Patsy answered. "I said he's stupid cause he flunked my grade in school. I never told no dirt on him!" Then she added: "My ma says he's got no ambition." I fully wished now that Mrs. Johnson had never expressed an opinion of the King family.

The second girl sneered arrogantly. "You tell your ma he got himself a job down at Melton's grocery last week. He's got more ambition than your no-count brother."

"Work four-hours-a-day; thirty-five-cents-an-hour," Ezekiel shot in. I tried to look impressed but Patsy remembered something:

"My brother ain't either no-count." She said, "Now you let us pass."

"You get out of our way now," I pleaded.

"You been tellin' tales on me an' Billy!" Lela insisted. Billy was the other of the two oldest Kings, probably not a year younger than Lela and a hulking fellow I was certain we didn't want to tangle with. The full import of Lela's accusation escaped us, but looking back it opens areas of speculation that would never have occurred to me at that age. Billy often helped around the house, splitting stove wood and working for grandmother in the yard. "My grandma says Billy is a real fine worker. She says he's a good boy," I said, but the Kings were unimpressed. Lela fixed me with a vicious stare.

"Billy's going into the navy next year, to fight like the devil at the Japs."

This caused Ezekiel to chirp in excitedly: "So am I!"

To our amazement, Lela suddenly reached out with her long arm and boxed her younger brother across the ears. One quick sudden movement. "You shut up," she said. "Now let them pass."

The other two moved aside a few inches and squinted with malice as we squeezed between them. "You should of hit her on her sore arm," the second girl said to her sister; we hurried our step. She yelled to our backs: "You better never tell no lie on no Kings!"

We walked several blocks in silence before I looked at Patsy. "You alright?"

"They was gonna hurt my vaccination," she whimpered.

"No they weren't, they just wanted to scare you. They wouldn't have hurt you really."

"They would, too. They're mean." We didn't speak of the Kings again that day but I remember in the afternoon we walked a mile through the less familiar area of town to avoid passing their house on the way back.

That was the only time we were confronted with any of the Kings directly and nothing really became of it. Also, Mrs. Johnson's claim of Ezekiel's shiftlessness was untrue. Maxie was the same age and he wasn't working at Melton's store. I don't know how to account for it, their father set them no example, but ambition was the one thing the King children had. When Lela was twelve she had a summer job with the local tomato cannery. Most of the children, one by one, as they were eleven or twelve, found work somewhere in town; in winters they split and sold stove wood; they were known as Good Cheap Labor. In December they entered the woods to poach cedar and spruce trees that they sold outside Hawkins Fountain and Melton Grocery. They had a business and bargain sense that amazed their clientele, amazed the heads of school even more.

Regularly each year a new King would matriculate in the first grade; if they skipped a year the following September registration received twins. They never dressed especially for school. It would have been wasted to present a good impression, a King never lasted more than a month in the first grade. Patsy once told me of Ezekiel. He sat quite still, rather sprawled, never once opening his mouth. He stared uncomprehendingly at Mrs. Barnett as she cooed over the alphabet and printed large white letters across the blackboard. During discussion periods Ezekiel mutely ignored the others' enthusiasm. When finally after several weeks the teacher called his name (they had been reading the letters across the board from "A" to "Z"), "Ezekiel King," she smiled sweetly.

Nothing. He stared at her as blankly as he had every day. "Would you read the alphabet for us, Ezekiel?"

"Ma'am?"

Mrs. Barnett glanced at her registration book and back to the boy: "You are Ezekiel King aren't you, dear? Would you like to read the alphabet as all the others have?" He showed no reaction; Mrs. Barnett smiled nervously. "If you'd rather, we could go on to the next student and come back after you've heard it a few more times," she suggested.

After a moment of silence Ezekiel pushed back his chair with a soft murmur against the floor and drew a long breath. "I'm about through," he said and walked out of the room. That was the last the school saw of him. They had learned when a King was about through with school the devil couldn't get him back again.

The Kings weren't ashamed of their stupidity but they didn't take a stubborn pride in it as some do. A King don't have much of a head for book readin' (they would tell you) but we've got a good mind for work. In truth most of the work they did required no mind at all, but it did call for diligence and they seemed not short on that.

As a crew, with even the grandmother, they descended on the woods during blackberry season and stripped it clean. They seemed to sense when the best day for harvest had come, and when it would no longer be profitable to go back. If someone in town wanted blackberries they carried a bucket or basket to the Kings' house and purchased them. I've heard the sight was something to see: the floor was covered with receptacles of every size. Buckets and tubs, bushels, crocks, and glass jars heaped brimful were spread over the entire floor. The house was given over to them so completely we often wondered where the Kings slept during blackberry season.

I say that the Kings were not ashamed of their inability to cope with education but perhaps that is not entirely true, for they were intensely proud of Alma. Alma was the youngest of the Kings; the last of the long-blond-hair and saucer-eyed line to come from the tarpaper house. Alma amazed the school fathers even more than previous Kings with whom they had come into brief contact. On the second day of school, the story is well known through town, Mrs. Barnett read the alphabet, pointing out each letter to the fascination of the first grade audience, and turned to make her annual enquiry: "Would anyone care to recite that for us?" The question received the usual nervous titter that moved through the room. Alma raised her hand and repeated each letter as Mrs. Barnett pointed it out from "A" to "Z" clearly. Mrs. Barnett checked her register, as was her habit, and smiled. "You're Alma King. Someone has taught you the alphabet already, haven't they, dear?"

"No, ma'am," Alma said almost apologetically. "Does it spell anything, ma'am?"

After that it became usual for Alma to be at the head of her class. She was promoted from the first to the third grade at the end of the year and the following year was passed to the fifth. She became at the rather amazing age of fourteen by far the youngest graduate in the high school's history. When the principal refused to graduate her at thirteen after she had completed all the tests satisfactorily he received the indignation of half the town and the full brunt of the King family's wrath.

Alma was presented with a scholarship from each of the three colleges in the area but she refused them. That summer she worked in the canning factory and the following September shipped off to a university in the east. I don't think it's important which one, but it was one of the best. She did not work her way through school; her family worked for her. Each week on Friday one of the Kings scrubbed up, dressed as fresh as possible and carried forty dollars to the bank where Mr. Brazeale made out a money order and mailed it to Alma.

She did not come back during the summer but continued school; after three years received her degree with honors in physics, mathematics, and biology; winning four prizes in the three fields. She began her master's in physics only a few weeks ago, earning her way now as she is employed in research.

She won the College Quiz Bowl for her school almost single-handedly. My grandmother writes that though the Kings had never visited her before, even the old lady, Alma's grandmother, asked to watch the program. The four children that are still at home were there too, and the mother and mother's sister who recently moved in. Mrs. King sat very proudly through the program; the four brothers and sisters made an enthusiastic cheering section in Grandmother's living room. The family is very excited about Alma's career and they every one plan to be there when she receives her master's degree.

But during the program on television it was the grandmother who seemed most proud. She kept a handkerchief twisted in her shaky hand, blotting at her cheeks. Probably she did not understand either the questions or the answers, but she listened intently to Alma's calm voice reciting. "Just listen to her," the old woman said softly, crying every time Alma answered a question. She would look at my grandmother, catching her breath and in a hoarse proud voice whisper: "Oh, Lord, just listen to her go."

The Polar Bear

From the roof of the building Joel could survey the whole kingdom of what was now his neighborhood. It was noisier, busier and seemed both exciting and frightening. From the roof, which was high-guarded by an ancient bronze ornamentation, he could launch paper airplane-things that Loren had learned to make in school (not in class, for they had been forbidden to litter the schoolground with them, but from another student who had been expelled for a week having been found folding one at his desk made from the girl across the aisle's arithmetic paper) and follow them whirl out over 76th Street or drift east toward Central Park.

Central Park: Joel gazed for hours across the building tops to the green strip edge of the park. Loren was to have taken him there during the summer vacation, but Loren had failed geometry and English in the eighth grade and spent his days at summer school, evenings playing with boys his own age. Joel had been forbidden to go alone; he couldn't see Emile. He didn't enjoy playing on the streets and screaming sidewalks.

When last summer they had lived across the street from the park, hot days were spent there wandering its circuitous lanes or climbing through crossing limbs of trees. "The scalloped leaves are oak; the pie-shaped on the long limbs are gingko. Elm trees are the ones that are dying." Emile had said that.

More than anything else Joel missed Emile, though he walked slowly, limping slightly, and Joel sometimes grew impatient, for Emile wasn't old; not ancient as a grandfather would be but more like a father, only Emile had dislocated his hip falling out of a boxcar in West Virginia. "Filthy state, full of dirty bums, poor people and coal mines. Never set foot there soon as I could walk again. Don't you either, hear?" More than anything else Joel missed Emile.

Though when he walked he swung his leg in a slight arch and tired more easily than a man should, still he stood tall and erect, lean and dark (always just barely in need of a shave), always with a sunny white laugh. Emile had said that he would be back in July and Joel crossed the last days of June off the calendar in his bedroom, looking up at it, counting every evening, his mind walking over the numbers across the wall until it came upon sleep. And then very often Joel walked still, only in bright sun with his friend; from north to south or skipping the short way in three giant steps, and across. More often than not they went to the zoo.

Joel first met Emile at the zoo; he had arrived too late to watch the sea lions being fed and had wandered past the bear cages waiting some time for one to appear from their concrete dens but they wouldn't oblige. Not to waste the day entirely, he wandered to the center of the zoo toward the spider monkey cage. A man was feeding the monkeys peanuts and without looking at Joel offered him one. "Don't give it to them, eat it yourself," the man said.

"I thought they were for the monkeys."

"Monkeys and boys are about the same thing, only they aren't much interested in eating right now. I think they don't want to spoil their appetite." The man turned and looked at Joel, frowning: "Besides, you look a little like a spider monkey yourself."

"I'm skinny," Joel said.

"Yes, you are, but that isn't bad, you're young yet. What I really wanted with the monkey was to get their ideas on evolution, but they weren't much interested in that either." Joel didn't understand. The man twisted the top of the peanut sack and handed it to the boy: "Here, maybe they'll do better for you," he said and started to wander off. Something, Joel couldn't have imagined what, made him follow the man.

"Where are you going now, mister?"

The man turned around and looked at him. "I just remembered that monkeys like cigarettes and it reminded me that I do too, and I don't have any," Emile said.

"Are you going to get some?"

The man grinned. "Well, let's say that I'm going to try to find one."

"Oh," Joel replied matter-of-factly. "Where do you live?"

The man took a penknife from his pocket and a small pointed stick from the other and began to carve the stick down to nothing. "I don't know why I should answer your questions or why you should ask them, but I live wherever I want to or wherever I am." He was walking out across the park now, Joel following half a step behind.

"Are you a bum?"

"Yes."

"Oh." Joel said again. "Do you like it?"

Then Emile had said something very strange. He had half turned and looked at the boy and said: "Look, monkey, we're going to have to understand one thing: I won't answer a question if I don't want to, and you don't have to answer me if you don't feel like it. O.K., partner?" So Joel had tried to remember not to ask questions.

Instead they had sat down in the brilliant sun, out on the grass. The man took from his shirt pocket a dirty Bull Durham tobacco sack and spread the top, looked in the empty sack and dropped it on the grass. "What I would really like to do," he said, "is to go all over the park and pick up cigarette butts, the long ones; and make the tobacco into pipe stuffing, but I think I'm too tired just now; maybe not too tired but too lazy. One thing you should try to avoid if you can is getting fond of tobacco; people, some people, let that one affection control their whole lives, did you know that?" Joel said he thought that didn't make sense. "It doesn't make sense but people do it. Like right now I'd like more than anything else to have a cigarette, but I think I might go to sleep and forget about it instead." He stretched out on his back and closed his eyes.

"Do you really do that?"

"Pick up cigarettes? Sure."

"Isn't it dirty?"

"Well, for a while I only picked up filter cigarettes," the man said, one eye lazily looking at the boy, "but the tobacco's coarser in them. Poorer quality, and then I got a couple of menthol ones so I switched to just anything except menthol."

"It sounds dirty."

"It's not dirty if you can't afford to buy them." Emile folded his hands under the back of his head. "Smoking is a dirty habit anyway."

"That's what mother says."

"Does she smoke?"

"Sure. Everybody I know does." Joel stretched out on the grass beside the man. "Can you feel the sun? You can feel it go right through you. It's going to be a hot summer, that's what Loren says anyway. Loren's my brother; he smokes—sometimes." Joel turned his head to look at the man.

"You have a brother?" Emile murmured without opening his eyes.

"It isn't like having much. He's four years older than I am and he's never home. I have a brother and a mother, but mother works." Joel started to ask if the man had relations, then hesitated.

"Why don't you lay still now and let me go to sleep in your hot sun, O.K., monkey? It's either that or getting up to find a cigarette and sleeping is easier, O.K.?"

"My name is Joel," the boy corrected softly.

"O.K., monkey," the man mumbled. "Now soft, alright?"

Joel was quiet for a moment. "What's yours?" he whispered.

"Emile. Now are you going to be still or do I have to get up and look for a cigarette?"

"I'll be still, I'm sleepy, too." Joel turned his head straight again and closed his eyes. Sunlight was red-orange under his lids. He shaded them with his hand. The light changed to green, and he tried to concentrate on sleep, but the sounds of the park crowded in on him. "Emile?" he whispered very softly but there was no answer. He lay still for a moment longer then sat erect. Emile slept while Joel unfolded a newspaper on the grass, weighted its corners down with stones. Then he walked back to the path and disappeared around the corner.

For over an hour Joel collected cigarette butts from the sidewalks and put them in a paper sack. He almost expected every matronly woman he saw to reprimand him, but no one seemed to mind or even notice. When he had picked up a great number he spread them out on the newspaper, tore off the burnt end and emptied the remaining tobacco into Emile's Bull Durham pouch. The string of the pouch he looped over Emile's thumb very loosely and drew it tight. Then he went home.

Given any ordinary circumstances that afternoon Joel would have been alive with conversation, at least for Loren, about the bum named Emile that he had met in the park and about gathering cigarettes off the streets. But that was the afternoon, as well, that Loren had gone to the ballpark for the first time. Loren and seven boys his age had held tickets for over a week in anticipation of the afternoon; he burst home rapturously explosive, carefully explaining, reexamining every play. Yogi Berra had hit a home run over the left field fence and that, in itself, declared the day an experience of a lifetime. In all, Loren's extraneous enthusiasm carried his younger brother away from his own experience. Enough to make Joel wish he were old and accepted into Loren's clique; enough that when finally Loren settled into an occasional exclamation, nodding his head sideways, of the general splendor of the afternoon, and asked Joel: "What did you do today?" Joel only looked up, lost in his brother's afternoon too much to remember his own. "What?" he asked.

"Where did you go today? Did you go over to the park again?"

"Oh, I went—" Joel began and thought of Emile. It wasn't like going to a ball game. Still Loren would be interested, would want to meet his friend; still—"to the park." He finished, "Nothing special."

Loren had taken his ball glove to the school lot that evening to meet the other boys and they played with vicious enthusiasm that night and for weeks every afternoon long into the evening.

The following day was Monday and it was evening before Joel found he had nothing to do. Already it was too dark for him to be allowed in the park, but in the evening he sat for some time looking out his window, down the building and across the street. Tuesday morning early, although Loren had been up and gone hours earlier, Joel walked across the street into the park. He wound through past the fantastically jeweled and calliopied carousel with its caricatured dancing animals. The galloping music turned in the air around him as he walked toward the zoo.

As he entered people seemed almost to be dancing, other children were running head on and around him. A mother physically dragged her squalling child from the area of a man who held a dozen captive balloons above his head. The park teemed with milling people, turning through lanes, crowding around the cougar and puma who returned their stares with bored tranquility. Joel had just entered the quadrangle of lilies and walkways around the sea lion pool when he saw his friend. "Emile!" he yelled across the square. The man saw him and waved as Joel ran up. "You stay at the zoo as much as I do."

"Hello again, monkey," Emile said, "you must live close by if your mother lets you come here all the time."

"I'm right across the street. You must live close by too . . ." Joel stopped as if in sudden discovery. "Emile! I bet you live here all the time, right in the park, don't you?"

"Not so loud," Emile whispered broadly. "You should know that everyone has to be out of the park by midnight."

"Everyone?"

"Everyone that the cops don't see. Or don't know," Emile winked.

"Do they let you stay?" Joel whispered. Then suddenly Joel grabbed the man's hand. "Come with me. I want to show you my friend."

"You have another friend who lives in the park?" Emile smiled and let the boy tug at his hand but wouldn't be dragged away.

"Not a person, my favorite animal. I almost feel like he belongs to me, guess what it is."

"O.K.," said Emile and the boy walked slowly across the court. "The lion," Emile said. "Every young boy's favorite animal is the lion."

"No, not the lion. Not a tiger either."

"Hum. Well, it wouldn't be a monkey."

"Was that a guess? It isn't a monkey."

"I give up," the man said.

"Don't give up so quick. I'll give you a clue: he's white."

"White all over," Emile repeated. "Then it couldn't be the raccoon and since we're headed for the bears' cages that only leaves me one guess doesn't it? That fellow there." Emile pointed to the polar bear's cage where the bear stood belly-deep in water, blinking out at his audience.

"Isn't he beautiful?" Joel looked to catch the man's reaction. "And he's smart, too. He's the biggest bear I've ever seen but he's the friendliest, too."

"He's friendly alright," Emile said.

"He smiles. Sometimes he almost laughs. I used to want to ride him," Joel admitted, "but I don't think so anymore; I don't think that he'd mind, though." Emile sat Joel on the iron pipe railing, took out his penknife and started whittling again. This time large x's across the stick.

"I've forgotten to thank you for the tobacco; I appreciated that."

Joel turned around on his perch to face Emile. "It took me hours to collect it."

"Well, see? The life of a bum ain't easy. Lazy as I was, though, I don't think I deserved to have someone wait on me. It was a surprise."

"Was it, Emile?" Joel glowed. "I had to wash my hands three times to get the smell off. I don't think I'll ever start smoking. Some people just let liking to smoke run their whole lives, Emile."

That had been the day when the man had begun to teach Joel to identify the trees and their names. "The one over there is a hard maple. If you watch in the fall that tree is going to be the reddest tree in the park."

"How do you know?"

"That's just its nature."

That had been the first day they ate hot dogs for lunch, sitting on a bench that later they went to every time they bought something from Amenz, the hot dog man. That had been the finest, freest day of Joel's life. But it was much like the others of that summer. During the weeks afterwards Joel became familiar with the park as he had never known anything before, and with Emile.

Emile knew everything. And almost everybody. He told Joel the names of most of the bums in the park, and introduced him one day to a policeman friend whose beat was the park. "Is he the one who lets you stay here at night?" Joel asked in a whisper.

"Now I wouldn't want to tell anything on a friend if he was," Emile grinned. "You don't betray a person's unlawful friendliness."

"He is!" Joel decided out loud, but his friend only continued to smile.

They sat one day watching a group of young Australians practice soccer on the grass. Emile knew the schedule for all the park regulars. When on Wednesdays and Fridays a tall colonel would come riding stiffly by on a rented horse, proud as a bronze statue, staring coldly ahead. He told Joel to the minute when the blond governess in white silk uniform and pug nose, leading a leashed pink poodle with one hand and a brat boy with the other, would appear around the bend of the fountain. "Now that's the type that will fool you when you start taking girls out. She won't order your most expensive thing on the menu, but it'll come high; she'll only have one drink and like as not she won't finish that. She'll probably not like the play you take her to see and she'll talk all during intermission about her brother-in-law's concession business in Atlantic City . . ."

"Come on, Emile," Joel interrupted, "you haven't done any of that, have you?"

"No." Emile considered for a moment. "But when a man's spent all his forty-odd years on the streets, in alleys and downtown, in the park and all over town; if a man spends his life like that, boxcar hopping and bumming the country and bumming the city, then he begins to get a feeling of what things are like. I know about that girl because I've seen her a million times. I've heard her voice, it's sharp like a crow; I've heard it arguing and chattering with another girl on their coffee break. Understand?"

"I guess."

Emile laughed. "Sure you do. Anyway that one, the nurse type with pug nose, will always make you take her home in a cab and she'll slam the door in your face."

"Always, Emile?"

"Mark my word. Now that one over there," Emile nodded to a trio of girls and nudged Joel softly in the ribs, "not the skinny one, God forbid, but the short one. That's the type. That one doesn't care where you eat because she's only going to want a hamburger and coffee (black) and she'll cry all the way through a movie and apologize all the way home. Then when you say goodnight, she's going to say there's not a drop of liquor in the apartment, but the refrigerator is full of cold fried chicken and if you want there's a half-bottle of sherry in the cupboard she uses to make meatballs or something. And when the sherry's gone she's going to turn down the covers and hand you a toothbrush she bought the afternoon before at Walgreen's."

Joel looked very skeptical. "Why don't you try it sometime, Emile?"

"Oh, I don't know. Number one, if I have to drink I'd rather have a straight whiskey, but I'd rather not drink at all. And number two, she'd do all of that for a man and not once know he was taking advantage of her." Emile stood up from the bench where they had been sitting. "And then I don't like sad movies, do you? Why don't we go for a walk; a long one. I want to show you Alice in Wonderland."

Alice in Wonderland, Hans Christian Andersen, the sailboat park surrounded by children, primped in crisp-edged clothing, with glowing faces, and Fifth Avenue. "Have you ever seen so many beautiful apartment buildings, Emile? Were they all once someone's mansions?"

"Not those. These were built as apartments; they're the grandest houses in the world, and they've got the world's best view of our park."

"Are all those men in uniform policemen or guards?"

"They're guards; doormen; you can bet your life they wouldn't let us in."

"I'll bet we could run right past them."

"Sure we could," Emile smiled. "I'll wait right here so I can catch you when you come sailing out."

The sailboat pool, Fifth Avenue, and the story of Cleopatra's Needle. These were all part of Emile's repertoire of descriptions, tales, and wisdom.

Joel had been coming to the park whenever he could meet his friend for nearly two months; still though it seemed much less: he had not spent every day there and once five days running he spent at home with a cold, resting, in theory, but actually spending much of the day staring out his window. So by mid-August when the heat sometimes blurred the air like a trembling sheet of cellophane, Joel could shinny up a tree and be completely lost in the arched foliage before Emile counted twenty seconds. "A thousand one, a thousand two, a thousand three . . ."

"That's too fast, Emile, those aren't seconds!"

"You're just getting slow, come on, it's good for your arms."

"Emile? Can you see me now?" Joel called from the top of a blotchy-barked cottonwood.

"No, but it's breaking my neck trying. Come on down, now. Slow, don't fall."

"There's one huge building across the street, it's about a block long," Joel called, beginning his descent.

"That's the museum, probably," Emile told him.

Already Joel was halfway down, testing limbs with his weight before stepping on them. "What kind of museum, Emile; pictures?"

"No, natural history; you know—bones of extinct animals and relics."

"The big ones?" Joel jumped to the ground and dusted off the knees of his pants. "The big ones, Emile? Our school class went there and saw that last year. All those animals died out years ago, did you know that?" He looked toward the direction of the museum. "There were all kinds of things like baskets and pots that Indians and things left behind."

"Something like that."

"Why do they do that do you suppose?"

"Do what, monkey?"

"Collect things that people made a long time ago and save them?"

Emile frowned down at the boy. "Well, I suppose that's the only way that we know how these people lived, Joel. We look at a pot, for instance, and say those people ground corn and ate bread like we do, and fetched water. We can tell something about how they got along hundreds of years ago."

Joel shivered slightly. "It's kind of creepy, isn't it?"

"Why's that?"

"You know, being gone and having your cooking things and arrowheads in a museum and studied by people."

Emile shrugged. "There is nothing so creepy about that. Some of the things that they left behind them are treasures today."

"You know what I mean," Joel insisted. "I mean do you think you'd want people to look at them?"

"I think I'd be proud if people thought that much about the things I've lived with and made. Don't you think you want to leave anything for people to see?"

"I guess if they wanted to it's different," the boy conceded and they were quiet for a moment.

"Nobody wants to just disappear without any trace of them," Emile said. "People scratch their initials and names in trees and walls and stones; the thing to remember is if you leave something after you, you want to make it so strong an army can't tear it apart. See? Tough and strong. Either that or don't leave anything behind at all."

"Oh, come on, Emile," Joel said, "nobody's going to put something you or me does into a museum."

"Well then, if it's not going to be kept by someone because it's strong, if you make things that are fragile, then you leave it with someone you love, someone who'll guard it for you. Maybe that's the next best thing. That's the best way to be remembered. Even like photography; understand?"

"No, Emile. But I'm trying to."

"Well, you just remember anyway and someday maybe it'll mean something to you." Emile drew a long breath and smiled at the very intent look on Joel's face. "Good lord, boy, I wish I was half as bright as you think I am, that's one thing I wish."

Toward the end of August one day, late in the afternoon, Joel asked his friend where he went during the winter. "I told you, a long time ago, remember? I live just wherever I am. Usually (of course, I can't stay in the park), I go somewhere in the south. Not too far, maybe Georgia or Florida, sometimes Arizona. I've been to all the states and that's something you want to do, but I know you will."

"Where do you like best?"

"Every summer I come back here," Emile said, "this is the only real city, you'll find that out, too. It's funny, people who live here leave in the summer and that's when I'm just getting here. But I guess they don't live in the park."

"Will you come back next summer?"

Emile was quiet for a moment. "I told you, monkey, I come here every summer."

"When do you leave, Emile?"

"It depends. God, you're full of questions today! Usually I go early, September, October; the one year I left late, November almost, was the summer I broke my hip in hell-hole West Virginia, but that was a long time ago. I was headed for Texas probably." They had been walking and Joel sat down on a rock beside the path now. "Emile," he said, "before long I'll have to go back to school."

"Do you like school?"

"That's not the point," Joel objected. "I will have to go back and mother says I won't be able to come running off to the park again, except maybe to ice skate."

"You'll be missing your polar bear?"

"They take it in in the winter. You aren't listening to me at all, Emile. Why don't you get a room somewhere and stay in New York this winter? You could. If you had a room you could stay here. You said you like New York better than Arizona or those other places anyway."

Emile laughed. "I said I like it better in the summertime, I didn't say anything about the winters here."

"Do you have to go away?"

"Yes, Joel." The boy was obstinately quiet for a few minutes. "Let's don't talk about it today," Emile said. "Nobody's leaving right away."

"I still think you could get an apartment."

"Tramps don't rent things, Joel. I couldn't get an apartment. I've only bought one thing in my life that was permanent and I'm still making payments on that—every week. And if my bum-buddies knew that I had that they'd laugh me outta the park. It takes a long time to get something paid for."

"What did you buy?"

Emile's answer was quiet: "Maybe I'll show you someday. I expect I will."

"What, Emile?"

"Now, damnit, monkey, stop asking questions or I'll have to invoke our agreement." Joel returned to his obstinate sulk and didn't even bother to ask Emile what "invoke" meant. The man reached into his pocket and got out a knife. He took a small white object from the other pocket. "I made you something last night so maybe you won't miss your polar bear so much this winter," he said. "Of course, I don't claim to be much of an artist, and your bear isn't much of a model, but I carved him for you out of soap. " He set the figure of the noble white soap polar bear beside Joel. Immediately the boy's mood changed.

"Emile! He's beautiful. Did you really carve it yourself?" Joel took the figure up in his hands. "It's exactly like him, Emile."

"Thank God for your imagination," Emile laughed. "It looks like a whole new animal to me. I used to carve all the time, that's the only occupation I've had," he laughed. "But soap is softer than wood and I couldn't think of anything else that was white."

"Can I really have him?"

"You don't think I want to carry a bar of soap around with me, do you? What would all my friends say?"

"Could you teach me how to make one?"

"You better find yourself a better teacher than me, son."

Joel turned the bar over in his hands. "It's really beautiful, Emile, if it's really for me, I'll keep it always."

"I can't think of anyone else would want a polar bear. But don't go forgetting and wash your face with him, alright?" Joel immediately swore that he wouldn't dream of that. He even added that he might decide to become a bum someday himself and never wash his face at all. "Well, put it in your pocket now and I'll bet anything your mother will be sore because you stayed out so late today."

It was late but on the way home Joel stopped to take the carving out of his shirt pocket and look at it, carefully turning it in his hands. When he reached home he wrapped the bear in tissue paper and put it in a drawer, unwrapped it again to look at it and finally set it on top of the dresser.

Days seemed, after that, to spin by with ever increasing speed. Joel's school was starting in two weeks, then one. "I guess maybe if you can, I'd like for you to come over to the park early tomorrow. I want to show you something," Emile said.

"What, Emile? We've seen everything."

And he looked as though he was going to laugh but his face reflected something else. "You mustn't ever think that you've seen it all, Joel."

"There you go again, you're always telling people things. I think you should've been a schoolteacher or something."

"You think so, monkey? I don't think I would have been a good teacher at all. For one thing, in general I don't—you won't tell anyone, will you? . . ."

"I know what you're going to say, I'll bet. Everyone says it," the boy interrupted. "You don't like kids. Nobody does."

"Teachers do, they have to."

"They may have to, but they don't," Joel said.

"Anyway, that's what I was going to say," Emile smiled. "Don't think I haven't thought about you. I don't know why we became such pals, except, maybe you look a little like a monkey and a little lonely. I think I decided you came to the park just to be around people. People and the animals."

"That's the only reason anyone comes here," Joel said and Emile didn't correct him. "Anyway are you going to walk back across the park with me, Emile? You never walk anymore, you just lay around like some old bum!"

Emile laughed. "You go on, monkey, and get home early for a change. Will I see you early in the morning?"

"What do you want to show me?"

"I don't know. You must try to be early, O.K.?"

"O.K." Joel ran down the broad path and turned just before it bent out of sight to wave.

The following morning was humid and intensely hot. All the air seemed to be hovering above breath's reach; people on the streets struggled visibly to gasp it like panting birds. Joel was surprised to see Emile sitting on a bench across from his house. He waved to his friend and crossed the street. "How did you know where I live?"

"I've seen you go in once or twice."

"Have you? I didn't know it. We live on the ninth floor and I had to run all the way down this morning; the elevator isn't working."

"Did you have to run?"

Joel considered this only a moment. "I guess not, only have you ever tried walking downstairs? I always run. Gosh, Emile, you look almost clean, you even combed your hair." He started to turn into the park, but Emile steered him down the sidewalk.

"I should look clean, it took me an hour to shave; even a bum has to shave sometime. And I wouldn't want you to be too ashamed of me; we won't be in the park today."

"I wouldn't be ashamed, Emile. Where are we going?"

"Well, first off, we're going to take a subway. Do you like the subway?"

"Sure. It's noisy, but it's fun. It's going to be hot down there today, I'll bet." They turned toward the Seventy-second Street station on Broadway.

"That's something I haven't been able to understand. The subways in Chicago are cool all year around; you'd think they were air-conditioned."

"How far is Chicago from here?" Joel asked.

"About eight hundred miles. We're not going that far." Emile paid their fare with six nickels. As they walked down the stairs Emile bent his head close to the boy's to be heard over the roar of a departing train: "Then from here we transfer at Seventh Avenue and head out towards Queens. Have you ever been to Queens?"

Joel shook his head and mouthed the word "No" over the sound.

Emile waited until the noise of the train had subsided. "It's nice. It's almost even quiet there."

The long white-tiled tunnel to Queens was indeed hot. The train shook violently, rocked as if in a vicious sea. Joel alternately sat down and stood holding onto the side of a seat to get the full effect of the tossing. For the most part Emile sat looking straight ahead or watched the slick white walls pass the window. At Roosevelt when the train stopped momentarily Joel took advantage of the relative quiet to ask how much farther.

"Are you getting tired, Joel?"

"It sure does throw you around, doesn't it?" Joel wondered for a moment what his mother would say if she knew where he was. It felt very different leaving the park with Emile. Somehow that had been their world and he had never seen his friend in any other surrounding. To dam up the spring in the park, or follow ground signals from high in a tree was one thing; or even imagining Emile alone riding a straw-floored boxcar high over the Grand Canyon. But being crowded into a train like this with dozens of people sitting all around didn't seem to suit Emile. Despite the adventure Joel felt, he thought Emile looked captive and almost frightened, as an animal might before it becomes used to its cage.

When they left the train and stood stretching on the sidewalks again, Joel became instantly excited; although the heat outside was exactly the intensity and closeness as below. Emile's fresh shirt was soaked through. But to Joel this was totally new; the houses were like those of a small New England town, or as he thought it might be. "Are we still in New York?" he couldn't help asking.

"It's a part of New York. I told you it was quieter out here. There are parts around here that's all industry, but here it's nice." Emile pointed across the street and began to lead the way. "We want to walk down that street over there."

"Have you ever been out here before?" Joel asked.

"Quite a few times, monkey. Remember the day you picked up the cigarettes? I came out here that afternoon. But I started a couple of years ago."

"How come you never took me with you before?" Joel asked but Emile didn't hear him.

For the first time Joel became aware that people on the sidewalks were looking at them. A woman wheeling a baby carriage pulled the perambulator to the curb and watched them pass. "They aren't as friendly out here, are they, Emile?" Joel whispered loudly.

"What? Oh, I suppose they are when you get to know them."

"They make me feel like I'm wearing a funny hat or suit," Joel said uneasily.

"They're friendly to their own kind of people."

"What kind of people are they, Emile?" Joel asked. Emile laughed but did not answer. They crossed the street and turned past an old ivy-consumed school building, closed for the summer, its playground laying bare, reflecting the sun. The houses slowly began to look older and were farther from the sidewalk. They passed a small dying park and Emile pointed beyond to a high stone fence encircling wide spreading elms. "That's where we're going." Two large ornamental iron gates stood open, flanked by bending marble angels. Through them could be seen winding roadways and lanes that crossed around endless mounds, and monuments scattered like dice across the grass.

Joel pulled back on Emile's hand as they stood at the gates. "Emile. This is a graveyard, you don't want to go here!"

"Yes, we do, monkey. I want to show you something."

"No. Do you know someone who's buried here? Let's go on."

Emile took Joel's hand again. "This is what I bought, Joel. It's what I was telling you about. Now come on, I want to show you."

But still the boy pulled back. "What did you buy? You can't buy anything in the graveyard."

"I bought a plot; you have to have a plot to be buried in, Joel; you know that. Now come on in with me."

"No. Emile, no! You didn't buy any such thing!"

"Joel, everyone dies sometime or another. Do you know where they bury bums? People who haven't got any family? What's the matter with you anyway, monkey?"

"I don't care! It scares me, Emile. I've always been scared of graveyards. I want to go back!"

Emile was quiet for a moment and they walked a few steps past the angels at the gates. He bent down and took the boy's shoulders, "I didn't know you'd be like this. Look at me now. I thought you'd be a man. Well, look where I point at least, will you do that? No one's asking you to go in if you don't want to, monkey." The boy raised his head and looked in the direction Emile indicated. "See that tall monument, the one beside the big ugly red urn? See it?"

"The white one?"

"That's it. The one that looks like Washington's Monument."

"I see it," Joel said quietly.

"Well, my plot is just past that; the unfashionable side of the street, I think, but I intend to play around Washington's Monument most of the time. I think I'll probably make that my Central Park." Emile looked down at the boy, who still stared across the graveyard.

"I see it," Joel repeated. "Can we go now? Please, Emile?" They turned down the walk and across the barren park. "I'm sorry I'm scared, Emile. Maybe next time I won't be, O.K.?"

"That's alright, monkey. I should have told you or something. I should have thought; probably all kids are afraid of graveyards. There's nothing wrong with that."

"Are you sure it's O.K., Emile?"

"Sure it is. Now let's go home."

Joel tried to think of something to say but they reached the subway again and started the long ride back. He couldn't say he was sorry again and Emile sat quietly watching the blank window. They did not go back to the park. Joel's friend stayed on the train at the Seventy-second Street stop. "You go ahead, monkey, and I'll see you tomorrow. Tomorrow or this afternoon, alright?" Joel nodded. He watched the train pull away from the platform and heard it stop in the distance for a moment, then fade slowly off. Joel leaned against the cool mirror of a vending machine and tried with his eyes closed to distinguish if the thin sound in the distance was the train he had just departed or another approaching from the opposite direction.

Joel did not return to the park that afternoon. The following day when he had forgotten about the graveyard, he could not find Emile. He sat on the railing, watching the polar bear's den until he tired of waiting for it to appear. The few days after that Joel was unable to leave home. He had registered for school, collected his books. The day before school began he had planned to go to the park, but a violent thunderstorm drenched the entire day. Joel stood for hours at the door of his house hoping to see Emile, but very few people passed on the streets; none of them friendly or familiar.

And then school. Joel had never told anyone of his friend so no one would have believed him if he told them he was lonely. His school seemed unbearably constricting and he wished very much to be back outside. For a stroke of luck his science class was studying trees and Joel made straight "A"s without studying for his tests. After school several afternoons he went to the park, carrying his books; sitting on the bench near the fountain, but he did not see Emile. Once, the third afternoon he went there, a man stood near the fountain, a bald man whose forehead reflected the sun. He stood staring, smiling each time Joel looked up from his book. "You seem to be looking for someone, child." Joel raised his eyes from the book again to see the man standing, almost crowding over him, throwing a shadow across the book. His glasses were thick, heavy lenses that magnified his eyes to look like painted doll circles, giving him the presence of some grotesquely enlarged insect. "If you're lost, I'll bet I can help you," the man said. Joel looked up again, squinting against the sun. Quite suddenly he felt pinioned, as an animal behind barriers. "You go away," Joel stammered. "You go away!" But it was the boy who squeezed past the man and ran from the park.

It was Friday afternoon, beginning October. Joel had been in school for three weeks. Already darkness was coming early and with it chilled winds; Loren had predicted a snow-filled winter, which they both would appreciate, and Joel knew his brother's predictions were always accurate. A few blocks from school Joel paused outside a small grocery. During the full of summer the sidewalks here were lined with watermelon and berries. Now the store displayed brightly glossy Indian corn and hanging clusters of violet onions like enormous grapes, pumpkins, and the dull, red orange of persimmons and brown of sugar pears and chestnuts. Several women were gathered near the door. A man in a white apron was weighing sweet potatoes into ten-pound sacks. Joel enjoyed the store; he enjoyed the apple and autumn smell of it. And Joel started to go in when he heard a voice that made him spin around in the doorway. "Hey, monkey!" Emile called from across the street.

Joel waved and dropped his books. He scrambled around the women's legs to retrieve them and went running into the street. A yellow-orange taxi swerved honking from the boy's path. "Emile!" he cried, running into the man's arms. "Why have you been gone?"

"Watch those streets, Joel. You nearly got killed just then."

The boy jumped back and looked at his friend. "Where have you been, Emile? I've looked for you everywhere!"

"I had to be away for a while, Joel; I wasn't feeling good."

"Were you sick? You look terrible, Emile; you need to shave again awfully bad."

"I'll bet I do."

"Can we go to the park?" Joel asked immediately. "I haven't seen the bear all week; longer even. I'll bet you haven't either."

"Yes, I have, I was there today," Emile said. "I can't go back there again now."

"Why not? We have time, Emile. I don't have to be home."

"No, we can't. I'm getting ready to leave now."

"Leave? Where do you think you're going to go?" Joel demanded.

"I told you, monkey; I can't stay in New York all winter. I've got to move on; it's late as it is."

"It is not late," Joel yelled. "You can't leave."

"Now don't argue with me, hear? I just wanted to see you and say goodbye before I left."

"Emile, will you let me come too? I can! I can ride a boxcar as good as anybody, that's all I want to do anyway. And I can eat beans out of a can like you said." Joel began to cry. "I can do those things too, Emile."

"Come on. Come on, monkey, are you going to let me say goodbye or aren't you?"

"No!"

"Then I'll have to go and not say it; if you want me to."

"Emile, I hate school! I don't want to stay here, I hate it!"

"Monkey." Emile stood up and took Joel's hand. "Now walk with me down to the corner, O.K.?"

"I haven't seen you in a month, Emile, and you want to run away," he murmured.

"Now come on, act right," Emile said. "You knew I was going and you knew you couldn't go with me; I'm not running away. I came to tell you goodbye, didn't I?"

"Yes."

"Well, alright."

"Why do you have to go today, why don't you wait till Monday and we could be in the park all weekend."

"Because I have to go today, don't ask questions, monkey." They stopped at the corner.

"When are you coming back?"

"I told you not to ask questions, didn't I?"

"Well, *when*? You can tell me that, can't you?" Joel looked up at the man.

"I always come back right after summer gets here. I always come back about July. Is that O.K.?"

"I guess."

"You guess." Emile laughed. "You guess more than anyone I ever knew. Now say goodbye and you better be getting home."

"I don't want to but I will. How long is it till July?"

"No time at all. Now you take care of yourself; God knows nobody else will."

"O.K. And you too, hear?" Joel said. He threw his arms around Emile's waist and squeezed him as tightly as he could. "Goodbye, Emile."

"That's more like it. Goodbye, monkey. Say, monkey." Emile squatted down again. "Do you still have the soap bear I carved for you?"

"Of course I do, Emile, it's on my dresser. I love it."

"That's fine. You run on home, now. Goodbye." Joel walked across the street and turned back. "I'll see you next July, now, hear?" he yelled. Emile waved goodbye again and Joel walked slowly home. He looked around only once and half-expected to see Emile behind him, but he was not.

Just before Christmas, Joel's mother found an apartment four blocks west for a lower rent and they had moved from the park. Even that short distance seemed to remove him completely. His mother had been quite satisfied that Joel would not be spending all his time in the park. And another summer would not be wasted there either. Loren would escort his brother there when Joel wanted to play; the two boys would act like brothers for a change. Only Loren had flunked geography and English and was attending summer classes. And still Joel was not allowed in the park alone. No. Definitely not again this summer. Not this year. So Joel stayed mostly on the roof of the building looking down on the screaming traffic and out to the park. Until July.

Joel had set the soap polar bear on the dresser. It had been there all winter where he could see it and remember his friend. Now, on Sunday, on the first of July, the day circled a dozen times on his calendar, he took the bear and wrapped it in tissue paper and placed it carefully in his shirt pocket. He walked quietly out of the apartment, down the steps and ran across Broadway toward Central Park.

It had been hot for weeks, very hot in New York and Joel couldn't imagine why Emile had waited until July to come home. But here in the park now, everything familiar as a recurrent dream, Joel did not find his friend. He walked the paths to every place they had visited, but he did not see Emile. He came to the carousel and the zoo. The polar bear blinked back at him; Joel felt the soap carving in his shirt pocket. He sat finally on a bench near the fountain; then when he looked up he saw a face he remembered. The policeman stood near a large concrete stairway; Joel ran up to him. "Mister?"

"Yes, sonny?" The policeman looked down at the boy.

"Have you seen Emile?"

"Have I seen who?"

"The bum, Emile. You know, he introduced me to you last summer. My friend, Emile."

"I don't think I know who you're talking about," the policeman said.

"Yes, you do!" Joel insisted. "Sure you do, he was my friend. You used to let him stay in the park at night. Emile."

"Oh, yes," the man frowned, "the one that limped."

"No! Yes! Yes, he did, a little."

"That's right." The policeman raised his cap and set it back on his head. "You're monkey, aren't you? You're the fellow who was always following him around. Are you some relative?"

"I'm his friend," Joel insisted.

"Well, I'm afraid I have bad news for you if he was your friend, son. He . . ." The policeman looked out across the park. "Well, he probably won't be back for a while."

"Yes, he will, he's supposed to come back today." Joel was now becoming angry and flustered. "He told me he'd be back the first day of July and that's today and he isn't here because I've looked all over the park!"

"I'm afraid he won't be back at all," the man said quietly. "He died."

Joel looked at the man blankly.

"He died last fall sometime. I hear he knew he was going to all along. He even bought a grave lot somewhere out in Brooklyn, so you don't need to worry."

Joel's face flushed red in anger. Tiny veins raised on his temple. His mouth formed several words before he finally located his voice: "In Queens!" he screamed violently. "He bought a graveyard in Queens but he did not either die! He did not!" People turned to look at the two, and the policeman spoke very quietly.

"If he was your friend, you should have known that. Now you just run on home or somewhere. Your friend died; any bum in the park will tell you that, you go on home now." The man turned and walked away.

"He is so my friend!" Joel screamed after him. "And he ain't dead!" The boy suddenly noticed that people were looking at him. "He ain't," he said only half aloud and ran out of the park.

He did not go home. He walked to the subway station, repeating he is not, he is not, over to himself. But on the train Joel sat quietly, holding to the bottom of the seat; even so the train pitched him from side to side. And when he got off the train in Queens he had no thoughts in his mind at all.

It had been hot and cloudy all morning, but now the sky was striped with gray and heavy black thunderclouds. Joel recognized the houses along the sidewalk. It seemed to be much farther than he remembered. The school, the wall; he paused for only a moment at the iron gates, looking over toward the tall white monument, then he walked slowly toward that area of the graveyard. Beside the tall monument ran a road that the caretaker used to move the cars on. Joel walked beside the road looking at the headstones. From one lane to another, being very careful where he stepped, he read the names. The stones were newer on this side of the road and smaller. Engravings had not begun to fade and the ground was still mounded on the graves. Occasionally a small bouquet had been placed at the monument, or a wire wreath. Suddenly Joel stopped. Directly in front of him, on the side close to the white monument was a thin flat stone of red granite with no date, no epitaph. Only one name centered in the stone.

EMILE

The letters began to blur in his eyes. "No," he whispered very softly. "No, Emile." But he knew better; he knew it was true but at the same time he could not feel the presence of his friend. He could not feel his spirit sitting calmly under the Washington's Monument as he had imagined. He looked down at the stone again, and once around the silent, eerie graveyard. Emile's stone bore no other inscription at all. "Emile?" Joel said. He looked at the neighboring graves and considered bringing their flowers to his friend's stone. "I brought your bear." He unwrapped the soap polar bear from the tissue paper and sat it above his friend's name on the red stone. "See? I saved it." Joel looked around the graveyard again. "I'm going now. I'm leaving," he whispered. "Why didn't you tell me, Emile?"

The Canary (A Fairy Tale)

Once, not too very long ago, but in a place very far away; far away on the moors and remote from surrounding villages, there was a town named Blue Willow. Perhaps the town exists today if you look for it closely. It was a very somnolent place that basked in sunshine all summer; and in winter, they say, a soft gray-blue smoke arose straight up from the many chimneys and lingered high over Blue Willow in one long amethyst cloud. And the town smelled of biscuits and cakes in the winter.

Now living in this quiet town toward the center square, where the fountain danced all summer and where horses drank and dogs waded and shook off their cool dampness in a brisk shower of raindrops in all directions, was a little woman with smooth soft hair the color of milk (tied at the back of her head in a loose round bun for she was a conservative woman who didn't visit about much). And with her lived a canary.

Now you may think it no unusual thing for a little aged woman with milk-white hair to keep a canary for company, but you forget that this quiet town was very remote indeed; and hidden, as it was, among azure hills and countryside, no bird of any consequence had ever found it. True, sparrows dusted themselves around the fountain and in farmyards, and smoky catbirds darted from barn to barn; but anyone hearing the shrill call of a catbird has probably been moved to throw stones; and alas, although sparrows are lovely brown and gray birds indeed, and were much appreciated by the townspeople, their song is pitifully small and even painfully unmelodic.

But, of course, the canary did not know he was the only songbird in the town or he might have sung more often. But he sat in his green wire cage and only in the evening, when the old woman put on the kettle for tea (for she was a very poor woman and had tea, alas, only with her evening meal) did the canary, listening to the song of the kettle, harmonize with it in his fine soft aria. Neighbors came in quietly to listen, and outside small boys stopped under the window and laid down their pointed sticks to hear the canary sing. But, of course, he sang only for his own amusement. And his feathers were the color of daffodils. Such a beautiful bird, in his green wire cage, and so lovely and soothing was his song that when sadness came to a family in the town (for it must be admitted that sadness comes to every family, even in a village so small and quiet as Blue Willow) the members of the family would gather at the old lady's house in the evening and listen to this golden bird. And the woman let them in, nodding quietly: for she was a wise woman and understood.

But one spring people seldom remembered to come to listen to the bird's song. Of course he sang just the same; in harmony every evening with the kettle. But this spring the people of Blue Willow were worried: the ponds on the outskirts of town were drying at their edges. The very shallow ones became non-existent altogether: their bottoms cracked in square designs and dried; and soon the gentle winds had erased all traces of the ponds. The wells began to shrink and the brooks grew pitifully narrow, for no rains fell that spring.

People in the town walked out into the streets and looked up at the bright sunny sky and shook their heads. For everyone knew up there lived Sean, who in summers and springs had been given charge of Blue Willow's weather. And the people of the town wondered why Sean did not cause it to rain. But Sean, who day after day looked down upon the sleepy, happy town and watched it every summer and every spring, was quite simply bored. If the truth had been known, Sean McCaffery (for McCaffery was his family name, but you could not expect the people of Blue Willow to be aware of that) was not a well-disposed man. For years past his memory he had each spring rained, and each summer shone brightly to make things grow, but this was far from his nature. This spring Sean McCaffery sat calmly looking around him, and above him, but not below. If the people of Blue Willow wished weather they could arrange it for themselves. This is not a proper attitude for a man in charge of weather, even in so far-removed and remote a location as Blue Willow, but nonetheless this is how Sean thought. For he was, if the truth were known, a very cold-hearted man.

So the days in Blue Willow grew only hotter and hotter with no sign of a change. The fountain in the center of the town grew still and dogs chased the sparrows from the tiny puddles that remained, but the following day those too were gone. And the townspeople held meetings and collected together to worry about the rains and about their crops, for if it did not rain soon nothing could be planted. But their appeals were unanswered, and they went about devising ways to ration the small amount of water that remained. For the wells, too, were scarcely one-fourth full and seemed to be failing more each day and soon there would be no water in Blue Willow at all. Animals stood by their troughs (for animals don't understand these things) and brayed for something to quench their thirst. And babies and small children, for they understand even less than animals if the truth were known, cried day and evening. And from nothing but exhaustion and worry their mothers cried, too.

But in the house by the fountain, which you will remember had by this time gone dry, where the little old lady lived; still each evening with the small share of water boiling, the canary sang. It was a very short song indeed, for the little old woman, no matter how well you like the song, could not allow the water to boil away. But sometimes, ruffling his feathers, which were the color of daffodils, the bird sang on for a moment: just to amuse himself and perhaps (for he was a saucy bird) to show his annoyance.

And of course the day came when there was no water remaining at all. And the townspeople were distraught beyond your imagination; but living as they were so remote from other villages they could suggest no improvement other than to continue to ask Sean to send them rains. And Sean was reminded of the weakness of humans and was pleased with himself for being stronger; for Sean, you will remember, was a very cold-hearted man. And in the little house there was no water to boil and no song for the kettle to sing. And the canary was very annoyed indeed.

But at last after hopping about his green cage for some time, several evenings in a row, he sat down to think. This took three days: anyone who has seen a canary will understand that their brains, in a head so small (and after allowing for the place where they make their song) must be very, very tiny and very slow to act. And this is what the canary thought: The song of the kettle is made from the boiling water. But since there is no longer any song, there must be no more water! And for a canary, you will admit, this is very astute reasoning. So when the little old lady came to open his cage the next morning, the tiny canary darted out! He flew once around the room and out the open door into a tree high above the village square. No amount of coaxing from the woman would make the canary come down. There the canary thought: If I sing because I like the song of water (and looking around from his high vantage he could see there was no water at all in the town) then is it not reasonable to think that if I sing, and the water likes my song, then it will come to sing with me? And looking up, cocking his yellow head sideways (for this is the way canaries must look up), he sang his low evening song and waited for water to answer him.

But nothing happened. It must be, thought the canary, that the water is very far away and cannot hear me. And you will remember he had never sung much anyway, and had never used even a tenth of his power (for although canaries are very small, some people believe that their insides are nothing except lungs and music box for they can sometimes sing very loud indeed). And with that the canary swelled out his breast enormously and began with amazing power to warble an incredibly complicated aria.

Men standing in their dry fields turned to look toward the village square. Women sweeping, for lately it had grown quite dusty in the town, ceased their work. Children playing and children crying quit their noise and walked quietly to the village square.

And very, very high above Blue Willow, higher even than where the smoke gathers in the sky during the winter, Sean McCaffery heard (very faintly at first) a song: a song so very sweet that he could not ignore it, and he unfrowned his forehead and bent to listen.

As old Sean listened he saw the townspeople gather in the square far below him. What a strange sight, he thought; everything there is suddenly so still. And what a very beautiful song, but wherever is it coming from? (For Sean was a bit nearsighted and could not see the tiny canary in the tree below.) It is a song I might have asked to hear very, very long ago when I was a child. (For Sean, even though he was a cold-hearted man now, had once been a child.) It is a song so reminiscent of my childhood, said Sean. So very sad and still so very lovely. And he began to cry. And below it began to rain.

And the people, seeing the rain, ran about and danced in the square. The canary was very happy to see that others wanted to hear the song of the water, but still the song did not come. It was not the same as that of the kettle, so the canary continued to sing. And above Sean continued to make the rain with his enormous weeping. And the streams widened, the wells filled, and ponds reappeared, so intense was the rain. While over it all was the beautiful sweet song of the bird.

But you will remember that Sean was a cold-hearted man. And as darkness fell and the day no longer warmed the town, his tears were cold and bitter as ice. But he wept so long as the music continued. In the tree the canary saw that his song was causing everyone to be so happy; but the rain was so cold now and he was so very tired.

People no longer stood around the square to hear the singing, but still he sang to make it rain. And above Sean was reminded how terribly cruel he had been and he cried all the more and swore never again to chastise the people for being simple and quiet.

But indeed they were not quiet now! Sean heard them laughing and playing in their houses below, looking out their windows and shouting for the rain to continue. He heard them happy in the cool, cool rains; he listened to them shouting gay thoughts and plans for planting the following day if the sun shone, and Sean swore to make it shine. He listened to their laughter from the houses, dry and warm away from the cold, hard rains. He listened to them so carefully that he did not even notice the song of the bird now. And did not even notice as the song grew weak, and neither did the people in the town. They did not notice even when the song stopped altogether.

SECTION 2
TRAVELS TO AND FROM THE CITY

1.

Shelton leaned back now into the itchy grey upholstery of the carseat and tried to make a comfortable seat. The fabric felt and smelled of carpet and once earlier when they had first pulled away from Springfield he had delivered a hearty slap against the brisley nap to exclaim an excited Boy! On our way! it had answered with a barrage of dust so heavy all the windows in the old Chevolette had to be opened, or opened as much as they could, for the first twenty miles. The negative imprint of his hand persued a pattern with the grey stripes. Wind, in passing through the windows had riffled through the clothes laid out straight across the back seat, tossing shirts onto the floor and one had flown histerically at an open window but had been slapped down before it escaped. Everything had been put back in order at their first stop and only the fosil of his hand on the seat reminded Shelton of the incident.
  "One hundred and twenty miles. Exactly."
  Shelton opened his eyes to see a luminous ghost disappear behind them at the perimeter of his vision. "Was that a sign?" He asked and pulled half erect in the seat.
  "One hundred and twenty miles exactly." Otis repeated. "Over half there; be there already if this heap had any juice left in her." Otis had a red nose; he had gone into a sneezing spell when Shelton kicked up the dust.
  "Sure you'll stay awake if I try to go t'sleep?"
  "Til midnight anyway. Long as the radio keeps talking to me."
  Outside the landscape had gone black on indigo; a rip-tooth edge of distant, and then close oak against sky. xxxxxxxxxxxxxxxxxxxxxxxxxxxx The faint warm glow of the speedomitor's orange disc xxxxxxxxxxbitxxxxxxk xxxkxx trembled xxxkxxxxindxx against the window, a distorted oval of heat that weakly illuminated his own reflection on the rushing darkness outside. Shelton sank into the seat again and shut his eyes. At least the radio worked. An anouncer's monotone announced the time as ten and onehalf minutes past ten. Nearly four hours; it didn't seem like it. xxxitan xxxxxxtix Extxxx A few more miles and they would be within range of the Tulsa xxxix stations, a better radio would pick them up now; one of the stations there had the tallest sender in the world. Shelton visualized it as Otis had described, xix vanishing right through the sky. It would be (   )dark when they passed it. He could still taste the vaguely nauseating breath of gasoline in his mouth. And the thin red rubber hose. In his inexperience at ciphoning gas he had scalded his tongue with the light liquid. Otis was expert. They had managed from one car or another parked along the dark unsuspecting streets in Springfield to collect, besides a near full tank, approximately five gallon Standard Oil can nearly full; Shelton had been belching the taste since they left. Two hundred ten miles. The trip would cost nothing but time, and time was a new luxury given them with his new diploma that May.
  With Otis it was different, his father was a drunk who had staggered off somewhere when xxxxxxxxfifteenxxkxxxixx Otis was twelve and never found his way back home; he had wandered through, seen, the country. Otxxix xxxxxxxkxxkxxinxxhxxdxxkxxxxxxxgxix His dresser top at home in Adair, or what was home now, was a tribute in gold-plated xxxxxxxxxx trophies: Third Place Basketball Tournament, Nashville High, 1951; First place softball team, Southwest Missouri League, Marshfield, Mo., 1953; Basketball, Sedallia, Mo., 1953; Springfield, 1954; Oklahoma City, 1955; Springfield again, 1955: tiny gold maxx figures forever jumping at a ball welded to their fingertips; they stopped time and action, remembering a dozen players and a dozen teams in triumph. he had never grown to feel at home And so Otis was used to roaming, drifting. But for Shelton this was adventure; his master, away and working, he would be soon; and free. For Shelton it had been endless nights of study for school and endless days of breakfasts with insipid and semblance of peace growing thinner between Shelton and his stepfather. And so Otis was running, running with both arms out to catch the air and raise up. He had never seen a city, a real city. He had worked, yes, at a local filling station since he was fifteen and hated it. He had had his own money, yes, what there was of it.

Fig. 3. First page, "Fish Kite" manuscript, undated; Lanford Wilson Collection, Special Collections and Rare Books, University of Missouri Libraries, Lanford Wilson Estate.

The Train to Washington

I THINK WHAT BOTHERED me most about Irene was that she was always calling her son a little son-of-a-bitch. Irene and I were never anything much more than friends, and after the fight at the Oyster Bar, I started coming in earlier in the afternoon when she would be asleep upstairs and Eddie was still in school.

I had first gone to the bar when I moved into the building next door. My apartment was a one-room, one-window affair four flights up: a very small, tall room of ugly rose walls and way off-white ceiling, but it was my first apartment in New York and I managed to be proud of it anyway. This was back a few years, a short while after the war, when even more soldiers wandered lonesomely around Times Square and the Oyster Bar seemed a favorite place with them. Back when there were more, but many more lights on the Square and a block and a half away the glare entered my room like sunlight. Then instead of looking only cheap and tired and gaudy the Square charged some great excitement, like the carnival it pretended to be but as an enormous carnival city. The hucksters were more clever, the pitchmen more outrageous and comical, the strip acts more daring and the drinks were so heavily and obviously watered you almost had to admire the proprietor's nerve; and because there were more soldiers on the street, there were women, with wide padded shoulders and skirts above their knees and their hair all up and down at once.

Every evening the Oyster Bar had some kind of commotion, and usually a fight involving at least five men and a couple of soldiers would be wrestling around on the sawdust floor. Old Al would threaten, in the same voice every night, to close the place; screaming out, "And then where would you go, eh? All you hoodlums? Where would you go then?" But you could tell from an underlying good humor in his voice that he knew they would go to any of the other dozens of bars in the area.

In the middle of this I sat at a booth with Eddie (the little son-of-a-bitch) taking it all in, waiting for Irene to come back to the bar. She had a room in the hotel above for commercial purposes; a hotel rather notorious for that, every girl who visited the bar lived there or at least had a room there. Eddie and I sat in the booth, sometimes with the next customer that Irene had lined up. ("Keep this one on ice, honey," she would say to me by way of introduction, "I'll only be a minute.") Some soldier waiting nervously, with embarrassed questions about the time and the kid and when did we expect Irene to be back, to which Eddie usually replied: "It all depends on the score. Sometimes an hour, sometimes ten or fifteen minutes." Coming from an angel-faced eight-year-old boy this never calmed the soldier, who was probably on leave this time in New York and probably from Omaha. Eddie looked tired and bored and asked a few impertinent questions and when the waiting customer in his fidgeting would knock over a beer Eddie would watch it run out across the table and onto the sawdust and intone a "one" and because the soldier knew he was going to be next, he usually spilled another before Irene returned. She came dancing in, kissed us all three on the forehead, took a quick drink of the Coke that always sat at the table and said: "Sorry I'm so long, darlings. Come along soldier, we've got to get you back to camp," and dragged him out of the booth before he quite realized that she had returned.

Usually instead of the next customer, Al, the owner, sat with us. He liked more than anything to sit back in the booth with a mug of his water beer in front of him and watch his establishment prosper. He ruled the place as the bouncer, his size being more appropriate to that position than to bartending. So enormously fat was he that he could not have moved more freely behind the bar, and when Irene would grab his hand, playfully pulling him toward the door: "Come on, Al, you're next," he would pull away, but gently, and say, "You wait, Irene. You just wait until I can lose some of this weight. Then you'd better watch out." Irene and everyone would laugh at this because in spite of his seriousness he had apparently been saying it for years.

Irene was an attractive woman. She was pleased and complimented when everyone thought Eddie was her younger brother rather than her son, but she always told them they were mistaken. She had probably lightened her hair a few shades and if you studied her face closely you felt she probably needed glasses. Her breezy talk and manner were a little confusing at first but you soon adjusted to being confused and, like Eddie, after you knew her she became less impersonal. She talked about her hometown, where Eddie spent the summers; when she was feeling especially self-critical she would sit for hours brooding about the future. Every few days she would decide to start putting money away to send Eddie to college but her lapses into planning or budgeting were soon overcome. She had a compact, a little round affair, that she drew out of her purse a dozen times an evening, a gesture you began to recognize; she would look into the lightly powdered mirror, bite her lip a moment, inspect her smile, set her teeth together and sneer fiercely, snap the compact shut and drop it back into her purse with a preoccupied sigh. This she usually did in the middle of a conversation as a kind of unconscious signal that she wasn't hearing you. Very often, though she looked directly into your eyes, you got the uneasy feeling that behind her attentiveness she was contemplating a hat.

And in her breezy way she called Eddie a little bastard, which, I assume, he was; and a little son-of-a-bitch; and it was disturbing, yes, but somehow ironic and amusing too if you didn't think about it. And Eddie was, disturbingly enough, rather like any other little boy, if maybe a little wiser when he talked to the soldiers. His mother's profession didn't seem to bother him that much; he went to school and talked endlessly about his teachers and classmates and asked the usual barrage of questions and advice. "See, this girl wants to be my girlfriend, and I guess that would be alright, but I have a girlfriend in Willard already, so what I wondered about, if I told Cynthia that I had this other girlfriend back home and how we planned to get married and all—what I wondered was—if I told her, then do you think it would be alright? Or do you think she wouldn't want to be my girlfriend then?" Willard was a small town not far from Washington, D.C., where Irene sent Eddie during the summer to spend his vacation from school with his grandmother. Although he had only been there in the summer, you could not help noticing he always referred to it as home. There were times when he didn't feel like talking about school or about anything it seemed, but I learned you could always draw him out of these moods by asking him what he intended to do next summer, or what he had done last. He had an Uncle John, who had been away the last two years in the service but would be back in Willard that summer. Most of Eddie's time there, it seemed, was spent either with his grandmother or Patsy or Marvin, his girlfriend and her brother who lived next door. He carried around with him a stack of dog-eared and crazed photographs of home, and like all photographs they said much more than they had been intended. His grandmother, a very elderly woman with long white hair pulled into a bun at the back of her head, stood proudly in front of a bed of tiger lilies at the side of the house. She allowed herself just a hint of a smile. The house behind her, in the photograph only incidentally, was where Eddie spent his summers. It seemed to me sometimes, as he talked on and on about the place, that I had been there.

The old photographs that stuffed his wallet passed before me creating a déjà vu sensation. I knew the driveway to the garage behind the house. The gravel was impressed with shell animals turned up from the bottom of a riverbed, and in late summer the drive was dyed blue-violet when the enormous mulberry tree above it dropped its overripe fruit onto the gravel. The house, the hard old house, would never wear out but seemed to have petrified. The great old house with a huge bulge across the length of its sagging roof, with worn washboard floors, its interior lighted by kerosene lamps with Japanese paper flowers floating in their bowls that threw wavering circles onto the ceilings, had stood for a hundred years at the farthest south edge of town where houses are scattered and there are woods of a sort, and a few small tobacco and cotton farms. His grandmother raised chickens, which he assured me was no easy task: "There came a tremendous storm last year. Usually grandmother can see a storm coming an hour away, but this one broke all of a sudden, with hail and rain and caught one of the hens and her chicks way out in the corner of the field." He gets very excited when he tells you, "and she covered all the little ones that she could, but there was eight of them that she couldn't and they drowned. Grandmother and me rushed out after it cleared and found them and Granny put them into her apron—did you know you could do that?—and we came running in and I got the oven going while she washed them in warm water and went all over them with her hands, trying to soften them up. They were stiff as a board. I mean they were really dead. And she brought them back to life. All eight of them. And we wrapped them up in warm towels and put them in the warm oven, with the door open, and we sat there in front of the oven watching them. And in an hour or so they were just as happy and alive as the ones the old mother hen had saved herself. Did you know you could do that with chickens?"

And he told about searching the woods for greens that his grandmother cooked with bacon ends, and picking blackberries, getting seed-ticks all over him. "So little, like mites, that I could hardly see them and Grand couldn't see them at all." And how she washed him down with kerosene and stood him in a big rattling galvanized tub and washed him again with lye soap to get the kerosene off. "And at night—see, we live across from the colored church—it's the old part of town, and we can hear them singing spirituals from our front yard. We pull a chair out into the yard and listen to them. There's no streetlight so it's pitch black; and the highway is about five miles away, across the valley on the other side of town, and some nights we just sit and look across to where all the cafés are and the filling stations with their red lights strung out along the highway and the cars are so close together, going into Washington, that it looks like a train. Their headlights look like windows on a train." And, "But it's going to be even better this year because Uncle John will be there and we'll do about a thousand things. We'll go hunting even."

All this was before the fight, and every evening I found myself sitting in the same booth. Sometimes Irene sat with us. We'd order a pizza or sandwiches from the delicatessen across the street and share them with Al, who was rather like a father to Irene and me, but not quite, and very much like a grandfather to Eddie. And sometimes Eddie and I in the afternoons would walk up into the park and visit the zoo, which was dull and very cold in the winters but he enjoyed it nevertheless. I usually stood shivering while he ran about the park, scooping up snow and trying a few snowballs and running out across some open area, looking back to see the long dragged footprints behind him. In the bar, Eddie seemed large for his age, with his world-wise chatter; but bundled up until he could hardly move his arms, running out across the snow, a small black figure on all the white, he looked not like a smart little man, but like any other very young boy, bundled up in a maroon mackinaw and red scarf.

He was not always alone. Once he joined a small group of boys in making a lopsided dirty snowman. They made several that winter, and I sat on a cold bench, watching the process. The beginning was always the hardest for them, with nothing much more than an overgrown snowball, rolling it firmly into the snow, yet lightly enough to move it along and pick up a thin layer off the ground; a thin layer at first but after the ball had grown larger, its natural weight rolled over the snow picking up all that had fallen, down to the leaves of the previous autumn and lifting a few of those which stuck to its outside. As they walked along, pushing the ball larger, winding it around the park, walking in the bare damp path of leaves that the ball left behind, it became heavy and heavier until they could no longer roll it over to make it spherical but had to heave it along in a straight path: so it grew round and flat with each revolution, picking up a layer of leaves, resembling, more than a ball, a fat white jelly roll. This then was the base of their man and another ball was started and rolled toward the first to be the snowman's stomach and a third for his chest. Where these three dark paths met in the white ground stood their snowman. The much smaller head they could carry to lift it on top. The face's features were stones; for the snowman's arms they used branches.

But when it did not snow there was nothing much to do except wander looking in the cold windows at the Halloween and Thanksgiving and Christmas decorations. We usually returned to the bar just as it was getting dark and the lights were turning on, seemingly by themselves. I should have been reading; I took books from school into the bar and never opened them. I listened to Eddie talk, which he did always, about school and the summer. One evening he asked me: "Have you ever made a bow and arrow? Because Marvin makes dandy ones. Better than the Indians. He even killed a bird with one once."

"No." I had to admit I hadn't.

He pondered this a moment and finally shrugged. "I imagine Uncle John has. We'll probably hunt with them sometimes. Birds and things."

In the area around Willard, Virginia, it is common for farmers to overturn cannonballs and Indian relics of every sort in their fields. Irene's brother, Eddie's Uncle John, had a collection of Indian objects: arrowheads and tomahawk heads, beads of clay and bone, and even the broken clay bowl of an old calumet. The games of the children run toward cavalry and Indian battles with charges and ambushes of the brigade. Their arrows sometimes have the real broken arrowheads that are found all over the town.

Eddie talked so much about Willard and his friends there that I wondered if he got along well at school, with the other children; but it seemed he wasn't interested so much in them: "Of course I couldn't tell them about Irene because I'd never hear the end of that. But nobody knows that in Willard either. It's funny when she comes home the last week of vacation, how we all talk about her secretary work and her boss, Mr. Sweeney," he laughed. "That's Al, who's so good to her and lets her take off a week every summer to come home." I supposed duplicity can come as naturally to children as it does to adults. Irene would simply shrug and say, "Well, no mother wants to hear that about her daughter. What would she say?"

When it happened toward the first of the year that John came into the bar, I had taken Eddie that early evening to see the revival of a Walt Disney movie. With all the other parents and older brothers and children, screeching children everywhere, we stood in the lobby of the Beacon Theatre, and as always I noticed how different Eddie seemed away from the bar, and with a group of children his own age. All down Broadway he danced around, being I forget which one of the seven dwarfs, and shouting about the witch and her mirror and making me promise to take him again before school let out.

When we entered the bar everything changed. Irene sat at the regular booth, several people were with her. She held a damp bar towel to her face, and when she looked up to see us come in she began crying again. Al, who was running about and had sent one of his customers to the market for a raw steak and another one to the delicatessen for a container of hot tea, looked up pitifully as a fat loving mother whose child has swallowed a pin. "Damn," he said, "you would come back just now when we finally got her to stop bawling. Just be glad that you wasn't here to see the fireworks." The tea came and Al sent another customer for the steak; the first one had apparently skipped with the five dollars Al had given him.

Eddie sat beside Irene and tried to comfort her. Irene cried and sipped the hot tea and cried again. She tried to cover her mouth and eye, which were beginning to swell. Between sips of tea Al fed her sips of brandy. It was Al who finally told us. "He sat here for over an hour," he said. "Just sat at the bar and had a couple of drinks, and Irene came in with a coupla fellows. How could I notice if this fellow saw her or not? But Irene, she was in and out with a coupla fellows or three maybe and this guy, after a while, he gets up when she comes in for the third time maybe; and he meets her at the door. And to me he looked like any soldier. But they begin to argue like sin and finally I caught on that this was her brother John."

"Uncle John?" Eddie repeated dimly, and tried to look at his mother's face but she nodded and turned away.

"So anyway," Al went on, "he starts yelling at her and he starts beating her around and before I could get there, Irene's on the floor crying and this John's run off like some scared pup with about three guys chasing him. They came back later and said he got away."

The steak came and Irene placed it over her eye as Al instructed. The brandy and tea had calmed her some; she tried to joke about it without being very funny, but to show us that she felt better. Eddie went across the street and brought her another hot tea. "Poor little son-of-a-bitch," she said, thanking him for the tea. "I'm just glad you didn't hear it, honey. John has probably the best right out in Virginia, and oh, Jesus, when he gets mad."

"He's very strong," Eddie told me.

"At least he won't say anything to Mama; that's something," Irene sighed. "As long as we keep away from there for a while. He's such a maniac." She took a sip of the tea and looked across at us and smiled. Eddie said nothing, but sat quietly, turning over a book of matches in his hand, carefully running his thumb over the embossed letters on the cover, and examining the structure of the inside.

Irene put her arm around him and hugged him tightly to her. "Poor little S.O.B. You won't mind so much not going to Willard this summer, will you? Honey? We can stay here and have as much fun, can't we?" I could see that Eddie was looking past her shoulder to the door, which was covered with a kind of bright decal to make the panes of the windows look almost like the stained glass windows of a church. But he was not looking at them or at anything definite, but just past her, as she held him tightly. His voice when he finally spoke was hardly there at all, but still it was sincere. "Of course not, Irene," he said.

She gave him another squeeze and he sat back into the booth. Irene looked at him for a moment. He seemed to feel our stare and shrunk closer into the corner. He picked up the matchbook again and turned it over in his hands. "Poor kid," Irene said. "Honest Al, you should have seen how he gets along with John. They had such good times; it's a damn shame. Eddie absolutely worshiped him." She reached into her purse and brought out the little compact; passed the heel of her hand over the powdery mirror and sighed, looking at her swollen eye.

The Water Commissioner

A FEW WEEKS BACK the late show was *The Farmer Takes a Wife*. I didn't stay up to see it, but I noticed an advertisement in the newspaper; the photograph was familiar. I don't often remember old movies. I'll watch an hour and gradually realize where I first saw it. And I don't remember any more about *The Farmer Takes a Wife* except that I saw the movie at the Ambassador Theatre in St. Louis.

It was my first trip to the city; I had only just graduated from high school in a small town a few hundred miles southwest of St. Louis. I rode to St. Louis in a milk truck; a man who lived across the street from me made regular runs to St. Louis and down to Poplar Bluff and although I believe it was against company policy, he gave me a lift. He let me off way on the west or south side of town, at Ohio or Utah or Indiana Street, in front of the dairy. I jumped out of the high cab with my imitation leather suitcase; Keith, the driver, called down to wish me luck. He also told me on what day and what time he would be back ten days later if I had not found a job, or if I had decided by then that I was not interested in metropolitan living, but that seemed impossible and I'm surprised I even remembered where to meet him.

It was around the end of May and in the rural community I had left they were worried that spring would not come that year. It had not rained and had not rained and crops could not be planted and rumors of drought were everywhere; not talk but rumors; everyone knew everyone's opinion: Clyde Warren believed it would rain within the week, old Mr. Williams was convinced it would not. But in the city, away from that, you lost interest in whether it would or would not; you felt very little involved and nobody talked about it.

I was disappointed in St. Louis; nothing worked for me. I was quiet and frightened and intimidated by almost everything, a typical farm boy in the big city. Though I did everything I could think of to conceal the fact, I must have looked like a terrible hick to everyone. The newspapers were full of jobs but I had no idea how I could get them. The advertisements gave phone numbers on which I wasted dimes, calling and hanging up as soon as they answered. A sense of resourcefulness, of which I had been very proud back home, completely deserted me here. And then, I did not like the looks of the city. It seemed filthy. They were, at that time, airing their dirty linen: it was the week of a city referendum which proposed a broad plan to reconstruct a good deal of the town, to clear and clean and rebuild at a breathtaking amount of millions of dollars. On many of the downtown street corners there were quickly constructed pine platforms draped in red, white, and blue bunting where people shouted into silver microphones about the shoddy condition of this neighborhood or that one, and what was being done in Philadelphia and what was being considered in Chicago, and how St. Louis was falling behind the times. Walking, looking at the buildings of the downtown which above the first story had gone all over charcoal-black and flat, and with the slightest wind sprayed a fan of soot down into the street, it seemed that there was still some hope with the referendum. Photographs and models of artist's conceptions were everywhere. The new St. Louis would be clean and sterile and shining and very modern. But the people would have nothing to do with the new St. Louis or millions of dollars of rebuilding and the referendum failed pathetically, and the platforms and bunting disappeared from the streets and with them, it seemed, almost all color from the city. But, of course, I was seeing it all through tired, disappointed, daunted visions of conquest. I did not know the public transportation system so I walked everywhere I went. I had decided to take a job as an apprentice in an advertising agency. It was just as well that I never applied, for I knew nothing about advertising and little more about art—I thought at the time I'd make a dandy illustrator, having been the best artist in my class at school. I had brought nothing with me to show that I could draw; I had not planned my trip at all. The one place I did find—a silk-screening house, where everyone was busy cutting color separations—I stood around looking amazed at their talent and speed, being generally in their way, getting knocked around, and finally I left without asking to speak to the boss.

I decided that I should be a window display artist. This when I saw an ad in the paper for one. The ad was for a shoe store and gave a phone number but I had learned that I could not speak to anyone over the phone without going into my whole history and sounding very frustrated and very silly, and they always had a ready excuse for me. I called information and asked for the address of the company, and was informed they could not help me. I pleaded. I told that poor operator my whole frustrating and silly story, I held her up for fifteen full minutes and she finally told me that I could find that information in the phone book. As it turned out the company was out of St. Louis proper and not listed in the phone book, but at least I got my dime back.

The idea of window design opened a new field to me. I tried every department store in downtown St. Louis. I filled out dozens of applications until I could hardly print legibly; the only encouraging experience was when a manager wasn't in. That time I was asked to come back. I remember him; he was very nice indeed. We stood on the mezzanine outside his office, overlooking the store's main floor. He talked for some time about how difficult it would be for me to find a job. I had discovered that, but he gave me several reasons that I hadn't considered. For one thing, I was ill-prepared; for another school was just out and everyone naturally hired local people before they considered outsiders. Most all of the temporary positions that would have held me over had been filled. In the end he should have only depressed me more but it was somehow encouraging to find someone who would at least talk with me, and seriously. And I discovered that when someone did I could speak with as much sense as I had thought I possessed before, but had begun to question.

I went through several bright ideas in that week. Each was about two days' work and came to the very same dead end. One, after I had given up advertising and window display, was banking. I was a fair typist, I convinced myself, and fair with figures and after all, anyone can count money. But the banks were terrified of me. They asked me a dozen times, as I filled out my application, if I intended to go to college. I said yes at the first one and was dismissed. It takes several months, they informed me, to break in a new employee and they would have to be assured of my intentions to stay for some time. At the second bank I said no, I hadn't the vaguest intention of going to college. I don't think they believed me. But I filled out another round of applications, this time emphasizing, instead of my artistic talent, my ability in arithmetic: my treasureship of the senior class (I was vice-president) and my general high regard for finance. I discovered the reason banks can present such a splendid and spacious lobby. Behind those high marble walls behind the cages, the office personnel and equipment is packed elbow to elbow to filing cabinet. I would not have been a good bank employee. I would have cracked in a week. Every time I came back out into the lobby, back out from that wall, I felt a palpable lessening of weight, a feeling of freedom, and when I stepped outside into the street I almost soared.

It was about this time—after the first four or five days, that is—that I probably decided I wouldn't find a job, and I started spending some of the scant money I had been hoarding to last me through the first few weeks. I went out to Sportsman's Park, everyone in Missouri is a Cardinal fan, to see a ball game. I went to what is the name of the large park there? Here I felt the fact that spring had not yet come for the first time. The ground was barren of grass—the whole park looked worn and used like a playground. All the animals in the zoo were the same dull brown color; they all had their winter shaggy coats still and I was very disappointed. The lions and tigers looked old and harmless. The reptiles were away somewhere and I went through the huge reptile house, examining habitat after habitat without seeing any of the occupants. The whole park seemed bare and common and tired. I remembered the referendum had had a special section devoted to restoring the park. It seemed hardly anyone had visited it since the world's fair, how long ago? Probably fifty years. The Jewel Box, that glass house I had read about and remembered from a play, was tiny and hot and filled with split-leaf rhododendrons.

Friday night (if I intended to catch a ride back with the truck driver I had to be at the cheese plant early Saturday morning, but I hadn't thought about that yet) I decided to go to a movie. I had been staying at the YMCA, which I had been told would be the cheapest place to find a room. I thought twelve-fifty for the tiny room just big enough for a bed and dresser and Gideon Bible was asking a great deal and taking profitable advantage of my Christianity. The "Y" advertised a pool and exercising rooms but I never found them. Like most "Y's" it had one large public bath on every floor. I didn't think anything about this when they told me at the desk, but later, around six o'clock when I decided to take a shower, I gathered the towel and the baby-sized bar of soap and set out through the labyrinthine halls toward the restroom. I entered the large room—finding it by following the sound of hard-running water—and stopped dead. An enormously fat man was standing bare and hairy directly under one of the showerheads, being pelted with water, letting it spray off him, in fact, wetting the floor of the whole room, grinning placidly at me, I swear to God, exactly like a sunning toad. I turned instantly and fled back to my room and locked the door. Dozens of trips were made past the bathroom as I waited for it to be empty. I developed the habit of walking into the room fully dressed, undressing and showering with the speed of sound, jumping out of the shower and pulling my clothes on over wet skin and running back to my room to dry off. All this and I could not have told you why I had been so afraid of the toad.

But where we avoid subtle dangers, we fall into the obvious ones with all the grace of a rhinoceros. The movie I had decided to see was the one I mentioned before. It played at the Ambassador Theatre, I believe it was, but I couldn't swear to it, anyway the theater was downtown a few blocks from the "Y." I had chosen that film only because it had opened that day and I knew it would be months before it would reach my hometown. I walked down to the theater. I walked feeling all the failure of my ill-prepared trip, the uselessness of it. I had dreamed of becoming a great artist here and, undaunted, when I realized I could not be that, I had thought I would become a great businessman, with a remarkable home and a remarkable wife and three or four remarkable children and a long black chauffeured Imperial. Well, I was sorry to see all that go, and I believe it was during the slow walk down to the theater that I realized I would not be an executive in another few weeks. But somehow, I still didn't think about going home. It is strange to say that now, because I had unconsciously arranged everything to allow me time to be at the cheese plant by the next morning, yet I had not accepted total defeat.

I bought a ticket and was told I would be in the middle of the movie and since this was a special occasion of a sort, I decided to wait; to eat first. I walked across the street to a sandwich shop and ordered a bowl of chili and a grilled cheese sandwich. The little shop was half-filled, that is to say there were about ten people sitting at the narrow counter or at booths alongside the wall. I don't remember what I was thinking, but I know I didn't notice the man sitting several seats down until he jumped up. He had seen someone outside on the street, I assume, that he knew and he went running out to the sidewalk, yelling after them. After a moment he came back in, grumbling to himself. He looked up at me and made some friendly joke. I laughed and he smiled and moved his cup of coffee to the place next to mine. He asked if I was from the neighborhood, and I replied (it had become almost a one-line pat answer) that I was from a small town two hundred miles away and was in St. Louis looking for work. It was a scene like the beginning of some bad play where the poor little boy bleats out his whole situation, background, and orphanhood before the curtain is completely up.

"Had any luck?"

"No."

He thought for a minute or so, then started telling me how difficult it would be to find work in a new place. I told him that had been my experience. He asked that dreadful question, "What can you do? What can you do?"

"Nothing." It had become, by that time, either nothing or anything. After a moment he introduced himself in a proper manner and said it might be that he could help me. In the seven days I had been in St. Louis no one had said that. He said it was possible that he could get me a job working in the city; some kind of manual labor if I didn't mind real work. I told the man I would gladly dig ditches, and it turned out this was just about what he had in mind.

For a city official, which he informed me he was, a water commissioner or utilities commissioner or public works director or commissioner of streets or something like that, he looked a touch seedy to me. Not trampish exactly, but just a touch seedy. There was a delicate little ring of neck that bulged out of the collar of his shirt. He had loosened his maroon knit tie to where the broad knot hung like a lopsided medallion over his chest, the tie trailing across his lap. He was an expansive and friendly sort; he asked a number of questions about my home, my parents, the kind of work I could do. He explained some complicated project just outside of town where he might be able to get me on as a laborer; I forget laboring at exactly what. He waved broad gestures with plump, short hands, dazzling me with a mass of red and white stones set in some complicated lodge ring on the little finger of his right hand. I said it all sounded very good, I would not be afraid of manual labor, the pay was better than I could have hoped to make even in a bank. There was a barrage of questions that I tried to catch and answer as rapidly as I could. He intoned them like a tired pitchman, in flat monotone. Did I have any old clothes, did I really intend to stay in St. Louis, did I drive a car, did I know the public transportation, could I read blueprints, had I belonged to a union, where was I staying, could I get up at six the following morning to be at his hotel by six thirty?

The possibility of getting up at six in the morning every day now strikes me as uninteresting, but at the time I was used to getting up earlier than that and it meant nothing to me. The point bothered him though. If I lived at the "Y" and had to go by his hotel, he told me he lived in a hotel, then I would have to get up earlier than that. I should be at his hotel, he now decided, by six; but since I didn't know the city that would be a problem. It would be much easier, he decided, if I stayed over at his place that evening and he could drive me out and introduce me to my boss.

I began immediately to think of reasons why that would be impossible. But he cooled just as fast. If I wasn't interested, etc. . . . Surely I couldn't expect, etc. . . . anyone to hire me without a recommendation. He could phone my boss, if I was afraid it would be a wild goose chase the next morning—he could phone him now. That way everything could be set. This appealed to him; he became excited again. It was difficult for me to readjust to thinking about living in St. Louis again, after I had come so close to giving the whole thing up. I had already decided that I did not like the city, and now I had to decide to stay. Mr. Penrod, we'll call him, suggested we go next door to the drugstore and phone the boss of the project. He was certain now that he could get me on. He was excited to be helping someone new to the city and I have to admit I got pretty anxious and worked up myself. He stood out on the sidewalk, impatiently, while I paid my check. In the drugstore he changed a quarter at the counter and crowded into a phone booth and closed the door. I walked back and forth outside the booth, hearing an occasional word. Through the tall narrow windows in the door I could see he continued to gesture with his free hand, broadly and accidentally hitting the walls of his little enclosure several times. Finally, he emerged, smiling, and slapped me on the back.

"Well!" he said triumphantly.

"What?"

"All done," he said. "I told him about you and he thinks he can use you. I told him we'd be out at seven."

"He can use me?" I was being steered out of the drugstore and pointed down the street.

"You'll have to stay up at my hotel, I'm afraid, though. Only way." Now he was very dogmatic. Now that the job was assured he was an agent with a bright new client.

I explained that I couldn't go anywhere just then. I had a ticket for a movie and was waiting for it to begin, which was very shortly.

"No sweat," he said. "I've got a few things I could take care of anyway. I'll meet you back here, outside the movie."

I said I didn't want to trouble him. I said I wasn't sure what time the movie let out. I said I could find my way to his hotel alright after I got out of the movie. I even said I wasn't too sure I wanted the job. His answer to everything I said was "nonsense." And he shook my hand, slapped me on the back again and said he would meet me after the show. He walked away very briskly. He did not look back and turned at the first corner.

I won't explain why I don't remember anything about the movie. I remember it seemed extremely short. I loaded myself with popcorn and candy bars and Coke and got very nearly sick. I had seen the last show of the evening and was one of the last to leave the theater. People were gathering under the marquee outside. A violent spring thunderstorm had started while we were inside. Looking back to the times I've gone to the show it seems like an unusually frequent occurrence to find it raining when I come out. I was instantly overjoyed. I edged through the crowd under the marquee and watched the marvelous, joyous rain bubble up in the street. It was running everywhere: down the gutters, carrying all kinds of debris; swirling around the drains at the corner of the street. Cabs raised a huge arch of water halfway to where we were standing. Very often, almost continuously the city was lit with a light neon blue. The people were a sorry sight. No one among them had an umbrella or raincoat. A few cars drove up to the front of the theater and a wife would rush out and fold herself hurriedly into the seat; people still standing watched the car as it pulled away. Then I heard Mr. Penrod calling my name from across the street. I looked over and sure enough, under the awning of a candy store was the water commissioner or public works director or streets commissioner, drenched to the skin, motioning for me to hurry across before the light changed. I stepped off the curb into the stream at the gutter. There seemed no point in looking for a narrow place in the water for it extended halfway out into the street for at least a block. Under the awning, all of Mr. Penrod's friendliness and good nature had disappeared.

I made one of my ineffectual comments like "Wet, huh?" and started to explain that I couldn't join him. He mumbled "Yeah," and started walking off toward the corner, completely unnoticing the rain. As I think about it he didn't mention the weather once. Of course, what was there to say? Nothing can look more absurd than two men sauntering along the street at the height of a spring thunderstorm, trying to ignore the fact that everyone else has taken cover. Mr. Penrod was still wearing his pallid suit; the knot of his broad tie had been pushed back into place. He had no raincoat, no umbrella; his wet shirt was transparent and stuck to his chest, exposing a holey T-shirt; the impression was of a man in suit, T-shirt, and tie. When we reached the corner (by now I was soaked as he) we stopped. The light was green; had it been red, there was no traffic. All down the street and sidewalk, which reflected the lights like buckets of dye had been spilled across them, there was not a person in the rain except us. Mr. Penrod stood with his hands in his pockets, perfectly calm, not intending to go further. I finally decided we were waiting for a bus.

Now whether I liked a person or not, if he was upset or visibly irritated with me, I had, at that time, a terrible compulsion to be pleasant to an extent I cannot believe today. As I recall that bus ride it is hard for me to believe that I sat, dripping onto the floor, rosily chatting about this building or that street name, or anything else that would perhaps bring him out of his wet gloom. Mr. Penrod stared out of the window or down at the puddle forming on the floor. Occasionally he looked at me, but I had to turn away when he did. It would be difficult to describe how comical he looked. His thin hair was dragging ringlets across his forehead, each strand dripping rain in his face. Once out of the downpour it was cold: all my clothes were sticking to me, when I moved my feet my shoes squished water. The air-conditioning of the bus was blowing against the back of my neck and I had to turn the collar of my shirt up to block it. The bus drove on interminably. There was no one waiting on the streets; the bus drove like an express through St. Louis; street after street, turning, turning, doubling back. I have a very good sense of direction, it had gotten me all over the city, but once I stop walking and begin riding I lose it. The rain had lessened to a drizzle by the time we got off. We walked three blocks and stopped on another corner. The buildings here were smaller, I had no idea where the downtown area was, even what direction I should start back. As I imagined, we were waiting for another bus. It carried us back into civilization. Not being able to ameliorate Penrod's mood I had fallen into a dreary silence, listening to the wheels of the bus on the wet street. Slowly he began to wake up. He was talking about something I didn't quite follow; I had no idea if the people he mentioned were personal friends or names I should recognize from the papers. I waited for a break in his conversation, trying to find a convenient place to tell him that I was turning back, but he continued, about the job, about some apartment he had been inspecting and considering renting, the district that surrounded the apartment building, the shopping possibilities. It seemed he grabbed at any string of thought rather than allow a break in the flow. When we got off the bus most of the lights had been turned off. I guessed it was around two in the morning; we had been on the trip for about two hours; Mr. Penrod had been building his conversation during the last hour without stopping. The bus let us off directly in front of a tall seedy hotel. Now again, as at the drugstore, he became the careful planner. It would not do to take someone up to his apartment, as he was paying for only one. It would be necessary for us to enter the lobby singly.

It is difficult for me to believe now, but not until we were standing in front of that crummy hotel did my dumb brain finally crystallize a clear and vivid plan. Not until then did I realize that Mr. Penrod could not possibly work for the city. The hotel was so pathetic and penurious I felt first very sorry for the man. He was very active just now but I wasn't listening to him. He would go up to the fourth floor where his apartment was—he kept saying apartment but a sign above the hotel, sputtering and dripping from the rain as though the water had all but put it out, plainly, or rather, dimly, said "Sleeping Rooms." He would go up to his floor and I would enter a moment later and go on up to the fifth. I would find the stairway and come down the one floor where he would be waiting in the hall. I said yes, yes, that would be fine. "You are coming up?" He looked horrified that I might not.

"Of course."

"You understand how to do it?"

"Yes."

"Good. Your boss will like someone who grasps things quickly, see? Now I can tell him truthfully that I know you're a quick thinker." I nodded, but he seemed reluctant to go ahead. He hesitated for a long time and began talking about something, but the impetus failed and he was quiet again. "Are you tired?" he asked finally. Truthfully I answered that I was very tired. I added that I was soaked and cold and probably catching a cold and if he intended that we leave at six the next morning we had both better get some sleep. He nodded immediately, so enthusiastically I thought he would not be able to stop. "Good, good; yes, yes. I'll go on up now. You come along in about a minute or two." He ducked into the doorway, and as he did there was just the slight sound of the word, "Goodbye."

How is it, having never been exposed to something, having never been warned, or even having seldom discussed it, we can suddenly be totally informed. I sometimes feel, psychologists be damned, we are perhaps creatures of instinct after all. I even knew then why I had gone to such circuitous means to shower. I knew that all of Mr. Penrod's promises were visions built like the Tin Woodman's sandwiches, out of air: he was in no position to recommend me to a job; he held no position for the city; he had not spoken to anyone throughout the long animated conversation behind the narrow windowpanes of the phone booth. His words must have echoed in the booth as he heard only silence on the other end of the dead line. What could he have been thinking as he nodded yes, yes, to that silence? Or as he stood watching the entrance of the theater through the rain. Since I first got on the bus I had known I would not go up to his apartment but until he ducked into the hotel and hurried over to the elevators I had not known why.

I had about three dollars in my pocket and although I had not seen a cab for some hours I imagined walking until I could hail one; taking it as far as the money would get me toward the "Y." My legs and back ached from the sitting cold and wet, hunched over in the bus. My head was thick, the feeling you get from being in a room filled with cigarette smoke. I walked to the corner and stopped. I would have laughed then, but as with any very complicated and wearisome practical joke, I would have cried just as easily; but I did neither. I stared at the red neon sign two blocks away on the front of the YMCA. I leaned against a light pole, its cool iron, octagonal surface still holding some of the rain, and stared down the street at the sign. We had been riding who knows what insane route through the city for two hours and doubled back to our starting point. It was just too feebleminded and pointless of him, and the pointlessness of it made me more tired than the trip.

I walked into the room with its bed, Bible, and dresser, all scaled down to Wonderland size, and packed, or rather stuffed—I've never learned to fold a shirt—my few clothes in the imitation leather suitcase and checked out of the "Y." I walked west, or is it north, which way does St. Louis face?—down, or across Washington or Olive or Market or one of the parallel main streets, away from the downtown area. I left at two-thirty with my wet clothes stuffed into the suitcase with my dirty clothes and walked to Jefferson Street, perpendicular to Market or Olive—and on Jefferson I walked, it seemed I was surely going too far, or Ohio or Iowa or some other state street. On Jefferson at five Saturday morning, after the rain, through the Negro section of St. Louis, it was like noon; it was like a picnic, a parade. No one slept. Everyone was outside, everyone was dancing and making love and shouting and yelling and singing and I was walking straight on, scared out of my mind for I had never seen anything like that before. I'd never seen payday celebrations, and I didn't understand it then but I do now. And the sun had been up and it had been light for over an hour by the time I found the cheese plant with the big truck waiting out front.

Fish Kite

Shelton leaned back now into the itchy gray upholstery of the car seat and closed his eyes: the fabric felt and smelled of carpet, and when they had first pulled away from Springfield he had delivered a hearty slap against its bristly nap to exclaim an excited: "Boy! On our way!" It had responded with a barrage of dust so stifling all the windows in the old Chevrolet had to be opened, or opened as much as they could, for the first twenty miles. The negative imprint of his hand remained, a leaf pattern on the yellow-gray fabric, and a fine layer of dust had matted the dashboard, settling back into the car. Wind had disheveled the clothes laid out in back and everything had to be put into order again at the first stop: only the fossil of his hand on the seat reminded Shelton of the incident.

"One hundred and twenty miles. Exactly."

Shelton opened his eyes to see a luminous ghost fly past the periphery of his vision. "Was that a sign?" he asked and pulled half erect.

"I said as soon as you stopped watch there'd be one. One hundred and twenty miles exactly," Otis repeated. "Over halfway there. Be there already if this thing had any juice in her." Otis had a red nose; he had gone into a sneezing spell when Shelton kicked up the dust.

"Sure you'll stay awake if I try to go to sleep?" Shelton asked.

"As long as the radio keeps talking to me I will." Outside the landscape had gone black on indigo: a rip-tooth of oak trees against sky. The faint warm glow of the speedometer's orange disc trembled against the window, a distorted oval of heat that weakly illuminated his own reflection on the rushing darkness outside. Occasionally, the highway passed enormous pyramids of rock waste from the lead and zinc mines interspersed with farmland and timber. Shelton sank into the seat again; the radio's tinny voice announced the time as ten thirty-five. Nearly four hours; it didn't seem like it. A few more miles and they would be within range of Tulsa stations, a better radio would pick them up now; one of the stations there had the tallest transmitter in the world. Shelton visualized it as Otis had described, a thin latticed spire vanishing into the sky with guy wires anchored half a mile from its base. It would be dark when they passed it.

He could still taste the vaguely nauseating breath of gasoline and the burn of the thin red rubber hose on his tongue. In his inexperience at siphoning gas he had scalded his mouth with the light liquid. Otis was expert. They had managed from one car or another parked along the dark unassuming streets of Springfield to collect a full tank and an auxiliary five-gallon Standard Oil can. Shelton had been belching the taste since they left.

Two hundred miles. The trip would cost them nothing but time and time was a recent luxury given them with their diploma that May. Shelton had lived in the little town, attending the consolidated school for five years, since his mother had remarried and they came to live with his stepfather. Otis had spent only one summer and his senior year at Athens. They had met the summer before when Otis and his mother moved there, and this was Shelton's first time away.

With Otis it was different, his father was a drunk who had staggered his way back home; he had wandered through, seen, the country. His dresser top at home in Athens, or what was home now, was a tribute in gold-plated trophies: Third Place Basketball Tournament, Nashville High, 1951; First Place Softball Team, Southwest Missouri League, Marshfield, Mo., 1953; Basketball Sedalia, Mo., 1953; Springfield, 1954; Oklahoma City, 1955; Springfield again, 1955: gold figurines forever jumping after a ball welded to their fingertips; they stopped time and action, remembering a dozen towns and teams in triumph, pulling into the public square in a chartered bus or convertible with the top pulled back—returning to a town where he had never grown to feel at home. And so Otis was used to roaming, drifting.

Shelton fell back into his nest, sensing the highway's surface on the springs. He had never been really away, never *alone*.

At Joplin, Missouri, Highway Sixty-sixty fades to the left, southwest through Kansas toward Tulsa. The highway divided their eleven miles outside Tulsa into four lanes. Motorists entering the city from this direction in the evening are treated as the highway rises just above the city to an incredible lake of lights. Quite suddenly Tulsa is before you. Shelton was not disappointed; at midnight with hardly another car about, they were laughingly tangled in one-way streets turning wrong directions, up down streets. It was late and after coffee at an all-night restaurant the old Chevrolet dipped silently into a large vacant parking area alongside a supermarket.

"You can certainly tell what the city's industry is." Shelton scanned the complex of buildings around: "Every building is Shell Building, Standard Oil Building."

Otis had moved to the back seat to stretch out. "When I was living in Oklahoma City a coupla years back, I remember there was oil wells all over town."

"In the city?"

"Sure. In parking lots and alongside buildings downtown. The Capitol building has about a dozen oil wells on its lawn. They have a few in Tulsa too, but not many."

"On the Capitol building?"

"Sure."

"That must have looked like crap."

"What's that building over there? The pointed one?"

"That's the Capitol. At night the top, that pointed top, changes colors, red and green and blue. They must turn it off now about midnight."

Shelton's gaze drifted from the obelisk over the silhouetted skyline. "When do we find a place to stay?"

"First thing as soon as we get up we'll go over to the Greyhound and clean up. All you have to do is walk down the street and look for signs that advertise sleeping rooms. We'll just have one room and maybe if we're lucky a private bath, don't expect the Waldorf."

"No." Shelton fixed his eyes on the thin red lettering of the Mayflower Hotel that seemed to float unsupported above the building's façade. "No, just a room is fine."

In the back seat Otis propped on an elbow, head against the car's windowsill: "What we have to do is after we find a room hit the pavement right away. If there isn't anything that sounds good in the want ads they have a place where you can go to get kitchen jobs in restaurants, even washing dishes. Till we can find something—that way we can have money coming in while we're looking."

"I wish I could *do* something."

"*Tell* them," Otis said. He had made the point a dozen times. "Anything they ask you if you've done it, tell them yes. You got to make people think they need you or you're out in the cold, nobody cares a damn if you need a job, they want to think you're going to make them money. They don't check references one time out of ten."

Shelton remained skeptical. "You," he said. "You could sell eggs to chickens. And get away with it. If I told someone I was a fry cook it would take him about two minutes to find out I didn't know what side to butter toast on."

"You'll be alright. A guy can talk his way through anything if he wants to."

"Sure. How much money do we have?"

"Four dollars."

Shelton began to laugh. "I don't believe it."

"Count for yourself."

"No, what I don't believe is that we did it. Two hundred and more miles from home with four dollars. It sounds insane. You tell someone back in Springfield you're going to Tulsa on four dollars and they'd have you locked up."

"They've got no imagination. Everyone in that crummy town can't see any farther than their nose."

"They can see as far as their stomachs, that's as far as they want to see."

"And that's why they won't ever get anywhere." Otis completed the thought as his own. "I want to get some sleep now. You can sit up front and chuckle to yourself if you want to."

"I thought you said you weren't tired."

"Try driving that crate and see if you don't wear down. It's like corralling a herd of elephants."

Shelton was looking toward the street: "A patrol car is driving by the parking lot about five miles an hour. Crawling like a turtle, looking this way."

"Don't pay any attention to them. As long as we're parked out in the middle of the lot they know we're not after anything."

"If they searched the car they'd find that gas can and hose." Shelton looked automatically toward the trunk, then back to the diminishing patrol car.

"So? We used it back on the farm to put gas in the tractor," Otis mumbled.

"Brother. I can't see you on a farm. Not to mention on a tractor."

"Why not? They don't know it. They think everyone from Missouri is a farmer anyway. We'll tell them it's yours and you used it. You know all about farming."

"We didn't have any tractor. It's alright anyway, they're gone now."

"They won't do anything as long as we don't look suspicious."

Shelton tried to curl up now on the front seat. "If anyone tells you a car is a comfortable place to sleep they'll lie about anything." He lay on his back, a doubled jacket for a pillow: "Are you going to write Edith and tell her where you are?"

Otis was nearly asleep, but he managed a grunted laugh. "Mom? Why would Mom give a damn where I am? Mom knows I can take care of myself. She'd probably be satisfied not to see me again for about five years anyway."

"My folks sure couldn't care less where I've gone," Shelton said hollowly.

"That stepfather of yours won't. If I had a stepdad like Carl I would have left when I was about ten years old."

"Yeah." Shelton blinked at the milky window that distorted the streetlight into halos and dreamed for an instant of having never met his stepfather.

"Still I'll write to them after awhile. As soon as I get straightened out and have some dough coming in. Besides I couldn't have run off when I was ten, mother never married again till I was thirteen. We just never got along. Right off. Right from the first he couldn't stand me and I couldn't stomach him. When the war was on mother used to go out with soldiers—when we lived in Springfield—some of them had dough, too. And after she married Carl I used to think that any one of those guys would have been alright. One admiral from Milwaukee owned a whole meat packing company. Sole owner; god, we'd have had steaks for breakfast. Another fellow owned a fishing-tackle outfit. Mother was beautiful then; lord, was she a knockout—you wouldn't know her now. So Carl drags us down to that damn one-horse town where people faint if a woman wears lipstick practically and within a year you wouldn't know her. I hated Carl more for that, I think, than anything else."

Otis grunted. "When I was living with Mom in Marshfield, there was a girl named Karen, lived with her mother. She and her mother moved to Tulsa about a year ago. I'll have to look her up while we're here."

"Sure. She good-looking?"

"Not bad; her old lady was a knockout. She used to come over to talk with Mom—they were in school together or something—and Karen would come along. We used to go out in the garage and make out while they talked in the house." Shelton laughed. "I think her old lady got wise though, 'cause she stopped bringing Karen along. Hell, I was only about fifteen; Karen's mother used to get flustered as hell every time I came in the house. I think she had pants for me. She'd have been damn good, too—she was a knockout. We have to get some sleep, it must be two o'clock."

"Yeah, I'm not very sleepy. I guess I must have slept half the way here. If you can find out where Karen's living we can go out and see her."

Otis had turned his face into his coat-pillow and his voice was muffled. "One time I drove the two of them and Karen's kid brother to the river in Marshfield, Potter's Landing. It's about ten slow miles and I just wore my trunks in the car. I thought her mother would faint she got so nervous."

Shelton laughed.

"I never saw a woman chain-smoke like she could. One after another. I'd have made it with her too if I could have got rid of Karen for a minute." Shelton blinked at the pattern of interlocking rainbows on the window. Otis yawned a mournful aria ending in a grunt. "We have to leave here before everyone starts coming to work." And added a half-said, as though in salutation, "Sleep."

"We'll wake up as soon as it gets light probably." Shelton turned in the seat. "Boy, steering wheels sure weren't made to sleep with. If I put my knees up I'm gonna blow that horn sure as hell." Otis was quiet in the back seat. "I'll have to write Mother some kind of postcard and tell her where I am. She'd have the Missouri State Police combing the hills for a month. But as long as Carl doesn't get canned and doesn't decide to rent a farm or something, God knows they don't need me around there. Every time Carl gets depressed about the cheese plant he starts mumbling about renting a farm somewhere. He has a cow and two calves in the back lot and he thinks he's a farmer. Buying grain and hay for them, he'll take about a two hundred percent loss every year. He feels like the farmers won't listen to him when he tells them how to feed their cows or build a barn unless he's got cattle, too. If he wasn't so damn simple-minded I think I could almost put up with him. Every damn thing he does is so small. You know what he does?" Shelton was quiet for a moment. An auto horn beeped somewhere far off, and he could hear the faint gearing of a bus or truck. He remembered with anticipation that he was well away from everyone. "He buys toys," he said faintly. "When he's in Springfield or Nixa in some five and ten store he brings back mechanical toys. Monkeys that climb string or a gyro scope and pull things like wobbling wooden ducks and horses and things. And once a bear that beats a tin drum. I mean he gets a kick out of them. He doesn't do anything with them. Sometimes he gives them to a kid across the street. But mostly they just lay around. You want to ask him what he wants them for but he just says when I get married and have kids or when his daughter out in Denver gets married—I guess he thinks he's going to give that junk to my kids. Every month or so he comes dragging in something else." Except for Otis's steady soft breathing the city was quiet now. Shelton closed his eyes and tried to remember the direction of the Greyhound station. They had passed it not far away but with wrong turns and stopping for coffee he had forgotten where. They would go there and wash up, and then they would find a sleeping room close to the business district, and then—the hard seat and coat softened under his head. "'Night," he murmured but it was hardly audible.

What was left of the night seemed gone in an instant. Shelton was awakened sharply with a drum beating at his head. He raised up face to face with a man on the outside of the window glass and only after an instant of shock realized he was a policeman, yelling, "Hey, come on, move on." Otis sat up in the back seat, swearing. Vaguely.

Shelton rolled down the window. "Yes, sir?"

"Come on, move on. What do you think this is, a motel?"

"No, sir."

The policeman rested his hand on the edge of the car door and looked inside. "What are you, drunk?"

"No," Shelton said. A worldly accusation always drew a mildly shocked expression from him. "Just sleepy. We got in too late to go to a hotel."

The policeman stepped back from the door. "Are you awake now?"

"I think so," Shelton half-laughed.

The policeman opened the car door and motioned. "You better walk around some."

Shelton climbed out of the car and spread his arms, squinting in the morning light. "I'm alright now. Thanks."

"No thanks, I just don't want you driving out of here into a lamp pole. You guys from Missouri?"

"Yes, Springfield." The policeman made a half motion to get out with a swipe of his arm. Only as he turned to Shelton, did he notice the patrol car parked a car's length behind, and for the first time as well he noticed the city was alive around them. With a shock he realized the parking lot was half-filled. Otis climbed into the front seat. The police car backed out of the entrance and squalled down the street. He stepped back into the car. "Boy did that give me a scare."

"Are they gone?"

"Yeah. My adrenalin was about a foot over my head."

Otis pulled the car into the exit lane. "I about cracked up when you said we got in too late to get into a hotel."

"I had to say something, didn't I?"

"Not that. It doesn't get too late to check into a hotel. What do you think they have night clerks for?" Otis checked the traffic and turned the car easily toward the bus terminal. "He couldn't have been very worried about us or he would have called you on that one."

Shelton had relaxed now. The view of the city was spectacular. Already the sun was drawing color from the sky and it would be a blazing day. "Why should he think anything?" he said. "With me stuttering like an imbecile and you with your baby face."

It seemed enough to explain their worthy and adventurous intentions, though actually Otis did not have a baby face at all. Strong and young, yes, but he appeared older than his eighteen years. He was tall and like most tall Midwestern boys he swaggered subtly, even standing stationary. But there was something very much more, perhaps in the squint of his eyes or twist of mouth, that suggested a paradox of innocence and worldliness. The one facial blemish lent weight to the visage—a thin brown scar low on his cheek that always remained a few shades darker than his complexion: in summer just barely visible, but visible—there on the tanned and crookedly smiling face; in winter quite salient—though his squinting warm blue eyes begged innocence, despite the former. People, without provocation, found it difficult to refuse him; for admittedly or not most everyone is drawn to attractiveness and admirable, subtly aggressive, health. Especially extreme attractiveness.

They made a fine pair, Shelton with his slightly undernourished frame, tall and almost bent, but springy and active; with dark circled and deep piercing eyes almost impudently scrutinizing and his easy, light-humored way. They made a fine pair, freshly dressed and shaved, walking along the shimmering sidewalks; standing on the blue-gray painted planks of the porch—the first house advertising sleeping rooms.

The house was white with a Gothic dowel work around its eaves. The porch railing had been painted that spring with the matte white coating that invites you to sit there and survey the wisteria on either side of the walk and the neighborhood of quietly curious houses, and repays the visit with a broad dusty white stripe across the seat of your pants. The ceiling of the porch, of a tongue and groove sky blue, buckled slightly. Two iron rings, four feet apart, as though they had floated like balloons to the ceiling and stuck there rusting faintly onto the blue, told that a swing once had been at one end of the porch. Whenever Shelton saw the vaguely lonely space where a swing had been removed he always looked to the clapboard wall behind where it had swung. The boards are invariably knocked with the corner triangular-shaped dents where some boy has tried to kick to a loftier height and had been restricted by the house. The dents always explain why the swing had been removed; once the chain jerks apart and the seat falls it is never repaired satisfactorily.

Otis knocked against the screen jamb. The center of the main door was set with the key of a twist-bell but the door stood open into the house.

"Yes?" The woman who appeared dimly behind the screen was wiping her hands on an apron. It was difficult to see into the darkness. The woman offered them no hint that she knew their business but her voice was cordial.

Otis answered her: "We're interested in a room for a month or so." The woman appeared to register understanding. She smiled and opened the screen with one hand and with the other made a gesture for the boys to come in and the flies to stay out.

"We saw the sign," Shelton said superfluously. They stood in the dark hall.

"You boys are from out of town?"

"From Springfield. We came down looking for work—just got here a few hours ago. But first we'll have to find a room."

She looked from one to the other and spoke to Otis, who had answered her. "You look very crisp to have driven all that way."

Shelton said, "We stopped at the Greyhound to clean up some. The road is pretty dusty. We drove."

The woman seemed impressed. She led them up a short walnut stairway to the room at the head. "This is the room. There's a bath, a large bath, next door." The room was furnished as any room in her house might be. Shelton noted with relief an ashtray was provided on the bed table. They sat on the side of the bed. Two windows commanded a view across the top of the porch they had just stood on. A pleasant breeze, of which the lady was proud, kept the thin curtains in restless movement.

"The room is seven dollars a week. Some charge extra for two, but I don't see any reason. Most of the doors downstairs are kept shut so you won't be bothered with my husband or me and we won't be bothered with your comings and goings." She sat in a chair opposite the bed.

"Normally we would pay for the week in advance," Otis said. "But we're awfully short. We can if it's really necessary, but we'd be able to eat better if you let us pay after the first week—or as soon as we can locate a job." He spoke casually and with immense trust. No request was troublesome to his easy nature. "I could leave my watch if you like."

The woman looked at them and smiled pleasantly. Shelton knew they were in. She would begin "two boys as good-looking as you . . ."

"Two boys as good-looking as you shouldn't have any trouble finding work. You'll have to pay me as soon as you find some. No, I'll tell you what," she corrected, "you can pay me fifteen next week for this and next." Otis had assured him it would be fine but it had remained an apprehension with Shelton. The woman introduced them to the bathroom and provided them with large white towels. She told them that the door was locked at midnight and asked that they not come in later. They said they would not and she withdrew smiling.

Shelton took in the view. Otis tested the bed and groaned appreciatively, kicking off his shoes, then jumping up to replace them gently on the floor and listen for a moment for a rebuke. None came. They had a room.

Walking toward Market Street, and the center of town, Otis bought a paper, and as they walked, turned the pages, blowing largely like billows on a lake against his face, to the want ads. It was mostly houses for sale, apartments for rent, property, situations wanted. One item appeared under Help Wanted Male: learn the business from the ground up, large eastern company opening branch here, interviewing possible customers in their homes. No selling. The paper flapped savagely in Otis's hand. Contact Mr. Schwertz at the Hotel Mayfair, Suite 1100.

"That's all?"

"No selling it says. That's the only one. I'll bet it's vacuum cleaners." Otis looked on through the paper. "That's the only one. It couldn't hurt to try." They went to a telephone at a drugstore and leaned against the wall. There was no answer in Suite 1100. "We'll try again sometime." They came back into the sun outside the drugstore and leaned against the wall. Many of the younger men wore boots and a large shady hat, cocked at individual angles, down in their face or back on their head, sidewise, in approximately the most attractive position. They wore suede jackets or denim; their manner and walk was slow and deliberate, almost a rehearsed swagger. Shelton looked down at the sidewalk and flattened a thread of tar with his heel. "Well, where to now?"

"That job wouldn't pay anything anyway. Door to door selling; nobody falls for that crap anymore." Otis squinted across the street. "Looks like we need a ten-gallon hat."

"Boots, too. I bet they're afraid of cows."

"They ride at rodeos, some of them. The rest of them probably don't know what a cow is. You hungry?

"Not very."

"Well, here's what I thought we ought to do. Since you've had experience in a restaurant you should go on and register with that place I told you about."

"The employment place. I'd sure better do something. I'm not hungry now, but I will be . . ."

"That's what I mean. And maybe I should try to look up this Karen and some of the people I knew when I was at Oklahoma City. We should know someone in town in case we need something."

"Which might not be too far off," Shelton finished. "Do you think you could find her?"

"I hope so. Maybe I can borrow some money off her till we get going."

Shelton nodded his head. He was wishing mainly that he had had breakfast. "Do you think this place will take me on?"

"Not there, they send you out . . . you wait in the office and they call in for help and they send you out. You'll probably won't wait more than ten or fifteen minutes. You can pick up maybe ten bucks for a day's work, not counting meals, so that's pretty good till we find something that's better."

Shelton gave an appreciative nod.

"And if nothing better turns up I'll join on too, and we'll both have something going for us until we can find better."

They got back into the car. Otis gave Shelton a dollar for something to eat and wished him luck. Shelton said he hoped Otis was able to find Karen. He got out of the car in front of a block of uneven two- and three-story buildings used mostly for storage and secondhand sales. The restaurant association's Employment Center was a small room in a half-basement office. A swinging shingle with an old-time pointing hand swung above a fire escape kind of metal staircase that descended to the level of the doorway and two large windows in the front office. The picture windows were cut in half horizontally, the lower half below sidewalk level, as if the building had sunk six feet into its foundation. They looked out onto an area used mostly for discarding cigarette packages and newspapers that collected the building debris from the street. The doorway was kept closed to the flies that buzzed over the area. The upper half of the two windows viewed a railing around the pit, and the legs of pedestrians on the sidewalk. One was confronted with a constantly shifting view of runover heels and running hose, flappy pant legs and lopsided high-heeled boots. Inside the office, chairs had been set back against the walls, chairs of the high school style, with arm desks. A desk was against the third wall, with a man behind it. He was perspiring and speaking on the telephone. The man glanced up as Shelton closed the door and indicated a stack of applications on his desk, motioning for Shelton to take one. Shelton did, nodding, and sat down at one of the school chairs. There were eight other men in the room. Some of them looked up when he entered, some of them seemed too involved with their magazines. They were, all but one, much older men, worn and unshaven, a collection you would expect on park benches, or in Springfield, outside the pool hall and around the third-rate bars. One man coughing sporadically into a copy of *Life*. Shelton assessed the men were waiting for a call. The perspiring gentleman behind the desk continued to try to sell an applicant to a hesitant restaurateur over the phone. A fry cook. The man looked at an application in his hand and then across to a colored boy sitting on the edge of his chair. "Has he worked a counter?" the man at the desk repeated loudly. The boy nodded. "Sure! Counter and kitchen, either one." The boy nodded again. "Well, I tell you what; you try him a day and let me know, he's a good risk, take my word for it. What's that? Night?" The boy was hesitant. "If it's necessary; rather have days, I guess anyone would. Well, then *try* him a night or two and let me know, O.K.?" There was a brief pause where the man studied a calendar across the room. "Fine, fine; I'll send him on over." A few of the men around the room nodded agreeably but the colored boy looked strangely appreciative and apprehensive.

"My wife don' much want me to start on even' work," he said testily.

"Yeah, neither would mine," the man said, writing on the colored boy's application, "but we take what we can get, don't we? You work out good, you can ask for days."

"Once you start even's it's the devil to get shifted." The boy shook his head and addressed the floor mournfully.

"Well, let's see how you work out before we turn anything down, don't you think? You go on out here this afternoon about five." He handed him a small receipt. The boy nodded, mumbling a mixed thank you, and went out the door.

Shelton only half followed the transaction; his attention was divided between the application and a large flat-bladed fan that jumped up and down over the man's head. It rotated very slowly, raising almost unperceptively as it turned until it completed the cycle, then it fell in an abrupt jerk a full four inches. The effect caused anyone watching it to flinch, expecting it to fall on the man's head.

The man took Shelton's application and read it through. "Kitchen?" he inquired.

"How do you mean?"

"You done kitchen work?"

"I haven't cooked," Shelton said before he remembered Otis's advice to say yes to everything.

"Who said cook? Bussin' and washin' dishes?"

"Sure, anyone can do that."

"Handle a dishwasher?"

"I suppose I could learn quick enough."

The man pushed out his fat lips and sucked them in. In the corner the cougher started up again so violently he had to put his magazine aside and take out a wadded handkerchief. The man behind the desk looked over Shelton's application again. "Well, we'll give you a try. I guess you'll work nights; you're single."

"Sure."

"You go over here and see Mr. Kaufman. He's the owner. We'll try you one night."

Shelton took the paper and read it. "This is dishwashing?"

"General thing. Dishwashing, bussin', cleaning up. You want it or don't you?"

"Sure." He folded the paper and put it in his wallet. As he started to leave the man looked up again and spoke but the cougher decided to hack again.

"I beg your pardon?" Shelton said.

"I said be a little early. The paper says five, but get there a little early. Kaufman don't like to be teaching a greenhorn on his own time."

After Shelton left the Employment Center he suddenly felt elated. It wasn't anything steady but it might become steady. It would hold him until he found something. He was employed. He was working and he didn't even know where. He took the paper from his wallet and studied it. The Shamrock Coffee Shop; the first thing would be to find it. The second would be to get something to eat. He wondered if Otis had had any luck locating Karen. More than anything, as he walked jauntily down the street, he wished he could tell Otis of his luck. He never did discover what the other men were waiting for at the Employment Center.

Shelton found the Shamrock Coffee Shop and things began to fall closer into perspective. It was a very small counter and stool café, located on what was probably a very good corner. It had large windows on either side of the corner door and a "U" shape counter. A large menu over the passage into the kitchen listed sandwiches and breakfasts and several complete dinners at rather a rock-bottom price. He walked past the entrance and stood under a small high window that seemed to be into the kitchen. Still, it was working. It was his first job in a city. Loud noises of spraying water and clanking dishes came from the window over his head. After a moment he walked on across the street for something to eat.

On the chance that Otis had returned to the apartment, Shelton decided to drop by, and to leave him a note. It was apparently true that their landlords didn't intend to interfere with their business. Shelton bounded up the front steps onto the gray porchboards of the house to see a very elderly man coming from the house. The man wore a dark suit and blue shirt over which, under the open jacket, you could see vivid Kelly green suspenders. The man's hair was the color of antique piano keys, that old ivory; and he wore strange blond shoes that matched the color almost identically. The man nodded familiarly, as if to his grandson. "Going to be a scorcher," he said.

Shelton skidded to a stop in front of the screen door. "Yes, sir, it sure looks like it."

The man slipped sideways out of the screen door and closed it quickly. "Flies are terrible this year. Going to be a dry one, when it gets this hot in June." He looked up to the sky-blue porch ceiling and murmured: "Clear as a chime. I said last winter we were in for a hot one. Hot and dry." He nodded pleasantly and sat slowly into one of the three wicker porch chairs, and took a silver flask from his inside coat pocket.

By two o'clock it was raining. One of those flashing, scattering showers that, even in the city, makes the air smell of summer and earth. Shelton saw it begin from his window over the porch roof and wondered if the old man would get wet. He had written a note to Otis, a rather long one telling of the job and the employment office, the location of the Shamrock Coffee Shop. He would have to work from five that evening until six the next morning; if Otis came in early and not tired, he was invited down to supervise Shelton washing dishes. The gentleman in the green suspenders was not on the porch when Shelton left.

Shelton found Mr. Kaufman behind the cash register, swearing. Apparently the waitress who was going off shift had neglected to put a new roll of tape in the machine and it had not recorded sales since noon. She looked on with a tired blankness as Mr. Kaufman threaded the paper through the register; but she only said: "Well, it may seem simple to you, but you aren't trying to do it and serve thirty customers and tend register at the same time." Shelton decided it wasn't the best time to meet Mr. Kaufman, but when he introduced himself to his new boss he was surprised with a sudden change in the man's disposition.

"You got here plenty early. They tell you to come at five?"

"Yes, they did. They said I should get familiar with things."

Mr. Kaufman waved his hand. "Ah, those dumb bastards down there, you shouldn't listen to them. They think it takes a degree to learn to wash dishes. You ever handle a washer?"

"No, but I suppose it can't be too hard." Shelton began to relax.

"It don't make any difference if you had, that heap I got isn't like any other washer anyone's seen anyway. I think someone overhauled a washing machine. You had anything to eat?"

"No. I didn't know . . ."

Kaufman raised his voice to yell to the waitress who had retreated to the coffee urns. "Pearl, tell this kid to grab something to eat. I gotta go out. Late already with that damn register." He motioned for Shelton to take a stool. Then he paused for a second and said: "Your name's Shelton, huh?"

"Yes, sir."

"You a Jewish boy? Shelton, ain't that Jewish?"

Shelton thought a second. "No. I'm Baptist when I go to church, but I don't go much."

Mr. Kaufman grinned: "English, huh?"

Shelton, still rather thoughtful, for he hadn't really considered his nationality much, and wasn't too sure, said doubtfully, "Irish, I think."

"Irish!" Mr. Kaufman slapped him on the back. "Sure, we'll get along fine, Shelly. Working in the Shamrock Coffee Shop. That ought to be right up your alley."

"Yes, sir. I hadn't thought of that."

Mr. Kaufman digressed into a more business tone. "Look, Shelly, I'm trying to get the hell out of here before the old lady comes in, so I'm going to leave you in control. You just keep the dishes cleared away for Jackie, that's the waitress, who'll be in before long, and keep a lot of the cups out front. She'll show you where everything belongs. Wally comes on at six, he's the swing cook—you're working to six, you knew that?"

Shelton nodded.

"That's fine then. Along about seven you sweep up a little and then you'll sweep and mop at four, before the breakfast crowd starts to come in. You just kinda follow anything Wally tells you to do. He'll tell you about the washer, he's the only one that understands it anyway. O.K.?"

Shelton had almost followed everything, he nodded again and smiled at the waitress who had come over to the counter and was standing in front of him. "Sure. O.K."

"So just get something to eat and wait around till Wally gets in and he'll tell you what to do; eh, Shelly?"

Shelton laughed, for one thing he had never heard the appellation Shelly before and found it strange. "Right," he said.

"Fine. Now I'm getting the hell out of here; I'll just leave you in charge. Pearl, clear out those Silexes before Jackie comes in, I don't want to hear her complaining about that again. I got enough to listen to."

Pearl smiled halfheartedly and handed Shelton a menu. Mr. Kaufman was out the back door, said something to the cook in the kitchen on his way through.

Shelton, not wanting to seem overly gluttonous just because the meal was free, ordered a hamburger and coffee. "Mr. Kaufman seems easy enough to work for, doesn't he?" he asked Pearl, who was busy at the Silexes.

"You get him in a good mood he ain't bad. Get him in a foul mood and you aren't working." She seemed not overly agreeable just now herself, so Shelton decided not to press her for an explanation. When she brought him his sandwich, it was nearly five thirty and she was nearly finished for the day. She said casually, "Wonder how long you intend to stay?"

"For a while, anyway. Why?"

"That job you got turns over three times a week."

"I don't guess anyone wants to be a dishwasher all their lives."

The comment meant nothing to her. "Day-washer would be the same thing, but they got some ninety-year-old jig that's been here since before God. Crazy as a loon."

Shelton was eating, but thought it best to be friendly now that she had decided to talk. "Really?"

"Batty as hell," Pearl said. "He thinks he owns the joint by the looks of it. You should go back there and see the pile of dishes he leaves for the night man. Says there's more for the day-washer so he goes home at four thirty and nobody washes so much as a glass until you come on at six. I tell you he's loony; everybody calls him Custer cause he's always sitting down."

"If he's that old, maybe it's best for him to sit; maybe we could all go in together and get him a wheelchair." Pearl liked this, she laughed and wiped the counter off with cloth, and laughed again.

"You don't know how funny that is until you seen him, Shelly. I swear he's older than God himself."

A few minutes early Jackie came in. Jackie was a carbon of Pearl, only about ten years older and with red hair instead of blond. She had a half-gold tooth flashing when she smiled, which was constantly. She nodded enthusiastically to Shelton when Pearl introduced them, shook his hand, gave him a wicked little smile, slapped him on the back and cracked a friendly little joke under her breath, which made her laugh uproariously again, but Shelton didn't manage to hear what she had said.

He laughed anyway, because she was good natured and comical. You could never tell when Jackie was serious, you could seldom quite understand what she said: she spoke softly and laughed loudly, but her expression usually told you if you should be amused or amazed. Jackie described almost everyone as relatively quiet and she was exactly right.

Someone appeared at the kitchen window long enough to scream: "Who the hell's going to wash these goddamn dishes?" Shelton jumped off the stool and turned around but no one was at the window.

Jackie made a motion for him to sit back down. "That's Wally, honey, you pay him no mind." Then she screamed, half turning to the kitchen: "He's here, stop your yellin.'" Shelton had already started for the kitchen. He soon began to discover why the job turned over three times a week. Wally had no patience with the regiment of dishwashers and kitchen help that had walked through that door. He was tired of explaining to them, tired of listening to them, talking to them, and most tired of giving orders. He looked to Shelton like anything besides a cook, like a ranch hand or road laborer. The heat of the grill had burned and tanned his face and arms; his hair was singed and dry and receded. Already he was perspiring, taking off his cap and wiping it across his forehead. "You got the bastard," he said when Shelton said the grill would be hot to work over. "Long about midnight you won't be feeling sorry for anybody but yourself. That bastard heats up the whole goddamn kitchen."

For all its sinister countenance the dishwashing machine was not difficult to master. It was a mammoth tin box with a canvas flap at each end. Dishes were scraped and rinsed in a large sink, then stacked into a wire basket, then pushed with a stick through the canvas flaps into cross streams of scaling spray and steam. After a few minutes the basket was pulled out of the machine through the flaps on the other side. This operation was the trickiest. It was accomplished with a long, straightened, wire coat hanger, with which you reached under the canvas flaps and fished for the basket. The machine leaked steam from a dozen cracks from both canvas doors; a puncture on top directed a panache straight into the air. You could see under the machine through a number of holes, missing bolts: The underside was an inferno of blue and yellow gas flames and red glowing metal grates. The wall all behind the machine burned with the reflection of the gas flames. Unlike almost every machine it never repeated the same sound twice, but set up a variety of unexpected sounds that fell simultaneously from every part. Somewhere in its insides every two or three minutes a deep twangy wire bellowed: "Pink Punk" as clearly as if it had vocal cords.

It took the first hour to clear away the dishes Custer had left from the afternoon, but every hour seemed like three. It became the longest night of Shelton's life. The brief chores Mr. Kaufman had mentioned were only a start. He swept and mopped the outside and the kitchen. He washed and scrubbed thirty pounds of potatoes and cooked them in a huge lard bucket, peeled them and sliced the hot potatoes for hash browns. From nine to one the café was packed and noisy. The heat in the kitchen was stifling; the air so humid cigarettes turned limp and wouldn't draw.

There was a window above the sink. The window he had stood under when he heard the spraying from the machine that afternoon. It looked out onto the beautiful skyline of Tulsa. Directly in the center was the bank building Otis had pointed out; its pointed top was lit with floodlights that changed very slowly orange to green to white. The view was so foreign from anything he had known, and exciting. But somehow, perhaps because he became so tired from standing, it made him feel very much alone. The slow change of color continued until midnight.

Green.

White.

Orange.

Off. And the skyline seemed to darken all over the city. Billboards vanished into black silhouetted walls, and only windows that remained lighted were the ones that marked the stairwells, stacked like tall rectangles of light. Noise on the street quieted and the crowd thinned until only a straggling bum or two came in between one and four. Shelton was tired, his arms ached from lifting the baskets of dishes, his legs ached from standing and walking on the slippery concrete. Otis did not come around, though Shelton kept a constant lookout for him. The constant heat and smell of grease and steam made him feel sick to his stomach and he didn't feel like breakfast. At five that morning, Mr. Kaufman drove up into the alley behind the kitchen. His first words were: "Where the hell's that boy?" He bellowed it out as he came through the back door. The door slammed shut as he yelled, "Shelton, how come you didn't mop up this kitchen floor?"

"I did, Mr. Kaufman."

"You did maybe, but when? It's too goddamned late now, people are going to be coming in here for breakfast. You cleaned up the front at least, didn't you?"

Shelton took a full breath and started to say something but the man cut him off. "Hell, forget it. I didn't expect you to remember anything." He walked through the kitchen and out into the diner.

"Boy, there's going to be hell to pay now," Wally said.

"I just hope he fires me, I'm not going to take his crap and all this work too for five dollars a night."

Wally motioned for Shelton to be quiet: "Take no notice of that." Wally was looking out into the diner. "He went right past her, didn't say a word. Went over to the coffee maker."

"Right past who? Is he drunk?"

"I manage that the both of them are drunk. Passed her right by, but you can bet he knew she was out there. Probably saw her when he came driving by."

"Who?" Shelton repeated and went to the round window in the kitchen door.

"The old lady. She came in about ten minutes ago. The one at the counter. She hasn't been here in about three weeks."

Shelton squinted through the steamed window: There was only one woman besides Jackie; or perhaps it was only the wide, yoke-collared, navy-dotted

Swiss dress that made her shoulders appear heavy. She was a plain woman with heavy make-up; in fact, only her long blond hair was attractive. "She's his old lady that he was running from this afternoon?"

The owner of the café drew a cup of coffee and walked slowly to his wife. He was behind the counter, standing in front of her. Shelton erased a little circle of steam to see through the window better. "Well, I hope you had an enjoyable time this evening," Shelton heard the man say. "Well, answer up, Lee, did you enjoy this evening?"

His wife didn't look up at first. Her voice was low and thick; you couldn't tell she had been drinking until she spoke, then her whole appearance altered. "Jackie, honey, could you get me a good cold glass of water?" Her elbows spread apart on the counter and she seemed to come apart and sway in a slow arch. Jackie brought the water without comment. There were four other customers having breakfast.

"I guess you didn't hear me, Lee. I was asking if you had a good time tonight?"

The woman finally looked up to her husband and said loudly and flatly, "Well, I'll be goddamned, if it isn't old Sam." Shelton winced at that and whistled under his breath.

"I guess you didn't notice me here, did you, Lee?"

"Well, Sam, I sensed your presence you might say, but I didn't notice it was you."

"You blind drunk lying bitch."

"No, Sam, you're just easy to overlook."

Sam Kaufman slapped his full sweaty palm onto the Formica counter making a roaring pistol crack that could be heard out into the street: Everyone jumped erect and poor Jackie threw a glass of milk into the air. "I asked you a goddamned question, now I'll teach you to run off on me! I asked you if you enjoyed yourself whoring it up all over south Tulsa tonight!" Shelton hurried back to the sink and started up the machine. Wally made a clatter around the grill. Above the noise they could hear the yelling continuing in the diner. Wally ducked his head to look through the window again: "Boy, one day he's just going to slap the shit out of her."

"Did he?"

"He's mad enough to. God she just sits there like the fuckin' sphinx . . . Goddamn! Here they come back here. I wish they'd stay out front. Look busy!" As Shelton turned back to the sink, Mrs. Kaufman came swinging through the kitchen door.

"Well, catch this domesticity! I'm glad we didn't disturb you boys. You're the new dishwasher, are you? Well, they get better looking every week." As Sam came into the kitchen she added: "What's the new kid's name?"

"Get out in the car, we're going home."

Shelton almost ran into the diner mumbling, "I got to get those dishes from out there."

"Don't run off, sweetheart, we'll have a nice talk." This last he didn't hear, only Mr. Kaufman's "I said get in the goddamned car." The back door slammed with such force it caused the door between the kitchen and diner to swing open.

Shelton looked down at Jackie, who was cleaning up the glass: "Good lord are they always like that? What were they, drunk?"

Jackie looked up in anguish, picking up the slivers of milky glass, but she flashed her half-gold tooth in a quick smile and said in one breath what sounded like: "I-don't-know-honey-lord-the-way-they-carry-on-you'd-think-it-was-the-holy-rollers-screaming-around-drunk-and-breaking-things. Scare the living-pants-off-me-hand-me-that OUCH! sponge, will-you-honey? God damn-THERE-I've-cut-my-finger!" She put her finger in her mouth and shook her head remorsefully as Shelton carried the basket of dishes into the kitchen.

It was five thirty. The last half hour had gone by unnoticeably enough, but the time until six dragged on endlessly. For one thing people began to come in for breakfast as light started to show in the sky. For another Shelton's duties shifted to cleaning up the kitchen: washing the washing machine, the sink; emptying the seven lard cans of garbage, filling all the silverware bins out front as well as the tables holding cups, saucers, and glasses. It seemed more running than anything. He was finished by six, but Custer had not arrived so Shelton sat out front where it was cool and had a cup of coffee. Pearl came back on modeling blond hair for Jackie's approval.

As Shelton sat he became more tired; he began to feel the ache in his arms and legs and chest and he cursed himself for not being in better shape. I think I haven't used my muscles in years, he had said to Wally. Wally left just before six as the day cook came on.

Jackie drew herself a cup of coffee and brought it around to sit beside Shelton. She slapped him on the back and drew a long breath. "Well-that's-what-I-call-a-Hair-Raiser, eh?"

"Yeah," Shelton nodded.

"Whatsamatter, Sweetheart, you tired? Long night, huh?"

"I'll say it's long. Twelve hours. They shouldn't let people work that long."

"They don't," Jackie said simply. "Against every law in the country. I guess he figures if you don't like it you quit, you know? There's always somebody else—still the tips ain't bad—ya-wouldn't-think in a joint-like-this, would you?"

"No."

"Ahhh, those truck drivers. Heart of gold, sweethearts almost all of them, I tell you the crap they put up with here with fights like that every night or so."

"They go at it every night?"

"No, but if it ain't him and her, it's him onta me or her onta a customer, hell, cut outta the same mold those two, happy as long as they can fight. Why don't you get on home, you look beat. You live around here?"

Shelton shook his head and it made him dizzy. "No. Springfield."

"Yeah, but you're staying around here, ain'tcha?"

"What? Oh, sure. Down on Mayberry Street. It's not far. I got a room with a buddy of mine. He was supposed to come around tonight."

"Ah, he's probably in bed where you oughta be."

"I suppose. Still, I should stay until Custer gets here, shouldn't I?"

"You're supposed to but nobody ever does. He's got that down to a science, he sometimes don't show till ten in the morning, still catches up in a half-an-hour. Why don't you get some rest? Did you sleep last night?"

Shelton opened his eyes wide to stretch them and thought a minute. "Come to think of it, I didn't get much sleep; not more than three hours, probably."

Jackie took his arm and forced him off the stool with a maternal nudge: "O.K., that does it. Off to bed. I'll tell them I sent you. You got no call staying here past six anyway and it's quarter past now." She half shoved him toward the front door.

"When do I get paid, Jackie?"

"Stop by when you've had some sleep. Aren't you coming back this evening?"

"I don't know. Yes, I guess so, but God, I didn't know it was going to be work."

"It's work alright. I'll see you tonight, scout."

It was still cool for the morning when he went out. The sky had faded from a bright salmon as the streetlights were turned out and was beginning to look hot and white. The streets, as they always are in Tulsa, were clean and reflecting the pale skies.

At the end of the block he saw Wally driving back slowly along the curb toward the café. Shelton stopped at the corner and leaned up against the window of a drugstore. Wally's car stopped a few yards from the café. In a moment Jackie came hurrying out and jumped in, slamming the door shut as the car squealed out. Shelton watched the car for another block where it turned west onto Houston Street. He smiled to himself and shook his head as he began to walk to the rooming house.

He looked up to the window over the porch, but could see only the white lace curtains moving with the upstairs breeze. The inside of the house was dark so he climbed the porch stairs quietly. Once inside the screen door he could see down the dark hall into the kitchen. The lady who had rented the room appeared in the kitchen door. "Oh, lord you gave me a fright. I thought maybe it was the morning paper but it don't come this early."

"No, ma'am, it's only me."

"Are you coming in?"

"Yes, ma'am."

The woman looked quizzical but didn't voice her thoughts. Instead she said, "I heard you talking yesterday evening to my father."

"Was I?"

"On the porch."

"Oh, sure." Shelton saw that he wouldn't get away easily; the woman stood in the door obviously waiting for an explanation. Shelton walked back into the kitchen and took a deep whiff of the baking aroma that filled the hallway. "You're making light bread, I'll bet."

"I am," the woman said proudly. "I'm the last of my kind, I'm afraid."

"My grandmother used to bake bread. That's about the greatest perfume in the world."

The woman pulled out a chair and motioned for Shelton to sit down. "Why don't you sit a moment and have a glass of milk? Perfume," she mused after a moment.

Shelton was very tired. It seemed things were happening in a dream. He wasn't really in his landlady's kitchen being served a glass of milk, he was upstairs in an aching sleep. "Yes, perfume," he said after a moment, but he seemed to hear his voice far away, as though someone were speaking to him. "My grandmother used to wear it—the baking light bread aroma. I think of Grandmother Tate every time I pass a bakery. I bet I always will."

The woman sat the glass in front of him and poured it with milk from an enamel pitcher. "Most women just bake for the county fairs; I do all my baking. I'll bring you up some of it." She paused. "Unless you're going right off to sleep."

"I'm afraid I am," Shelton said and put his hand around the cool glass. "I've been working all night."

"Have you?" The woman was obviously delighted.

Shelton nodded. "Not much, but alright until something better comes along, I guess. I washed dishes all night. Uptown at the Shamrock Coffee Shop, you know it?"

"I wouldn't know it. I hardly ever go uptown. I wouldn't know one place from the next."

"You wouldn't want to know this place; but it'll do until something else comes along." Shelton got up from the table and reset his chair. "Thank you for the milk, I'll sleep better now; but I've got to turn in." He walked back to the walnut stairway.

The woman followed him a few steps. "I'll wager you wouldn't have had much trouble sleeping anyway."

"No, I'm just going to push Otis over and pass out." The woman laughed. "Do you think you could knock on the door sometime this afternoon about four? In case I don't wake up?"

"I'd be happy to. You sure didn't waste any time finding work. That speaks very well of you." She padded back into the kitchen.

Shelton reached the top of the stairs and pushed the door open. The room was as he had left it the afternoon before. His note was still on the dresser, the bed made the same. Shelton read his note to Otis and shrugged, but he was too tired to do much but sleep.

It wasn't necessary for the landlady to awaken him, but she did knock. "I'm awake, thank you." Shelton called. He was sitting on the side of the bed.

"There's a call for you on the telephone." He opened the door.

"A call for me?"

"Are you Otis?"

"No, but I'll take it. I can take a message for him." He walked down the stairway wondering how anyone knew where they were staying. The telephone was in the hallway.

"Hello?"

"Otis?" It was a woman's voice.

"This is Shelton, I can take a message."

"Well, where is Otis—is he supposed to be there?"

"Yes, ma'am, he is, but he isn't here just now. If you leave me your number, I can leave a message."

There was a pause while the woman weighed the idea.

"Where could he be reached?"

"I don't know; he didn't come home last night actually. Could I ask who's calling?"

Another pause. "Didn't he just get in town last night?"

"Yes, ma'am, we did."

"Well, he couldn't have given his number out to too many people, could he?"

"I suppose not, but you could give me your name; I'll have him call you."

"You just tell him someone called; I'll take my chances that he's tired this morning and hasn't made too many stops."

Shelton had a sudden thought: "Are you that girl from Marshfield? Is this Karen?"

The woman's voice came back sharply: "No, I'm not that girl from Marshfield."

"Well, why the mystery?" Shelton said as he heard the phone set on its receiver at the opposite end of the line. "I'm sorry," he said to the dead line and hung up. When he started to climb the stairs he noticed he wasn't as sore as he had expected. He rewrote his note to Otis, adding what information he could about the phone call, and left the house by four thirty.

At seven that evening Otis showed up at the Shamrock Coffee Shop. Jackie came back to tell Shelton he was out front. "Where the hell you been?" Shelton asked as he came out.

"Better ask where I haven't been. God almighty, is this a wild town."

"Yeah? Did you get any sleep?"

"I got some. You sure drew a hellhole to work in, didn't you?"

"Well, maybe jobs are scarce. You should see me peeling potatoes along about three o'clock. If I stay here they'll be asking me to cook too and wait tables."

"What are you paid?"

"A lousy five bucks a night and I earn it like nothing you've ever seen. Where the hell have you been? What did you see that's wild?"

"I looked up Karen in the phone book and went out to pay a call out there."

Shelton interrupted. "Some woman called you."

"Really?"

"Oh, come off it. How'd she get the number?"

"It was Karen's mother."

Shelton almost screamed: "Her mother?"

"I told you she was hot after my pants. Seems Karen's been married for about two years and moved off to Phoenix."

"So you took care of the old lady for her."

"Old lady, hell. She'll teach you to respect your elders. God, what a night."

"What happened?"

"I'll tell you when you get off."

"Good, I'll quit now then. You want to burn a fuse back there? What happened?"

"Well, what do you think happened? I shacked up with her. About fifteen minutes after I found the house. Right in the middle of the afternoon." Otis held three fingers like a catcher giving the sign to the pitcher.

"Christ. No lie?"

"Well, why not? I tell you, I been around, but don't knock it. Then I left along about eight o'clock and went downtown and stumbled into a bar. And I swear. Swear, just the first bar I walked into off the street. . . . "

"How the hell you get money to go into a bar? What's the age limit in this state, anyway? Seventeen?"

"How should I know what the age limit is? Anyway, the first place I walked into, they usher me right on through into the back, and whammey! You've never seen such a gambling palace in all your life."

"Gambling palace. Oh, sure thing. I've got work to do."

"I swear. Crystal chandeliers."

"I'll bet. Where did you get money to stay in a gambling palace with chandeliers all night?"

Otis grinned his slant-eyed grin and drummed the counter a few times like a bongo. "Slick."

"I'll bet."

"Slick as falling off a log."

"I'll bet."

"Karen's mother gave me twenty."

Shelton had a towel in his hand. He threw it on the floor now and walked a few steps away from the counter and back. "Damn!" he said half to himself, but he was smiling. "You mean I break my back in this dump, twelve hours for a lousy five bucks, and you screw all night for twenty?" Otis laughed and shrugged and Shelton began to laugh, too. Shelton turned to Jackie: "Hey, do you think I could get a cup of coffee for my bum friend? He's had a hard night."

"Sure thing, honey." She brought the coffee, cracking a joke under her breath which neither of them quite heard, and slapped Shelton on the back, and returned to cutting butter into pads and serving them onto squares of paper.

"Well," Otis drawled when she had retreated, "I told her I was just passing through and she gave me a little dough to hang around on."

"Well, god damn. And DON'T TELL ME! You blew it on the gambling tables."

"Not tables, on the floor."

"With crystal chandeliers they're playing cards on the floor, yet."

"Dice."

"Anyway, you blew it."

"I suppose so, but don't worry about it, there's more. That gal isn't poor exactly. I had a pot of over a hundred dollars for over an hour."

"I don't want to hear it. Where'd you stay?"

Otis drew a long breath. "Wel-l-l, along about midnight—"

"After you'd lost the hundred and the twenty—"

"After I'd lost the works, I snuggled back to mother till the bars closed."

"Another three whacks," Shelton speculated.

"One. Then, there was a very nice girl—a little young, but not exactly green—that I'd met at the bar, and after she got off I gave her a lift home."

"And got some sleep at her place."

"And got some sleep at her place," Otis repeated.

"But not much."

"Not enough anyway."

Shelton shook his head. "Do you know what that does to me? Do you have any idea how our evening entertainment varied last night?"

"You're not mad are you?" Otis was still grinning.

"I'll tell you what I'm not. I'm working here tonight and then I'm not working in this hole anymore."

"That's what I came to tell you. I read your note at the house and doubled over."

"Really? Well, I doubled over a washing machine in back that blows steam in my face."

"When do you get off?"

"Do you think you can take it? Six in the morning."

Otis whistled. "Well, my young working friend, I thought maybe I'd go back to the crystal chandeliers this evening and have just a little fun. Would that make you feel bad?"

Shelton thought a moment. "Where did you get the money this time, the young thing from the bar?"

"Only ten, from Mother Earth, she really wants me to stay. Seems she's been having dreams about me all these lonely years."

"Lonely, hell. Sure, go back and lose the ten, but don't expect me to stay here after this one night."

"That's what I said, there's no sense in you slaving your youth away. You might need it for something worthwhile someday." It was agreed that Shelton wouldn't work after the night. When he told Mr. Kaufman, the man gave him his ten dollars without a word. At six the following morning Shelton left the Shamrock and went back to the house.

Unlike the evening before it had been a hot night, more typical of the hot sticky Midwestern evenings. Otis was stretched out across the bed, his feet tangled in a sheet that he had kicked off. The curtains hung motionless in front of the open window. As Shelton closed the door Otis half raised his head, squinted toward the door, grunted, and turned over. Shelton sat on the side of the bed to take off his shoes, and looked over at Otis. "Holy Christ, what'd you do, have a wet dream or something?"

"Go to sleep," Otis half mumbled, then raised up again. "Wha? What the hell are you talking about?"

"You've sweated all over the damn bed; it's soaking wet."

"You're telling me. It's like a steam bath."

It seemed as soon as Shelton shut his eyes Otis was shaking him by the shoulder. It was something he wouldn't remember clearly later; a half-dreamed sequence he couldn't be certain really happened. Otis was dressed and was standing over him. "I gotta buzz over to Marge's place; are you going to sleep all day?"

"Who's Marge?"

"The mother image. She called."

"It's too hot to screw, what are you going over there for?"

"Don't worry about it, she's got air conditioning."

"Yeah, like Meramec Cave; what time is it?"

"After three. Are you getting up?" Shelton had closed his eyes again and almost drifted back.

"What time?" He finally managed to say.

Otis was at the dresser when he opened his eyes again.

"After three; you sleeping all day?"

"Yes, go away."

"I'm gonna need some gas. I'm taking five of your ten, O.K.? I'll pay you back."

"What happened to the dough from Mother Earth?"

Otis laughed. "Well, I boozed it up a little last night, mostly."

"Sure take it, but bring it back." He closed his eyes again and heard the door close quietly. In a moment when he opened his eyes it was like awakening in a totally strange place; the feeling you get as a child when you go to sleep in your own room and in the night go to your parents' bedroom and awaken there the following morning.

He dressed and only remembered Otis leaving when he saw the money on the dresser. He wandered that afternoon, up toward the business section, looking in windows and reading posters outside movie theaters. Once he passed a drugstore and saw a turning rack of postcards; pictures of the city by day and at night in glossy Kodachrome, and miniature posters of montages of the state: oil wells and derricks; there was a picture of the hideous dark capitol building in Oklahoma City and banners of "Welcome to Oklahoma" and "Greetings from Tulsa." He bought a picture of the bank building at night. He turned the card over to the side for a message and stared at the blank space for several seconds without remembering what he wanted to say, then put the card in his shirt pocket. In a Ben Franklin dime store a kid was squalling and being pulled away from the toy counter by a fat overpowering woman; still she was having a time dragging the child away. The counter was piled with cheap, tin mechanical things: cars and trucks with soft plastic wheels and tractors from Japan that had caterpillar treads and a winding key. At the corner of the counter were three Charlie McCarthys that danced in a loose-limbed staccato tap on a tin drum. That was the toy that caught the child's eye. The metallic tapping could be heard all over the store like rain on a roof.

Shelton walked into the stores mainly to keep cool. The outside air was hot and heavy and secondhand. As he wandered down a quieter street, a street of auto lots on one side and recreation parlors facing them from across the way, he was thinking about Otis in the air-conditioned home of Karen's mother. He wondered what the woman looked like. She would be beautiful. Otis always came up with the prettiest girl in town. There had been a near scandal when he dated the preacher's daughter once, but the girl's parents quietly put a stop to the romance and probably none too soon.

Shelton was standing in the cool draft from a bar. The smell of beer, which usually seemed stale to him, was inviting this time. Tulsa does not serve mixed drinks; it's a dry state and Oklahomans are confined to getting drunk in public on beer. The bar was dark after the sunlight and cool as a cellar. Shelton bought a beer at the counter and carried it to a booth across the room. The table and high-backed benches were lighted with a wall jukebox.

When he became accustomed to the darkness he saw there were only a few people at the bar. He sat in the long row of booths by himself. There was a girl at the bar who looked at him a moment, then turned back. I wonder if she knows I'm underage, Shelton thought. He decided though that she was underage as well and couldn't say much. It was only then that he began to feel courageous. He hadn't entered a bar by himself before. For one thing he didn't carry a false I.D. as Otis did and if he was questioned it could only lead to an embarrassing scene.

When the woman came over to the booth, Shelton saw that she was not underage after all. It was the way she wore her hair or the effect of her makeup and the dark bar lighted only with red. "Why the long face?" Her voice was sweet and childish.

Shelton had watched her walk across the bar, thinking about her age. "I don't know, did I have a long face?"

"Like you'd lost your best friend. I hope you're not the sort of boy who likes to sit alone and cry in his beer."

It was the word boy that bothered Shelton. "No, not at all; I'd like your company if you'd care to sit down." He didn't really want her there, but she had practically invited herself.

She sat across from him. "Good, there was no one to talk to over there. Christ, you're young; how old are you, anyway?"

"Twenty-one."

"You can tell me, Joey'll sell anyone over eight and a half if they've got the money. Sixteen?"

"Eighteen," Shelton said quickly. "But I only had a birthday last April."

"Aries."

"Yeah. How'd you know?"

"It's a hobby of mine. When the horoscope says danger I don't go out on the street."

"My mother's almost like that." In a moment Shelton walked back to the counter and bought another round.

"You didn't tell me why you're so glum looking," she asked when he returned.

"Am I still?"

"A little bit."

"I don't know, then. Maybe I'm thinking about looking for a job tomorrow."

The girl nodded. "That would do it, alright. Did you get canned?"

"I quit. It wasn't anything special, I only took it for a coupla days anyway, but I should find something. There isn't much to do here in the summer, is there?"

"Or any other time. You sound like a freshly disillusioned out-of-towner."

"From Springfield," Shelton filled in. "Are you from Tulsa?"

"Nobody's from Tulsa."

"Did you find something to do?" He thought maybe that he shouldn't have asked her, but her reply was simple enough.

"Oh yes. I found something to do. The money's good and the hours aren't too bad. I work here and live in, as they say."

Shelton had never found anything so easy to ask in his life; it seemed the natural question, and the girl had practically told him already. "Are you a prostitute?"

The girl laughed softly. "Well, as long as you call it a 'hostess' I won't mind."

It was a strange kind of pointless conversation. Her name was Ann, she was from Deerfield, Oklahoma, and had been in Tulsa four years. The first year she had worked as a carhop, the second as a waitress, receptionist, barmaid, and then for Joey. "I started out as a real hostess-barmaid, but it didn't last long."

"Haven't you ever been back home since then?"

"Lord no. I haven't even wanted to. Not even when my dad died; or I should say especially not when my dad died."

"I guess not."

"People are either born to live in the city or the country. It never works when you try to change, and I was born for this. Well, Springfield is a large place, isn't it?"

"Oh, it's big enough. I'm not really from there; we lived in a town south of Springfield that you wouldn't have heard of."

"Where's that?"

"Athens. It's about population three hundred."

"Sounds like Deerfield. Everyone sitting on the porch to see what's happening in town, and nothing ever is."

Shelton smiled. "It's a lot like that. But it's peaceful if you like that sort of thing."

"Oh, it's peaceful. Deerfield is peaceful, but I'm one that doesn't like that at all." Ann stared for a long time, without saying anything. She wasn't looking at Shelton, but over his shoulder, to the back of the booth. Shelton knew she was thinking about Deerfield and would liked to have said something, but he couldn't think of anything at that moment: one of those long sad pauses that can end a conversation, even a friendship, when both people are thinking their separate thoughts. Finally, she said: "So tell me about Athens."

"You know about it. It's like Deerfield."

"Not the town, about your family. Did you finish school?"

"Yes. Just last month. And my family isn't much to get excited about either."

"Is anybody's? I think sometimes the way we do things is all wrong. You know, a mother and father and three kids in every pot. It doesn't work. I don't know what we ought to try next, but families just haven't worked out."

"I know mine is screwed up," Shelton said. "I've got a stepsister out in Denver I haven't even seen. And a stepfather in Athens I wish I'd never seen."

"What happened to your real dad?"

"I don't know. He's living in Pennsylvania somewhere."

"Well, you shouldn't feel bad then, you've got two."

"My mother's alright," Shelton said. "But I never got along with Carl. We never did understand each other, you know?" The girl nodded. The beer made him feel expansive and easy: "I don't mean he beat me or even chewed my ass much, but we just never got through to each other."

"It's always like that."

"Well, picture this. Here he is a man forty-god-knows-how-many-years old, eight probably. And he wants to have a farm. He's working for this goddamned cheese plant as a field man—you know what a field man does? Well, they go around and keep all the farmers happy and tell them how to get higher production and more sanitary conditions, so they can get better prices; and cut them down to size when they start pouring the milk cans half full of water—that sort of thing. So what does he want? He wants a farm or else the farmers won't pay any attention to what he says. Well now, that makes sense. Everybody knows farmers don't want city men coming in and telling them how to run their business. Right?"

"Right, I guess."

"Damn right." Shelton leaned back into the corner of the booth and spread both hands out on the table. "So what does he do? Does he get a farm? No, he's got a little one-car garage in back and a fenced-in lot, so he has two full-grown bawling cows and a calf penned up back there like a couple of chickens."

Ann laughed.

"And that's his farm," Shelton explained. "And that's exactly what he's like about everything. If you ever eat out he figures exactly ten percent of the check for a tip; for a treat he'll take you riding out to some broken-down farmhouse and ask you if you'd like to live there. You know; no plumbing, no heat, no john. What am I supposed to say, it's heaven? Then when you tell him what you think of the place, he blows up. Won't say a word for a coupla days."

"He sounds like a real jewel."

"Oh, he is." Shelton made a broad gesture. "And you know what his hobby is? He builds little windmills. You know, like you've seen along the roadside at those clip joints? Wood hillbillies with their arms blowing around like windmills, or a bloodhound's head with his ears flapping. Saws them out of wood and paints them. He has a little jigsaw on the back porch. And then when he goes to some other town he comes back with some kind of damn plastic toy, like a teddy bear or something."

"A toy," Ann repeated.

"That's what I said. And don't ask if there's a kid in the family because there isn't except for him. He has them stacked in the closet and all over the place. Says he's saving them. God knows what for. Says when his daughter out in Denver gets married, she'll have kids and they'll have a lot to play with—well, just between you and me, I wish she'd hurry up, because they're stacking up around the house and there's not going to be room to walk before long."

Ann laughed at the gesture; Shelton was holding his hands above his head to indicate depth. "But that's not too bad," she said. "I like toys, too. Almost everyone does. I have a teddy bear upstairs and a kewpie doll."

"He doesn't play with them or any of that, he just stacks them up. I'm not saying that toys can't be interesting. Fascinating! But he's just sort of absent-mindedly busy with them and brings them home. It's hardly ever for some purpose. Once in a while we can get a kick out of them—like fireworks. That's the only human quality he has, he brings home fireworks for the Fourth of July. We all used to go down by the river at night."

"I used to love to do that. That's the only thing I miss about the country. That and hayrides."

"Yeah, the Fourth used to be fun. Fireworks and a kite. One time he brought home—I don't know where'd he'd been; Springfield, I guess—but he found one of those enormous Chinese kites that are shaped like a big red fish—with scales and eyes and tail and a big open mouth; but it's a kite, made out of tissue paper, and we had the whole town over at our house watching it."

"I've never seen one of them in the air."

"They look almost like they're swimming. It's really beautiful in its way, you know? But this damn thing—it was going fine for about an hour and then the wind shifted and the damn thing dropped like it'd been shot down. Fell straight into an old elm tree in front of our house. Tallest tree in the county; no lie, if someone asks where you live you could just say 'up at the top of the hill by that big tree on the other side of town' and they'd know where you meant. It was about the biggest tree in the county. So this damn fish got stuck way at the top; you couldn't begin to get it down. So we pulled the string, you know—and everyone was yelling directions and suggestions and naturally the string broke, with it still up there. We threw a couple of rocks and probably busted it up a bit. The thing that pissed us off was you could see the damn thing so plain but you couldn't get it down. Here's this big red fish up in the top of our tree like it'd been caught in some underwater plant, you know? But it never did fall out. By the time fall came around it was so beat up by the wind it was just a whole mass of like pink ribbons—you know, like confetti, flapping around. Like a flag almost. Every time I came home from somewhere I'd look up to that tree before I went in to see if it'd blown out."

"Is it still up there?"

"Hell, it's probably rotted by now. But it sure looked funny for a while, before it got so ripped up."

"I'd like to have seen it. What'd your dad say?"

"Carl? Oh, he just laughed. Hell, we had more fun with that than about anything."

"Hey, Shelton?"

Shelton put his chin in his palm. "Yeah?"

"How would you like to come upstairs?"

"I'd like it. That's all I've been thinking about since you sat down, but I don't have any money."

"Oh, for Christ's sake, I don't charge everybody."

The beer had worked on Shelton like truth serum. "I never have, you know."

"I didn't think so."

"You didn't?"

"That's why I wouldn't charge—because you're not going to knock me around like some lumberjack."

"No one would knock you around, would they? You're too—"

"Too what?"

"I don't know—too soft. You'd bruise or something." She took his hand and led him to the stairs in back. Joey looked up from behind the counter, shook his head, and yelled: "Hey, businesswoman?"

"Mind your own business."

Shelton was drunk. The ceiling was hung with a hundred Japanese lanterns of every size from tiny to three feet across. Her bed was painted pink and had a faded rose chenille spread across it. The rose-patterned wallpaper was blistered and peeled back in places, showing an older paper of apple blossoms on a pale blue field. Shelton closed the door behind them and leaned back against it. He was swaying a bit, but smiling, looking around the room. "Good god."

"What's wrong."

"What's wrong? If I wasn't a little drunk I'd think I was drunk, you know what I mean? You bring someone who's sober up here and—well, I don't know what he'd do." Shelton had to duck under some of the lanterns.

Everything in the small room was painted pink: the dresser, the frame of an oval mirror hanging beside the door. The floor was covered with a soiled rose rug.

"Well, if you don't like it—" Ann smiled and pulled the drapes across the room's only window. It was dark. Shelton was sitting on the bed, kissing her. With the beer blurring his mind and the long talk down in the bar, and the long walk before without talking to anyone, wandering alone trying somehow to share Otis's experiences, Shelton felt now a palpable warmth move over him; an excitement, that he took to be love.

Everything was experience by touch, slowly. He was holding her gently, carefully. She had unbuttoned his shirt and it was on the floor somewhere. They were lying diagonally across the bed as Shelton began to undo her blouse, feeling her body through the cloth. He was easy and relaxed but she seemed tensed; she twisted in his arms. He heard the blouse rip and felt it pull away from her: she had torn it off and heaved it at the wall in one violent motion. Everything went wrong. Instead of relaxing she was fighting at him, biting at his neck and chest, making strangling, panting sounds. He took her shoulders and tried to pull her up to him but she twisted away, her fingernails at his back and belt. The top of his pants ripped and again he attempted to pull her up to him but she fought away. In a panting animal voice she was saying over and over "Let me! Let me." Shelton tried to get off the bed, but the waistband of his pants shackled his legs together. Her face was against his stomach, contorted and red. He pulled at her again, her hands were locked around his waist. He heard himself say no and felt the girl's earring cut across his belly, then her warm mouth was around him. Shelton felt nothing but panic and suffocation; all desire had turned to repulsion. He pushed her away with both hands on her face and sprang up standing onto the bed, striking at the lanterns that were all around him. She was screaming something, but he wanted only to run away. The mattress waved under his foot when he stepped back and threw him backward over the end of the bed, hitting his arm against the wall and dragging a cluster of enormous pink lanterns down with him. The mirror hit the floor beside him and crashed in a thousand pieces across the rug. In an instant he was out the door, in the hall; holding up his trousers with one hand and with the other slamming the door, shutting off the sight of her. Even as the door shut he saw her leaning toward him with both hands gripped white around the pink bar at the foot of the bed. Her face was wild, screaming unintelligibly; her neck cabled with veins. There seemed no air to breathe in the hallway. His only thought was to get outside, but as he ran down the hall, turning at the stairs he could hear Joey's voice from below yelling, "What's going on up there. Answer me, Ann." Shelton ran directly into Joey's grip at the bottom of the stairway. "What's going on?"

The room seemed to be rocking around him. He sensed only vaguely that the bartender had a strangling grip around his neck and was pushing him toward the stairs again, yelling up to Ann. Shelton thought later that he must have lost consciousness for a second. They were at the stairway and a moment seemed to have passed, for Joey's question seemed to reverberate in the air as they waited for Ann to answer.

"Let him go. Kick him out," he heard Ann yell from her room and felt Joey's arm release its pressure on his neck.

The bartender spoke softly to him. "Are you alright, kid?" Shelton saw the door across the room and started walking toward it, not looking back. His only desire was to get past the door and outside before his legs failed him; before he passed out again. He had to force his legs to move toward the light at the window. "Are you alright?" he heard Joey ask from behind him. "Do you want your shirt, kid?" He walked through the doors into the white wall of heat outside. At the corner he took hold of a parking meter, leaned out, and vomited into the street.

Shelton did not remember walking back to the room. When he awoke it was evening. It had rained and was cool and a strong wind was blowing outside. In most sections of Tulsa on summer nights you can hear insects singing in the grass and crickets call and answer across the yards, just as they do in the country. In the early evening lightning bugs blink around the houses and out in the gardens. Shelton got up and put on a shirt. There were bruises on his shoulders and a broad scratch across his stomach where he had felt Ann's earring.

He was lying on the bed again when Otis came in. "I was hoping you'd be here," Otis said even before he shut the door.

"Yeah, I fell asleep."

Otis seemed uneasy. He lit a cigarette, and sat down, then stood up again and walked to the window. "Hell, this town is totally dead," he said finally. "I've been around all afternoon looking for work. They can hire Mexicans for next to nothing, they don't want to talk to someone who wants a decent salary."

Shelton was looking straight to the ceiling. "I understand they need a dishwasher at the Shamrock Coffee Shop." He said it jokingly, without malice.

"That was a lousy deal, wasn't it?"

"Yeah. I pity the guy who has to keep that job for long. What happened to your girlfriend's mother?"

Otis sat on the side of the bed. "You want to know the truth? She kicked me out. She neglected to tell me she had a husband who was coming home tomorrow."

"Oh, Christ! Must have slipped her mind. So what do we do?"

Otis was quiet for a minute. "I don't know," he said finally. "How much money do you have?"

"Nothing. Just that five you took."

"Not that either. That's shot."

"Christ. I thought you were getting something from your woman."

"Well, I thought so too, but it didn't work out that way." Otis went back to the window. "There's one thing for sure, there's no reason to hang around this town. We've got seven fifty rent due in three days, too."

"Coming from where?"

"Coming from nowhere. We won't be here if we leave right now."

Shelton sat up on the bed. "God, I'd hate to do that to her."

"Do you see anything else? You want to go back to the Shamrock Coffee Shop?"

"No."

"Well, look." Otis began walking about the room, a habit when he was planning something extemporaneously. "We haven't got enough gas to get us back, but we've got some. When I was driving around this afternoon I found a big truck lot, there's about twenty trucks just sitting around waiting to be driven off."

"So?" Shelton said uneasily.

"So how did we get here? That's the way we can get back. Every one of those trucks have about a sixty gallon gas tank filled."

"We're not going to go through that again, are we?"

"Well, do you see any other way? It's not like in Springfield; here we can get it all from one tank and be gone in about fifteen minutes. We still have the hose and the can . . ."

Almost before they had decided to leave they were packing the shirts together again. Once Otis asked Shelton what he had done that afternoon. "It was too hot to go anywhere, I went to a movie."

"Oh."

"It wasn't very good."

"Hey, Shelton, what are your folks going to say when you come back?"

"I don't know. They'll probably say I've been gone four days and I'll tell them I took a vacation. What'll Edith say?"

"I don't know. I might not stay long. I been thinking about going out to Phoenix maybe. How's that sound?"

"Hot."

"You're welcome to come along."

Shelton shook his head. "You aren't going to Phoenix in the middle of the summer."

"I don't know." Otis took the shirts and they walked quietly out of the house, and down the block to where the car was parked.

The truck lot that Otis had seen that afternoon looked foreboding at night. The big diesels were parked in total darkness behind a long garage. Otis drove around the block twice. On the third circle around he turned the car into the driveway and cut the light. He pulled quietly to the back of the lot behind one of the trucks and stopped.

Everything went smoothly for the first fifteen minutes. Otis had pulled close enough to the truck to siphon gas directly into the car. Shelton stood watch a few feet away at the door of the car. The tank was full and Otis got the five gallon can from the trunk of the car, letting the gas flow into the ground while he was gone instead of starting fresh with a wet hose. The can hit against the car and again against the truck, making a loud hollow sound.

"Hey, keep it quiet at least."

"Well, I'm trying to."

"It doesn't sound like it."

"Is there anything coming?"

"No." Shelton had just said it when a long beam of light flashed across the top of the truck above them. "Holy Christ," he whispered under his breath and crouched down.

"What is it?" Otis was squatted by the front tire of the truck. He had whispered the question. There was a long pause when the only sound was the echoing of the gas pouring into the empty can while they watched the spotlight move through the lot.

"A cop," Shelton whispered. "He came in from the other side, I didn't see him."

Otis crawled up beside Shelton and looked at the patrol car. "They probably have regular rounds through here. At least if he doesn't see us he won't be back."

"Yeah, if he doesn't see us. Oh, Christ."

"What's wrong?"

"My leg hurts."

"Try to forget it."

"Sure. Can't you shut that damn thing off?" The noise of the gas draining into the can continued, not quite so hollowly as before.

"The tank's about dry, it should quit before long."

"What's the sentence for stealing gas?" Shelton asked, snickering quietly.

"Oh, shut up." Otis looked out toward the car. It had stopped in the middle of the lot. "It looks like they might be here a while."

"Swell."

"I was thinking. . . . "

"It's about time."

"Not about now," Otis whispered. "About when we go back. I thought maybe we could just stop long enough to get the rest of our clothes and go on somewhere."

"Like, where?"

"I don't know. Kansas City, maybe; or even Chicago."

"Sure, well, I hope you have fun."

"I wasn't kidding," Otis said.

"Neither was I." They were quiet for a minute. Then Otis whispered: "I hear Kansas City's one of the prettiest towns in the country."

"That's what you said about Tulsa, but I haven't seen you admiring the view."

"Be quiet." They were both watching the patrol car; they crouched in silence for a few minutes, then Otis said: "You know I told you Marge kicked me out."

"You told me."

"She didn't. I didn't go over there."

Shelton didn't look over at him, and he sensed that Otis was still watching the car. "Where did you go?"

"I went back over to that bar I told you about."

"The one with the chandeliers."

"Yeah."

Shelton didn't say anything for a moment. Then: "And I suppose that's where my five bucks went."

"Yeah, that and more. Quite a lot."

"You didn't have any more."

"No, but when I was there the night before I told the girl my dad was this big-shot lawyer in Springfield—you know, kind of soften her up?" Otis paused and Shelton waited, still looking out across the lot.

"So they thought they knew who I was and they thought it'd be safe to take my marker. They let me stay all afternoon. You should have seen me play it. I even bought the boss a coupla drinks."

"Marker," Shelton repeated. "Is that I.O.U.?"

"Yeah, same thing."

Shelton looked at Otis, but could not see his face although it was less than two feet away. He had been staring at the spotlight, which made it seem darker between the car and the truck. "How much?"

"Three hundred dollars."

"Holy Christ!" Shelton said it aloud. They both crouched down farther and looked toward the car. It began to move slowly toward them.

"Of course, they don't know it isn't any good yet. They know I'm underage, but they'd be ways of collecting if I was a lawyer's son. The three hundred and more, probably."

"I were you, I wouldn't hang around Springfield very long either."

"That's what I said, stupid." Their voices were even quieter now. "Why don't you come along? We could stop long enough just to get clothes."

"Come off it."

"What's wrong, you wanted to come down here—you were game enough."

"To get jobs, sure. . . . "

"Well, damn it, there's jobs in K.C."

"I wish you luck in finding them, then; I've had it."

"Come on." Otis spoke easily, even in a whisper.

"I said I've had it! Look, damn it—I'm cramped up in the middle of the night stealing gas from some trucking company in a town where I don't even know one person. And I'm scared to hell and in about three minutes we're both going to be in the Tulsa jail anyway, and if we aren't, my knees are covered with gas and my arms ache from sitting here and my knees are cramped!" The spotlight paused just over their heads. Otis made a loud hissing noise for Shelton to be quiet. They could hear the call radio from the patrol car. As he listened Shelton noticed the gas behind him had stopped running. The car pulled slowly by them and around the building. Both boys breathed heavily and stretched out on the ground.

"Nothing." Otis finally breathed.

"What?"

"Nothing happened."

"Only I lost about four year's growth."

Otis got up and dusted off his pants. They put the lid on the gas can and eased the trunk shut. "So what about it? Are you game for Kansas City?"

"I told you. You can drop me in Athens and go on if you want to."

"If we didn't like it, we could come back."

"Otis, I'm not interested!" Shelton said loudly. "Why the hell did you leave an I.O.U. at that place, anyway? Why did you go in the first place? I'm sorry you're in trouble, but it doesn't sound like fun anymore."

"O.K., I'm sorry I asked you along."

"I just don't want to hear any more about Kansas City. Borrowing money for that is about the dumbest thing I've ever heard of." They got in the car and Otis slammed the door hard and loud.

"I said I'm sorry I mentioned it!" They sat there in silence for a few more minutes, then pulled the car ahead in darkness. He only turned on the lights when he reached the streetlight. Shelton rolled down the window and looked out. Otis was angry; he was driving too fast, but traffic was light and they reached the highway. Otis did not speak but kept his concentration on the road; Shelton watched the landscape flow by. Neither boy spoke. They would drive in silence the whole way back, and they would not speak the following morning when Otis let Shelton out at the bottom of the hill and watched him walk up toward the house.

SECTION 3
SKETCHES OF TOWN LIFE

Fig. 4. Lanford Wilson, Ozark, Missouri, 1955; photographer unknown; Lanford Wilson Collection, Special Collections and Rare Books, University of Missouri Libraries, Lanford Wilson Estate.

The Rimers of Eldritch

No one was much surprised when Eve Johnson died, they had never expected her to live in the first place: a girl as sickly as Eve could never bear children, her own mother had passed on giving birth to Eve. When it was discovered Eve was pregnant everyone sighed, shook their heads and waited out the end. There was nothing much to think about it either way; since she had not been married they would have enjoyed thinking the devil had had his say in the matter and claimed his own, but it was difficult to believe the devil could use Eve once he claimed her. And besides there were circumstances which made it doubtful that the devil would have had anything to do with her. So the people of Eldritch preferred to wonder what happened to Driver Junior and the miner.

His name was Edmond but the people called him Driver Junior; it was a cruel joke, more heartless because people didn't realize it hurt him, or if they did they would never claim to understand why. They had called his brother Driver and it seemed natural to call the younger Driver Junior, though the two were nothing alike. Driver raced cars in Rogersville at the stock car races. He was a powerful man; handsome and friendly. On Saturdays the whole town's population excepting a few of the older people who waited on the porch swings, nodding, would pile into four cars and a pick-up truck and follow the bright green and yellow car into Rogersville. Driver towed the car behind a '49 Plymouth Plaza. He was the hero of the town. He was brave; obviously he had more courage, more strength. He was easygoing. When the races were over everyone went to the Hill Café for a beer and to listen to Driver's account of the race: laughing usually and in good strong voice, he sped them back around the tracks, this time driving. Then they followed him out of the café and the line of cars trailed back the fifteen miles to Eldritch. They entered the village with horns blaring and hissing after the green and yellow car like a string of geese. Henry Olson, turning from the gaggle into his yard, giving the horn a last blast, always pressed too hard and the sound of the horn blared through the night, growing fainter and fainter as the battery weakened. That was Saturday afternoon and Saturday night; and that was Driver. It was natural to call his younger brother Driver Junior, and people started it long before Driver was killed in the races. The green and yellow (green because no one dared to paint a racing car green) car was just rust, sitting in the middle of Main Street, in front of the old Lyric Theater, sitting where it had stopped when the chain broke as they pulled it back through town, the tires flat and half-rotted away on the rims, the car's top smashed down and front wrinkled up like a stomped paper cup. No one had removed it from the broad dirt street; cars went around it and in summer there was an island around the car of weeds and grass. Everyone looked at the car, not sadly but resentfully.

Driver Junior had not joined the town much at the races and although they thought little of it then, they remembered it now. He was a poor show for a brother of Driver's. He was thin. He was pale. His voice was gentle and although pleasant, not rousing. His bones were not huge, his face was not handsome: beautiful in some vaguely insulting way, with long lashes around overlarge brown eyes. Driver Junior was plainly delicate. He had nearly his brother's height but none of his bearing. Yet he was not disliked; in a village as small and quiet as Eldritch everyone is liked. It had been expected that Driver Junior would leave Eldritch after school; but Driver Junior had little ambition and was not inclined to leave then. After seventeen, when he was out of school, he worked at the grocery and slowly people began to forget they had expected him to go.

Few boys then stayed in Eldritch. They drifted off to better possibilities—and girls, too, left town at an early age. To marry or to work at the factories in Rogersville or Springfield. Eldritch was a dying town; it had always been a dying town. No one kept a yard, the train had abandoned the line that passed through the town twenty years earlier. The Lyric Theater had been built when the area was rich in coal but long ago even the boards had fallen from its windows; the coal mines themselves stood at the end of the Main Street, stark and black, rip-toothed, high but slowly falling, almost bearing down. Less than a hundred people remained in the town but the number had stayed constant for two generations.

Driver Junior worked at the grocery, at the counter and on deliveries. He went by foot as the town was not large and orders were never heavy. Half of the houses had fallen down; but here children played games, played house with huge rooms to occupy, and hide-and-seek with places to hide forever. He enjoyed seeing the games and used sometimes to explore the old mining buildings or attics of the empty stale houses. Through town he nodded to people swinging on their porch. To Mrs. Appleton, Mrs. Olson, to Cora Johnson and her thin little granddaughter Eve. He stopped often to talk with the girl and sometimes after work the two went walking through town, below the town into the woods and around the mine. People they passed nodded and smiled but afterwards shook their heads. "Don't know what they see in each other if you ask me. Bit-off little cripple like that. If you ask me Driver Junior would be better off going to Rogersville for a girl." No, they would tell you, he wasn't handsome. But he had a tender way about him. Yes, they would say: Eve was sweet but a cripple is a cripple. They would remind you though, always, that she had a lovely face. But her shoulder blades stuck up through her back like bird wings. Her legs were uneven and terribly thin, causing her to limp, so the two walked slowly.

No one heard their conversations, no one wondered. They could only see Driver Junior's lips delicately forming words and see Eve nodding enthusiastically. He spoke quietly; she spoke with great animation. She was frail, and looked as they walked, waving one arm in the air, if he hadn't held her other hand she would have flown away altogether; in circles like a lamed bat.

It was probably good, people finally conceded, that they liked one another, for both were withdrawn from other people. Still it was on Driver Junior, whatever happened that early evening, that the blame eventually fell. Eve had always stayed at home, she had never gone out before.

What Driver Junior said about Eve was puzzling. Everyone knew she was only a child. A child in mind. But Driver Junior found this charming. She wanted to be an elf, he said; she sometimes thought of herself as one; and dreamed she was flying over the village and down across the valley with a bag of frost, seeding the buildings and stark trees with a coating of hoarfrost that sparkled in the mornings and didn't melt till noon. In the fall sometimes she was a tiny burrowing animal, thrashing around through the wood's leaves. Though she was twenty her mind was twelve, they told him.

It is not unusual in Eldritch for miners to come through. Some towns in the area still have small mines; and on occasion coal miners come to look at the petered-out mines of Eldritch. They get drunk at the town's one bar-café and leave the same night; so no one thought much when another miner got drunk that night. A stranger in town enables the bar's steady customers to hear a few new stories and tell of the rusted old car out on Main Street and of Driver.

No one had thought anything of Eve and Driver Junior wandering off into the woods; but suddenly, just after twilight Eve was running erratically down the Main Street, screaming in her thin child's voice. People appeared on their porches. Cora Johnson ran down the street to meet her granddaughter. No one knew what had happened; the girl could say nothing coherent, she could only cry or scream. Some were already dismissing it as some kind of fit when Driver Junior appeared. He had been crying and seemed almost as hysterical as the girl. The girl had been raped, he told them. A miner had come upon them in the wood, he said. Yes, they nodded, there had been a miner in town that afternoon. Yes, he had been drunk; he had left (some swore) off toward the wood. He had appeared suddenly in the woods, striking both Driver Junior and Eve, though apparently not hard, as there were no marks. He had tied up the boy and raped Eve in front of him. If there was more to the story Driver Junior did not tell them. For three days it was all the town talked about. The county sheriff was notified and posted a description of the miner. People from the town searched for the man, without avail. Driver Junior had not joined the search, but they understood. He did not talk of the incident, but sat a good deal in the storeroom at the back of the grocery.

Eve did not come back on the porch, and Driver Junior did not go to her house. They were not seen together after that. Not even after a few months, when it was learned that she was pregnant, did Eve come back to the porch. The fifth day after the incident (accident, it was termed) the miner was seen in town. Of course by this time every stranger in town was the miner and was reported. This miner was seen once by Mr. Carey when he closed the grocery. He telephoned the sheriff in Rogersville and told Driver Junior to go on home. Mrs. Olson also saw the miner, with someone else, and it was later assumed to be Driver Junior himself; but the boy's mother disowned it. Mrs. Olson said two men—the miner and a boy that looked like Edmond—drove down the street in a new car. They turned onto Main Street and in one plunge rammed the old rusty racing car off the rim of its old wheels (the car fell apart like a bag of parts spilled over the street; a door, a broken headlight, a pile of unrecognizable rust), backed the new car into the road again and swerved around the wreckage, both laughing wildly. All Driver Junior's mother would own was that her son was gone; packed and gone, and she felt certain the boy was in terrible trouble somewhere.

Green Grow the Rushes

The days immediately following the flood were very warm—a thick sweet atmosphere clung to the valley in a vapid attempt at recompense. Lon sat by the bridge that spans the mill pond and watched the sediment settle to the bottom of the river as it cleared. He perched high on the rocks beside the highway and peered down into the wavering reflections. One leg tucked tightly against his chest, both long thin arms doubled around it. His chin rested on the pointed knee, the other leg dangled in an insouciant manner above the water. He rubbed his chin slowly across the tightly stretched denim patch on the knee, making a short rasping sound. The early morning sun shone very brightly through the warm air and reflected in the silver spotlights that played across his wide cheekbones and pallid blue crystalline eyes.

To Lon's left the river flows over the low sluice and makes a sharp turn against a high limestone cliff that juts out over the swift water, then follows the cliff in an easterly direction until it is lost from sight among the hickory trees. To the right, up the river, lies the shallow fertile Finley Valley stretching out not ten feet above the river's surface. Close to the bank for perhaps three or four miles up the river from the dam grow an assortment of cedar, maple, oak and wild fruit trees strung together by large tangling grapevines and low rushes.

The valley spreads down from the wooded area perhaps a mile and a half eastward before the sharp rambling hills begin to rise above it. From the hills one can look down on the valley, neatly sectioned by crossing wire fences. The small farms fit compactly against one another; the buildings, mostly on higher ground, line against the dirt road.

The Collins farm is the second along the road. A shiny metal mailbox leans forward toward the lane. A driveway with wispy oil-stained grass growing in a long row down its middle leads past the white frame house to the outbuildings behind it; a barn, a tool shed, and an old pump house.

Lon climbed down the large irregular boulders that are stacked against the steep bank beside the bridge and stared out across the field.

He entered the lot from the rear, crawling between the two tightly stretched strands of wire. As he came between the barn and the hen house, Mrs. Collins emerged from the back door of the house, drying her hands on the course printed material of her apron. "Lon? For Pete's sake, Lon, where have you been? I've been calling you all morning. Dad wanted you to go into Springfield with him."

She descended the steps and walked toward him. "I was down at the river," Lon answered simply.

"Well, what were you doing down there? I can't for the life of me see what you get out of sittin' there all day."

Lon, not answering, walked on up the back steps. He paused at the door to remove his mud-laden shoes, set them neatly against the wall and went through the kitchen into the small living room.

The screen door whined painfully and his mother entered the living room. "Don't just sit down now, Lon, don't you think you'd better do something?"

"Do what?"

"Well, what have you accomplished all morning?"

"Nothing," he said lamely.

"Well, you could clear out the calf stall and bed her down with some fresh straw. Or the loft, it's needed it for a month now." She paused a moment. "Well, Lon, you know your dad won't like it to come home and have you just sitting around." She returned to the kitchen, "Go on, now, it won't take you long."

Lon came into the kitchen, "Use the old straw?"

His mother smiled, "Well, I suppose so. Ronnie called while you were gone."

"What'd he want?"

"I guess just to talk to you—said he was going to have a party this Sunday if you wanted to come."

"He has a party every week," Lon said and opened the door. Mrs. Collins turned from her pan of potatoes to watch him through the screen as he put on his shoes.

"Do you think you'll go?" she asked.

"I don't like his parties."

"It might do you good to get away from the house once in a while."

"They're no fun, mother."

She looked after him as he crossed into the sunlight and walked toward the barn. He's so thin, she thought. Good shoulders, good bones, eats like a horse and doesn't gain an ounce; moves around too much, always wigglin' and squirmin'. Ain't right for a boy of nineteen to be so nervous and fidgety. Ain't right young as he is.

A thin band of potato skin curled from the sharp edge of the paring knife and dropped with a gentle splash into the pan of water.

Lon entered the musty-smelling feed room from the side door. Sunshine fell from cracks between the boards in narrow yellow pinstripes across the floor; tall walls of churning dust sparkled in the light. "I couldn't stand another of his stupid parties!" he said aloud. "It's a waste of time." He took a pitchfork from between two nails where it hung on the wall and shoved it into the loose hay that had accumulated on the dirt floor.

He finished with the feed room just as his mother came out onto the back steps to call him for dinner. The two ate alone that noon. "I imagine Dad will be pretty late getting home," Mrs. Collins said matter-of-factly.

"If I know him when he goes to town, he'll stay all day."

"Well, he hung around here waitin' for you two hours this morning. You're gonna have to learn to be more responsible, Lon." Her line of thought was interrupted by a long moan from Lon. "Well, it's true," she snapped again, "you just don't take any interest in things."

"I take interest in the crops," he said.

"Well, you can't raise corn all winter."

Lon pushed his chair back from the table.

"Where're you going?"

"Down to the river."

"Lon, that's just what I'm talking about—running off like that. You just cleaned out the feed room, you haven't touched the calf's stall."

"I'll get to it Saturday." Lon walked through the kitchen, gave the screen door a slap and it screeched open. He jogged down the steps and out across the feather-strewn barn lot.

It had been almost a year ago, when the early spring warm had begun to draw the first tender blades of grass from the earth, that Lon began to be really disturbed about himself. He started to realize that he could not face people. He had developed the habit of walking down to the rows of trees that lined the bank of the river. Seldom did anyone come there. He walked from the bridge, where the trees began, along the narrow overgrown path and sometimes out into the cornfields of the valley. He watched the long attenuated ears as they grew from the cornstalks, tucked his thumbnail into a tender kernel and let the thick creamy liquid spurt out on the back of his hand. He watched throughout the summer as the grains slowly hardened from their milky green to a bright and wrinkled gold.

As the autumn frost crept up the valley Lon had walked through the cellophane crackling that crusted the woods. The crisp ochre sun shown through the translucent leaves with a red warmth. He continued to walk after the first snows began to flake down through the branches and squeak at his boots. Little splinters of ice formed along the bank of the river, stretched and crisscrossed out into the water.

Now on this bright spring noon Lon's mother stood at the kitchen window and watched him climb over the lower strand of the barbed wire fence. I can't for the life of me see what he gets outa sitting down there all day, she said to herself.

Lon ducked under the low budding branches of a maple and walked down the path.

A girl sat swinging slightly in a loop of the large shaggy grapevine, her smooth white arms contrasting sharply with the bark of the vine. Lon stood still for a moment, not knowing exactly what to do. He was startled by her presence and felt very uncertain about himself, but more than anything else he was offended by the encroachment.

She turned around suddenly as he stepped on the brittle, crusted path.

"Hello." Her voice was thin and startled.

Lon nodded.

"I seem to have missed the flood—I'll bet it was really something." Lon noticed as she smiled that she was an attractive girl in a way. Her small round face was set on an incredibly thin neck—two very large brown eyes completely dominated her face. Rather like a young calf, he decided.

"Yes, it was." He spoke very uneasily. "Well, the water was all the way out to . . ." As he turned to point to the fence of the muddy cornfield, he realized that from where she sat she could not see the valley through the dense wall of trees. "Well, maybe three-quarters of a mile that way."

"Oh, that far?" She seemed genuinely interested.

"Well, the valley is awfully low," he said. "You can see on the tree trunks, here, that it was only, well, about five, five and a half feet deep." He rubbed his fingers on the line the muddy waters had left against the bark of the skinny oak.

"I'll bet it was terrible."

"Oh, no, it wasn't terrible at all. It was really quite exciting." His voice trailed off into almost nothing toward the end of the sentence.

She gave a gentle little shudder. "I think it'd be horrifying."

He took a few steps in the opposite direction—it wasn't, though, it wasn't horrifying at all—it was huge, powerful, it was beautiful.

"Do you live here?" she asked. He turned and looked at her, thinking again that she looked like a fresh young calf.

"Yes, we have a farm up the valley a little."

"Oh, how wonderful. What do you call it?"

"We don't call it anything. I mean, it's just a small farm." He found himself becoming somewhat embarrassed. "I mean it's not a big ranch or anything like that." Again his voice weakened toward the end of the sentence.

"Oh."

"Say, I didn't tell you my—well, I'm Lon Collins—I should have introduced myself."

"My name's Carol Brown. You can't forget a name like that, can you?"

"I'm afraid I'm pretty good at forgetting any name."

The girl stood up suddenly and walked around the looped vine to the path. "It's so pretty here with all the trees and grass and all . . . I'll bet the path is just lined with wildflowers in the summer, isn't it?"

Lon considered this for a moment, and then said honestly, "Well, no, not exactly; there are an awful lot of daisies in the field, but here—well, violets; there are a few violets sometimes."

"Oh, I bet it's beautiful. Would you like to walk up the path for a minute? I'm just dying to see where it goes."

But Lon was shaking his head before she finished. "I'd like to but I really don't have time . . . really." He found himself groping for an excuse. "I have to get back to the house pretty soon; we milk at five and Dad gets—oh, oh, good God, he went after grain today—Jeez, he'll expect me to be there when he brings it in!" Lon turned instantly and ducked under the low branches and was almost hidden by them before the girl realized what he had said.

"Well, I wouldn't want you to get into any trouble." She squatted slightly to afford herself a better view under the branches. "Well, goodbye," she called as he ran stumbling over the rugged furrowed field.

Lon kept occupied the remainder of the evening with various obligations to the farm. He never thought of the girl again until later in the evening when he had gone to his room to read. His eyes moved across the words of the page but his mind did not recognize them. He was thinking of this interloper that had suddenly interrupted the seclusion of his river retreat. "Now what the hell could she get out of sitting down by the river?" he asked aloud. "If she thinks it's so horrifying, why the hell did she stay?" Where does the path go? He thought, good God! Up the river! Where else could it go?

The next afternoon Lon walked cautiously around the large rocks at the bridge where he could see down the deserted path. He felt very much relieved when he saw that the girl had not returned. He sat near the bank of the river and absently tossed little stones into the water, watched the rings interweave as they spread.

"Hi, Lon. Gosh, do you come here all the time?"

He jumped to his feet and whirled around so quickly he nearly lost his balance and fell backwards into the river.

"Gosh, did I scare you?" asked Carol.

"Good, God, I'd hope so!"

"I'm sorry. I didn't even think."

"That's all right, I guess I was dreaming. Where did you come from?"

"Up the river. It's beautiful, isn't it?"

"It's really prettier in the summer." He crouched down by the edge of the water. "Everything's real dense and thick then—almost like a jungle."

"You didn't answer my question." She sat down beside him. "Do you come here all the time?"

"Oh, I guess I didn't hear you—yeah, I walk down here almost every day," Lon said, feeling very uncomfortable since she had sat down.

"Gosh, I'd think you'd get awfully bored after a while."

"Oh, no, you only get bored with things that are always the same. The river's not like that at all."

Carol didn't say anything for several moments. Then, "Do they go swimming here?"

"What?"

"I said do they go swimming here?"

"Oh, no, the bottom's too muddy here. There's a place on up the river with a rock bottom."

"They swim there?"

Lon nodded. "They swim and drink—throw parties—sometimes at night you can hear them laughing or singing—screaming."

"Oh." She was quiet again, then suddenly: "Oh, look! Look, Lon, in the water." She leaned against his shoulder and pointed excitedly into the murky water. "See it? Well, look, silly."

"What?"

"A fish—see it?" The little blue perch gulped at the surface of the water and suddenly darted away. "There it goes!"

"Oh, yeah, I saw it—a perch. If you look carefully you can see them all the time."

"Really?"

"Well, haven't you ever seen a fish before?"

"Sure, but not like that—not in a river, just swimming around . . . not just swimming around like that . . ."

Through the remainder of the afternoon they sat by the river talking. Lon found he no longer resented the girl's presence; rather, he felt only very uncertain about himself. The casualness of the girl's manner made him feel all the more strained and self-conscious. He found that she was staying with her mother's sister, in one of the very large and expensive houses near town, while her parents were getting a divorce and some sort of settlement was arranged. He thought it all very complicated but smiled and tried to understand when she told him. In turn, he had related the difficulties, disasters, and happiness of the farm . . . the flood, the siege of tornadoes two years before; the advantages of rotation planting; the taste of homemade ice cream and its difference from commercial ones. And in this manner they spent the afternoon.

The following day when Lon walked down to the river Carol was standing at the edge of the field by the trees. "I could see you coming across the field," she said. They walked through the trees to the path. "I got a letter from Mom today. The divorce is final now. I'm supposed to live with her in St. Louis, I guess. That's what she said."

"Swell."

"I don't like St. Louis. It's an awfully filthy place."

"It won't be bad."

"The buildings are just black from coal smoke," Carol reiterated, "the streets are dirty, the people are dirty . . ."

"It couldn't be as bad as that."

"Would you want to live in a place like that? Cooped up in a swarming place like that? All the people and noise, and oh, God, the smell is terrible. Have you ever lived in a big city?"

"No," he said honestly.

"It's terrible."

"You'll get used to it."

"If it doesn't kill me."

Lon laughed and they wandered on up the path. He looked down and watched the little dirt clods crush to powder under his shoes as he walked. "When are you leaving?"

"Mother said to come back tomorrow morning," she said slowly. "My aunt was just furious when I told her I was coming down to the river . . . she wanted me to stay home and pack."

They stopped for a moment and sat down on the bank. Carol picked up a long blade of grass and absently pulled it in two along the center spine. "I wanted to stay a little longer," she said.

"Couldn't you?"

"Probably not . . . I think my aunt's tired of me already," she laughed. "I thought maybe I'd get to go on a weenie roast—isn't that silly? And I wanted to go on a hayride. When you're in the city all summer long, roasting in the brick ovens, you dream about things like that. And swimming in a river." She turned to look at him, studying his face.

"I guess living on the farm like you do, you don't realize how wonderful something like that is."

Up the river a catbird suddenly shrieked in its high shrill voice.

"I guess it's just another party to you. It's funny you know? I suppose you think about the city the same way."

Lon listened to the catbird cry to the sun for ending the day too soon. Its piercing call echoed down the river as it hurried to build its nest, lacing the rough twigs into the structure, moaning to itself for having found its mate too slowly.

"You never can tell, you might really like city life if you ever go," Carol was saying. "I've got used to it here in no time . . . the river and the trees . . . talking to you; walking down the path." Lon felt the muscles in his arms and shoulders begin to ache and tense. The slight dampness of the ground chilled his body. "Love must be very much like that," she said. "You know? Just getting used to something and not wanting things to change . . . to want to hold on to something as long as you can." The aching twisted down against his spine and ate at his stomach with a gnarling scraping tension.

Suddenly he jumped up. "God, it's getting late, I didn't realize it was so late."

The catbird laughed at his weakness.

Carol stood up. "I've got to be getting back to the house," she said. "I've got an awful lot of packing to do."

They started back along the path. "It's a shame you have to go so soon," Lon managed to say.

"Yes, it is . . . I tell you, I'll write you a letter as soon as I get there and tell you how terrible everything is. Then maybe you could answer."

"I never was any good at writing letters."

"You might drop a card or something when the violets bloom." They reached the beginning of the path. Carol started up the slope to the highway and turned. "Well, goodbye," she said; "maybe I'll see you again someday."

Lon nodded. "Goodbye."

Carol reached the top of the slope and looked back. "I . . . I'll never forget the river," she called.

"The river won't forget you," Lon answered. He looked up the highway for several moments, then turned and walked back down the path. The scuff of his shoes was noisy against the crust of the packed dirt. And far up the river the catbird screeched at the reddening sky. . . .

Chalk Eye

It was conceivable that I should get a job with them. The campaign, the real heat of the campaign hadn't begun. At the time I didn't know who headed the planning; but it didn't really matter. I was asked to wait in the anteroom. Someone will see you presently, the receptionist murmured, and I waited with several others in fat leather chairs along the opposite side of the room. Someone else came to the desk and spoke to her. "Oh, sir," she called to me, "were you waiting for Mr. Carson?" "Does he do the hiring?" I asked. The woman looked over her glasses as if to say that if I didn't know the people connected with their esteemed candidate for governor, I hadn't much business applying for a position with their campaign. "Mr. Carson," she said finally, "is the organizational chairman." Then she looked at me intently. "Surely you've at least heard of him." Any further comment drifted away as a group of congratulatory men came from the far door, smiling and shaking hands. A man who had been seated beside me got up and walked toward the group.

From that distance I could easily sort him out. The same smooth browned skin, the black-slick hair, the always-laughing face and perfect teeth. I found myself before the receptionist's desk again. "The one in the light suit," she said pointing with her glance, "the tall one. Mr. Carson." "Yes," I said. "I remember him now."

"He's very young, but it's no secret he's in line for the state's attorney general appointment," she whispered. I must have looked startled. "Once we're in office; providing we win," she added. I sat back down on the too-comfortable chair. Some of the men had left, others, including Mr. Carson, had gone back into the other room.

2

Neil Carson. One name; Neil Carson, and my mind went weaving. Weaving back through the schools and corridors, through the days of roommates and class time, crackers and cheese, through the rowdy time of playgrounds and gravel, through the dim light of apartment houses, lattice and smoke, thrown up against my mind like still-shots of black and white of some dry vacation. Thrown up against my mind like sand. Weaving back to the time when I had known Neil Carson. It was as simple as that and I was there. Flashing of light about me, in memory.

There was a tall dark brick wall on which the kids had scribbled undecipherable four-letter words and amazingly provocative diagrams in blue chalk. I can remember the wall; and over it when I was at the other end of the yard, a tall chimney that puffed black smoke all summer. The back of the back of the house. I recall the frightened trembling of the tin-shaded light above the back door when the elevated train rushed across the top of the wall, and the fleeting shadows bending across the back of the building; the strange vibrating underfoot—and most vividly of all, the crashing sound of the train. Sometimes I would listen until the train would be so faint in the distance that I was never sure just when the sound disappeared altogether. I remember the yard and the outside more vividly than our small apartment, which now seems very dark and vague, although I know that in the bedroom that I shared with my mother there was a glass lamp on the dresser and beside it the little ceramic statue of a man playing a violin. These recollections come in flashes, when least expected. I won't deny that times before when I have been walking down the street, I have suddenly thought of the large green sofa and the rich wine colored pillows, and the smell of coal; and I am puzzled for a moment—the image goes away and I can never quite retrieve it as clearly.

Beside the wall was a shed. A ramshackle affair it must have been, for I know that the sunlight striped down from between shingles on the roof, and fell across the dirt floor. Dust swirled in tall walls of light that divided the inside into "rooms" where we played. The shed was filled with discarded furniture and trunks, wicker and crumbling leather and a wealth of stacked newspapers nearly filled the space, except for our tunneled rooms and passages.

Betty was the girl's name, and I remember her more clearly than any other one thing about the place, only for years when it all came back to me, I couldn't remember the boy's name at all. I could clearly see in my mind the back of his wrist, where he had cut N.G.C. into the skin and filled it with indelible ink; but the name had eluded me. I can remember coming out of the blinding sunshine into the shed. "Betty?" I would call inquisitively.

"We're playing house," the boy would answer. "You stay away."

"He can watch, can't he?" Betty would always say.

"It's no fun then."

"Then he can be the iceman and come back later!" she would say to him, and she would giggle, the silliest little intimate laugh. I often tried to make her laugh that way when she spoke to me, but she never did. When I talked to her, she was very maternal and dignified.

"Sure, kid, you can be the iceman and come back later . . . go away now. You go look for some ice now." I was persistent, I know, and would generally barge in anyway but Betty would scream, "Go away, or you can't come back again! We won't let you deliver your ice here!" And it was always that that stopped me. So all in all I never saw them; only through the shafts of light that we call walls, in some dark place with torn holes of light darting about them.

I was the iceman, and in those days the actual iceman was the children's hero. Not that he looked or liked the part. No horse—only a slammed-in pickup with wavering high side gates that we chased down the road robbing it of splinters and bits of ice. Bittersalt and turning icewater, numbing our thieving little hands. All the while out here shooing us away like sparrows from the chicken yard, in a rush of pitched Italian. He was our hero. It all comes back in a vignette of still shots; as though turning through a photograph album of laughing faces. It all comes back with the sound of laughter and bells from the tamale vendor and the vocal roar of children being airplanes across the top of the wall; jumping into the incinerator filled with leaves with the scream of bombs. It all comes back to the trembling of the green tin lampshade and the train across the wall, blasting toward the distance.

The shortest walk is a distance to a child; ten feet through our newspaper tunnel was a journey halfway to the middle of the earth.

Mary was twelve, I remember that distinctly, and the boy was sixteen, with black hair across his face and his shirtless back burned dark brown. His boyish face hasn't changed since then. And there was no doubt who was boss in the tenements of children. Someone to shrink from, hide from. I remember him laughing, but a mawkish laugh. Playing in the sunny yard and atop the wall one day, someone spied a chink in the brick wall that seeped water from somewhere on the other side. A trickle of water ran down the wall and soaked into the ground. Just above the chink someone had drawn a large blue-chalk eye. "Look, it's crying," Mary laughed, "look, the wall's crying."

Another girl tucked her hands behind her and stared at the eye intently. "What do you 'spose it's crying about?"

"Maybe someone hit it!" someone suggested and we were all gathered around by now.

"Maybe it laughed so hard it cried," Mary offered.

"Walls can't laugh."

"And it can't see with that eye," the boy said, laughing at us.

"You don't have to see to be able to cry," Mary said, "blind men can cry." But as a whole we didn't argue with the boy much, and it was more or less always his opinion that prevailed.

During that hot summer it seems as though we lived from day to day completely undisturbed. From the house to the shack. Airplane buzzing in the backyard. Lazy and happy; it seemed we were alone. Children without parents almost. Working parents out or home tired, worried with frowning faces. So we enjoyed it most outside; out in the sun or the cool shack.

But suddenly, of course, the sun was gone. For me the sun was gone. I lay beside the ceramic violinist, my head throbbing with a fantastic fever; and still I shook with cold and pain and my throat couldn't utter a sound. For a day my mother stayed with me as I laid trembling. And the following day the house was screaming.

The mad disorganization of an ant-castle suddenly stirred was all about us. The questioning, the crying, the children caged in their rooms, slammed doors and clicking keys in the lock plates.

The yard lay quiet in the sun, alone and burning with heat in its loneliness. A blue-uniformed policeman stood at military attention in the yard. Occasionally he mopped his face, raised his hat, and fanned the top of his head. A swarm of activity around the shack the first day. Nothing the second. Then they were back the third, yelling among one another and digging around the building. Searching the yard, and beyond the yard.

3

Of course the things that come most clearly to our minds are the things we would rather skip over. The memories we attempt to beat out are the ones beaten more indelible; they swell and lodge more securely.

I entered the shack from the loose boards around the side, crawling between yellowed stacks of old papers. This was our cave. During explorations, we crawled through yellow paper walls with ropes tied around our waists. One must be quiet here, for danger lurks all around in these ancient crumbling catacombs. Silently I reached the top of the stack, among the beams of the roof. Then I heard their voices and realized they were at the other side. I crouched and peered down toward them. Never had I spied on them for fear of being seen by the boy. Now I hid my face and lay very quietly against the papers. It was intensely hot and close near the roof of the building. I could barely hear their voices again. Only Mary talked, house talk that I didn't make out. Slowly I stretched out flat and looked through the dusty end table legs, turned upside down and between old once-wicker-bottomed chairs. They were crouched in between the furniture, an old glass bottomed lamp with a bead-fringed shade glistened in the sunlight over their heads.

I hid my face again, and might have gone to sleep, or passed out, so long I lay there tensed. Then suddenly they were shouting. The boy was yelling and I saw them through the chairs, Mary slapping at his face and bare chest. He backed off a little and I saw him full; his face twisted and red. "Little bitch!" he hissed in a lizard voice. "Little bitch!" He said over and over and ran in toward her. They were out of sight. The tables bumped and jammed up against one another and a pile of chairs came tumbling down toward them; but the boy kept hissing, and Mary shouting back. I pressed myself hard against the stack of papers. I saw only his arm and hand. The beaded lamp raised high, singing excitedly in the voice of Chinese wind chimes. He brought it down in a wide arc, swift as lightning with a crash of thunder behind the chairs. Again it raised, throwing off a shower of beads that flashed in the sun like multi-colored fireworks and made hail-sounds, rattling through the shack. Again it crashed behind the chairs, and again the flashing shower and hail sounds. I pressed my face down into my hands but the shatter of glass echoed over and over again throughout the room, each time louder. Only the noise of an approaching train drowned it out. The shack shook violently through every board, as the train passed. The sound grew slowly softer. Farther and farther into the distance, I strained to hear it; fainter and fainter then gone altogether and everything was quiet.

Pictures of our neighborhood were in all the papers. Diagrams and maps of the shack. There was a picture of Mary; her legs bent like a rag doll. The bold headlines screamed, "POLICE LOOK FOR SEX FIEND" and "Derelicts Questioned in Murder of West Side Girl." Not too long after that, the Carson family moved from our neighborhood. We moved too the following year.

All that was fifteen years or more ago. But there are things that bring it all back. It happens to everyone.

Around the office were pictures of the esteemed candidate for Governor. Red and blue lettering and huge blown-up blue photographs. I left the room, with the receptionist staring stupidly after me, sputtering, "Well, since you've waited this long . . . I'm sure . . ." I shut the door quietly behind me and walked down the shiny buff-marble hall to the elevators and out into the afternoon street. I don't like to leave a room without some sort of an explanation, it's not my nature to miss an exiting line; but just at that moment I couldn't think of anything to say.

Drift

Toward the end of October but with April eyes he came here; never going into town but stopping at the group of buildings on the hill above, looking for a moment to the neon red above Hilltop Café before he entered. From the south up Route Sixty-five he had hitchhiked without even a change of clothes. He was young, maybe eighteen, with fine sandy hair that fell across his face across gray eyes.

Roslyn took him in. Took him in and as chance handled it his name was Buddy. Roslyn who had been left the café when her husband, Bud, walked off; who stood behind the counter serving the same menu for years to truck drivers passing on Sixty-five and people of the town who came up late after the place below had closed. Took him as a dishwasher and to help in the kitchen though she had managed before; stood ignoring the rumors through town when she bought clothes for him, when he was never seen away from the hilltop.

And gradually the face of the café changed. Metal awnings were added to windows, the building was repainted a fresh white. Toward winter drivers from the highway saw Buddy behind the café, splitting wood or working to level the ground before the freezes came. Roslyn had driven to Springfield for new tablecloths and to order menu covers.

By Christmas, which had always been like any other winter day but this season was decorated with lights and a tree and green banners of Noel, Buddy was serving customers; spending more time in front. And slowly, I guess the rumors became quiet, until finally very little was ever said. He stayed with Roslyn in her small apartment above the café and the café closed now promptly at ten each night. People did talk of the change in Roslyn. She began somehow to look younger, gaining a vitality in her walk; she was gayer than anyone remembered, even attractive and always laughing. She joked now with the truck drivers and they became friendly with Buddy. Often he played cards out front with them on very cold nights early before closing when business was slow, while Roslyn talked from the kitchen or through the window between the kitchen and diner. Several Sundays they went driving, sometimes to a movie in Springfield; arriving home late, laughing. I once saw them cheering a parade like any lovers away from acquaintances.

People around town who had at first whispered now mentioned that Roslyn had managed to lose weight and looked healthier than she had before he came, and Buddy didn't look at all like the kid who had drifted in that fall. I suppose no one could help but notice.

In fact they seemed so happy there it was a surprise to everyone when toward the beginning of spring without a word he left. Without a sign, leaving everything she had bought him. When people inevitably asked where he had gone she shrugged it off as unimportant and went on with her business: "He drifted in, he drifted on," she said. Still now the café closes at ten as it did during the winter. Only people say it would be an easy hit for someone wanting to carry off what they could find there some night. That's what they say, no one's tried it. They say the door is unlocked.

SECTION 4
SKETCHES OF CITY LIFE

Fig. 5. Lanford Wilson, Sixth Avenue, across the street from the Waverly Theater, New York City, February 19, 1966; photographer, James D. Gossage.

Mama

From the window of my apartment I can look out to the house next door. Perhaps three feet has been maintained between the buildings for an air shaft; and during the summer days when the rooms begin to become insufferable all the sounds of the building across the way come through my open window. Directly across from my window is the room of a character I had seen before a number of times in the neighborhood. Not being one to especially notice individuals, no one, nevertheless, could avoid some shock at meeting him on the streets. He was male, or at least it's to be assumed he was male, but you could tell only from his dress and hair. He wore tight pants—skintight, and soft almost blouselike shirts. He never seemed to go outside without a full face of makeup—still he wasn't a pretty boy—he was garish, grossly overweight, and he wasn't young; one would probably guess thirty-five after close inspection.

The fact that he turned heads and drew comments from almost everyone on the street bothered him not at all. He walked very quickly, never looking to either side. At first I think I was annoyed at discovering he was a neighbor and when I heard him in his room—he seemed to spend a great deal of time there—I usually withdrew from my window and turned on the small electric fan. Once, though, sitting in the dark of my room I saw him come in very late, talking. I believe I was curious to see what kind of friends he had for I stayed at my window. But he walked directly to the bed, cooing almost in a soft voice. His words were distinct but it took several minutes for them to register, so strange was the conversation, or so foreign to anything I had expected. He was speaking in a kind of child talk, looking back to the bed several times at a bundle of light blue blankets. "Mama warm you up some milk honeybaby. Must be starved," he was saying. "Run around and come home to her babydoll, what naughty Mama I am." During this, of course, he was heating something at the stove. Later I saw it was a bottle being warmed in a pan of water, but at first I couldn't see clearly.

That first night he pulled the shade on his room, and I heard only muffled sounds in the same child talk as before and saw only his shadow pass across the window. In the weeks that passed, however, I saw him prepare the bottle regularly at the same hour every evening, talking lowly and lifting the bundle up to cradle in his arms. Some evenings very softly he sang a slow mournful lullaby, high and sweet as a choir. At first I thought of a puppy, as my mother would have treated a newborn pup or kitten. "Very own baby, honey," the man crooned softly, "baby sweetheart," and sometimes playfully tickling and laughing. One evening after a week, however, I saw a tiny hand and arm come from the bundle and the man very gently tucked it back—later he cradled the infant in his arms saying it was too hot for covers and what a good baby: "What a dear sweet baby don't cry about the heat. Mama keep it warm in winter for her baby, keep it cool when it gets hot so her baby don't cry." Several times though I thought I did hear a soft infant's crying, covered quickly by profuse shushing and much cradling and rocking.

One evening the man brought home a small dress and several times washing, diapers and the sort, were hung about the apartment. "Dirtiest little tyke in town, aren't you, only? Keep Mama so busy she can't hardly think about work anymore—mean ol' boss is cross to Mama when she's thinking about her baby boy." But very often after the end of July the shade was pulled halfway down and I saw only the man's shadows weave across his window and heard only soft, muffled cries and softer comfortings. It had occurred to me, of course, to notify someone though I had no idea whom. "Mama would just die if she ever had to give up her baby—if she lost her little baby, do you know that? Does baby know that? Does baby know how Mama loves him?" But still you wonder about an infant, a really small child, however well behaved, being kept by such a man; though I had seen him buying baby food and condensed milk at the grocery outside his room and no one visited them. Then once after he had come home and heated the bottle I saw him rushing about the room: "Mama's got to go to the store or we won't have anything to eat. Forgetful Mama walked right past the grocery and didn't remember to get baby something. Be good boy till Mama gets back, will you sweetheart? Someday Mama will take you along and you can go to the store with Mama." He left the door ajar.

The thought occurred to me instantly. Just a simple curiosity. I was in the front of the house by the time he came out. The door to his building was the kind that locks automatically so I had to buzz a room at random to get into the building. Once in, as the house was very similar to mine, it wasn't difficult to find his room. There was the noise of someone leaving a room from an apartment below that froze me where I stood. I listened as the steps went down the hall toward the front. The room itself, through a crack of light that striped out into the hall, was very similar to my own. I pushed the door open. The walls were a light ivory, the room was furnished with curtains and a more feminine décor than I could have noticed from my window. It was littered with cosmetics and bottles and dozens of cans of baby food lined the shelves of the pantry. I pushed the door open slowly to see the bed. The infant lay asleep, it seemed surrounded with stuffed animals and plastic rattlers that you see at the five and ten stores. I heard the man's voice in my mind almost more clearly than I had from the window: "If Mama lost her baby boy, Mama would just die; does baby know that? Does baby know that about his Mama?" The infant wasn't asleep, I walked over to the bed, slowly at first before I saw with soft pain, somehow the object whose welfare I'd been worried about was a doll. A doll with painted face and painted eyes that whined "Mama" when I raised its head.

Fuzz on Orion's Sword

It was after eleven when the 8:10 train arrived from Boston. For a long while Leonard studied the blackboard: there was a desk raised like a lower-court judge's platform with a large schedule of arrivals and departures on the wall behind. A man totally unconcerned with the progress or tardiness of his trains wandered from side to side of the board, chalking new times in the squares. The 8:10 was erased, slowed down, three times. Leonard imagined the train's progress as if following a player once around a Monopoly board: Move to Salem Heights, go back three squares to Jotham Bridge; Jotham Bridge snowbound, lose one turn. For a long interim there was no anticipated arrival time posted at all: the black square, or rather, the gray smudge gave him the eerie feeling that the train, his sister, and a bottle of J&B she had promised him had atomized somewhere between point of departure and destination; been rubbed out, as it were, by some cosmic, dusty felt eraser; leaving perhaps a dark melted area in the snowy upstate landscape. Or perhaps the train had landed on Chance and drawn a card reading go to jail. He accepted the possibility with wonder but doubtfully.

Restlessness won out after a while and he wandered out of the waiting room, leaving the train unattended. The station was not crowded for all you hear of Grand Central. Most of the people stood about in lines to the ticket windows on the far side of the room. There was a small circle around the brass information desk and another, somewhat larger, allowing themselves to be mesmerized by a slowly revolving Nash Rambler. He lost his way back to the waiting room, wandering through brightly lighted halls of bookshops, hat shops, shoe shops, record stores, and strategically placed refreshment stations. When he found the room again, Yvonne's train was back on the tracks and due to arrive now at 10:45. Leonard had a cup of coffee at an adjoining café, in view of the blackboard. He looked through the newsstand's merry-go-round of paperbacks until the nervous little proprietor asked him to please buy something or move on. The last word on the train's arrival, posted while Leonard sat over a second cup of coffee, was 11:15 so Yvonne finally appeared in New York a few minutes early.

The survivors of the vigil began to stand up, stamping out cigarettes, and folding up their worn-out newspapers, brushing ashes and chocolate crumbs from their coats. There was not a large crowd but with greeting friends and carting luggage around, once people began to file into the room, they managed to create the proper waiting room feeling.

Yvonne and Leonard saw one another at approximately the same instant, or rather, they both threw an arm into the air as though someone above had pulled a string. She ran up to him and threw her free arm up around his neck. By now people were greeting one another all around them with dampened enthusiasm: waited for hours—God, what a ride—froze all the way—

Yvonne was covered neck-to-knee in a ridiculous raccoon coat and toe-to-shin in pointed black leather boots. Leonard gave her a fat, brotherly hug: "God, you feel frozen."

"I am frozen. No heat for over an hour and that's the last damn time I ride a train. You look great."

"So do you. Is your hair lighter?"

Yvonne tucked her arm under his. "Of course not."

He took her suitcase, a tan leather Samsonite one-suiter, and directed her out of the room into the labyrinthine corridors. "It's anyone's guess how to get out of here, I dropped bread crumbs but some pigeons followed me." He smiled, "A year in Boston and already you look like you were born there. I'm surprised I recognized you."

Yvonne elbowed her brother in the ribs, a reflex action automatic even after four years' separation. "Like hell. Whatever your ideas about Boston, it's wishful thinking."

"On the phone you said you loved the place."

"Of course I did. David was standing on my shoulders like the Spirit of the Mayflower or something." Leonard snorted. They walked up the long ramp toward the Forty-second Street entrance at Vanderbilt Avenue. "One thing I'll give Boston," Yvonne was saying, "they have the best fish markets in the country. Shrimp and clam and eel and god knows what kind of ocean denizen."

"And you finally decided to like seafood."

"No. Too bad. I can't even walk down the street."

"You'll learn."

Yvonne screwed her face into an expression of faintly nauseated refusal: "No luck. I tried when I was out on the coast. All the kids at school were poking some kind of smoked oyster at me. I just hated them for it. I was sick all four years." They emerged finally into the bright not-winter, not-spring sunshine. "Can we walk? Just a ways—it isn't too cold is it?"

After a week of quasi-spring weather and light winds, Thursday had turned cold again and a soft, damp snow had fallen intermittently throughout the evening. On avenues the snow was felt only slightly and even on the side streets proprietors could easily clear their sidewalks—with shuffleboard strokes of a snow shovel, piling it in a low bank against the cars at the curb. This morning, Friday, was a little warmer again, sidewalks were beginning to dry in places or were freshly wet around patches of ice that had begun to melt, but the streets were still awash with a shallow daiquiri slush that cars slopped up onto the curb. In another half-hour Midtown would be crowded with people rushing off to cash their checks and take an extended lunch hour, but Leonard and Yvonne could wander along just now. "And you can point out all the landmarks along Fifth Avenue, like Cartier and Elizabeth Arden; you really can't imagine what a relief it is to be able to walk on concrete again. Boston is snow to the knee, try to look demure with a boot full of slosh sometime."

"Very well, Cartier—how about Saks?"

Yvonne considered. "You might run me around Saks once or twice; is that too terrible? Not seeing you for four or five years and then telling you to take me somewhere to look at clothes."

"It's pretty bad," Leonard agreed. "But I was expecting it."

"Really, I only want to look today. We can save tomorrow for shopping and we can spend a fortune. I intend to spend most of it on myself, but I know damn well as soon as I walk into a kid's department Bobby will have about ten new outfits and I'll go begging. I'm a sucker for toy shops."

Leonard smiled. "How is Bobby? I keep forgetting I'm an uncle."

"That's alright, Bobby keeps forgetting he's a nephew. You two will have to get together sometime. We sent you a picture of him, didn't we?"

"No. Not in two years. I have a constant image of your bare-butt son flopped down on a blue blanket looking roughly the size of a half-grown cow and weighing in at about four hundred pounds. I believe he's even chewing up a plastic hippopotamus and grinning, like a—"

"There's a new one. I thought we sent it to you."

"No."

"What did you do with the one you have? Did you hang it up?

"I did not. I put it in the bottom of my sock drawer. What's he like now?"

"I guess he was a bit fat then. Now he's skinny and tall; he's going to be tall." She paused a second. "And probably like every other four-year-old he's advanced for his age. And he's beautiful, I have to say that, he looks like me. David won't admit it but of course he does. And he's noisy and normal and he's bright."

"Is he?"

Yvonne tugged at her brother's arm. "Well, don't say it like that. Of course he's bright. When the devil are you coming to Boston? It's just as close for you as it is for me."

"I guess so. I thought you'd need to be liberated more often than I would, though."

"That's probably true. Still you should at least see the place. David's asked you up a dozen times. He'll drag you all over the apartment and down into the basement—he's got this tool room and a lot of equipment his father gave him. Christ, it's almost embarrassing: they got us the damn apartment and all the furniture and a million dollars worth of power saws and they've crammed so much junk into Bobby's room the poor kid doesn't have a place to sleep, let alone walk around. David's anxious for you to come up. I know he'll bore you to death before you're in the front door, but you really should come sometime." They reached the corner of Forty-ninth Street and stopped at the curb for a light. Leonard had met David only once, a few months after the wedding, and had been neither really impressed nor disappointed in him. It bothered him that he couldn't remember now exactly what David looked like, if he was medium or tall or had brown hair or black. He decided to wait until his sister volunteered the information. Right now Yvonne was saying, "And it's not a bad apartment either; at least we're settled. God, Bobby was turning into a regular banshee running from one army post to another and everyone looking like his father to him: there are so many soldiers overrunning the apartment all the time I wondered if he really knew which one of them belonged there. If he stubbed his toe or something he just fell into the lap of the closest one at hand: calling everyone Daddy. I felt like the girl in the green hat."* The light changed. "You'll like the new place. It isn't Nob Hill or anything. Don't expect us to live there."

"I didn't suppose you would."

"Why not? You needn't be so smug about it; we're not poor. Just a kind of over conservative, middle-of-the . . ."

"Nob Hill just isn't in Boston is all."

---

* A possible reference to the wild war widow heroine of Michael Arlen's 1924 best-selling novel *The Green Hat*. —Ed.

"Are you sure?"

"Of course I'm sure, it's in San Francisco."

"Well, what is it if it isn't Nob Hill?"

"Beacon Hill."

"Damn."

"Why?"

"Damn. I just wrote Susan Browny—remember her?" Leonard nodded—"that we had a perfectly lovely apartment with this charming view of Nob Hill. Do you think she'll know I'm wrong?"

"Probably. She's been there."

"When? Not since I've been there she hasn't."

"San Francisco."

"Oh." Yvonne paused, then added, "Damn," but shrugged it off. "Well, she knows I couldn't remember the name of a hill or anything else." When they reached Fifty-second Yvonne decided she was ready to take a cab. "That suitcase must be dragging you down by now anyway."

"It's not too bad. For you."

"I'm feeling suddenly all-over gritty and cold and like I've been on a train half the day."

Leonard hailed a cab for them. He carried the suitcase into the back seat with him. "Is that a terribly smart neighborhood?" Yvonne asked when he gave the driver his address.

"Not anymore, lady; used to be," the driver answered. He pulled out into the traffic. Yvonne and Leonard exchanged a glance; Yvonne bit her lip.

"We're visiting a friend," Leonard spoke up. "Elderly lady."

"Grandmother," Yvonne said and looked out the window as they turned into the park.

"Yeah? One of those types. Well, it's O.K. if you like it. Used to be swank, you know?"

"That's what she told us."

"They let it go to the dogs, though. It ain't really bad in her block but over west of there . . ." The driver glanced up into the mirror.

Leonard became interested in the view. "She mentioned it was near the park."

"Yeah. It's not too bad on the corner there, but over west they let it go to the dogs."

Leonard set the suitcase on the curb and paid the driver. Yvonne was drumming across the top of the car. "I'll bet dollars to doughnuts that's a planetarium, isn't it?

"Where?"

"Across the street, stupid."

"Oh. Yes. And don't ask me; I haven't."

"Of course you haven't."

Leonard nodded to the doorman. "Wonder if Grandmother's home?" he said under his breath as they reached the elevator.

"Yeah, those types."

Leonard's apartment was at the corner of the building on the eighth floor and was a spacious what is usually called three-and-a-half-room apartment but was actually two and a number of quarters. A smallish foyer with a hall closet and a 1920 lighting fixture he hadn't decided quite what to do with hanging in the center of the ceiling opened onto a very high, large living room that faced the park. The bedroom, straight forward, faced Eighty-first Street. To the right of the foyer was a square little kitchen just under the size for a comfortable breakfast table. There was a bath off the bedroom that also opened into the living room, "To avoid having to build another half bath," Leonard explained. The ceiling in the living room was high with heavy dark molding. A fireplace opposite the windows was flanked with dark bookcases set into the wall; the fireplace itself was a marble monstrosity of the same genre as the lighting fixture in the foyer. He had occupied the apartment just over a week, so it lacked any personal coloring except several of his architectural renderings that were framed and hanging in the bedroom, and books that crowded in toward the fireplace. A large sofa in the living room could double as a bed when needed. The one bedroom was large enough for a high, tilted drawing board where he occasionally worked. Leonard had left the windows opened a few inches to avoid getting the rooms overheated and the heat had been turned down, so it was a little too chilly when they first came in.

Yvonne opened the suitcase across his bed and began to shake things out. "I've become an absolute monger about clothes," she said. "How do you like this one?"

Leonard had picked up a magazine that had lain in its mailing wrapper for several days and was opening it. "It looks like a long brown T-shirt."

Yvonne frowned and slipped the hanging straps over the ends of a hanger. "Well, it's Pucci and he's great and it's silk-jersey and you'll love it. And besides it cost David a fortune."

"How large a fortune?"

"Well, over seventy."

"Christ."

"Marked down, I might add. *Way* down."

Leonard laid the magazine on a table at the end of the sofa and went into the kitchen. "When weren't you?"

"Wasn't I what?"

"A monger about clothes."

He was bringing a drink into the bedroom when she said: "Well, *damn!*"

"What?"

She was standing at the window, her hand holding the curtain aside. "There's that damn green dome again."

"Where?"

"*Across* the *street*, stupid. It takes up your whole view."

"It does not. I've got the park and half the West Side and the goddamned Hudson River if you stand on your toes and squint."

"Then it takes up *my* whole view."

"What have you got against planetariums?"

She shrugged and let the curtain fall back in place. "Nothing, I suppose. I just didn't really *need* it."

Yvonne carried the drink into the bathroom with her and sat it on the glass shelf under the medicine cabinet. She showered and changed into a robe, a roomy satin affair built strictly for comfort, and fat rabbit slippers that had been a "present" from Bobby. She carried the glass back into the living room.

"Christ," Leonard said, looking up from his chair, "I'd forgotten what a vision you were slopping around the house."

"I'm not, really," she said innocently. "Not anymore. I'm the inside cover of *Bazaar* around the house. Today I just feel like slopping around. At least you're used to it."

Later Yvonne sat across the room on the sofa, her feet out in front of her on a low table. Leonard was saying, "So we all signed but, of course, they're tearing it down anyway."

"Hmmm. Do you know what they'd have done if they had it in Boston?" Yvonne mused.

"It makes you feel pretty stupid when you're talking about the one thing you're supposed to know and they don't even consider your opinion as worth listening to."

"They'd have turned it into a National Shrine or something," Yvonne said, following her own thought. "You have no idea how those people are."

"A shrine would have been better than what we got."

"They had to dig a subway or something through the park," she continued. "Maybe it was the Commons, I wasn't there, they told me about it. And this ground was so goddamned consecrated they moved it—the topsoil—somewhere until they had this subway or sewer laid or whatever it was, and they carted it back. Spread it out inch for inch where it had been. Or so Doug says."

"Who's Doug?"

Yvonne removed her feet from the table and tucked them under her on the sofa. "How do I know? Clare Allendale's nut brother. He's vice chairman of some committee."

"All Dougs are vice chairmen of some committee. My boss is a Doug."

"Same guy as Chicago?"

Leonard nodded. "You want another drink?"

Yvonne set her feet back on the floor and straightened the front of her robe. "No. I think I'm nearly ready to see something of your fair wet city. What can you show me that's dry and inside and warm?"

"Sardi's?" he called from the kitchen. "I can't afford it. Next time."

"Well then, cheap and dry and warm and inside?"

Leonard came back into the room. "What would you like to see?"

"Do you know what I'd like to see?"

"What?"

"That is, if you wouldn't make little critical asides about the construction of the place."

"I won't, probably. What?"

"Guggenheim Museum."

"You sure?"

"I saw a picture of it in *Time* magazine and it can't really look like that."

"O.K. But I'll tell you right now, it does."

Yvonne stood up. "Not another word or you'll spoil it. I remember you very well at a dozen other places and—"

"I wasn't saying anything."

"You were *going* to, I could see it coming."

With all the added spirit, reinvigoration, that had been apparent in her voice, Yvonne managed to delay an hour, wandering about the apartment in her slip. It was just after three by the time they left.

In the cab, crossing the park, Yvonne said, "You should really have been out in California." She was looking out to the bare limbs, stark, above the sweaty black stone walls on either side of the street. "I thought several times California was the place for you instead of Chicago. You always seemed the leisure-loving type. If you know how to live like that, California's the place to do it."

"How was school?" Leonard asked. He was half listening to his sister.

"Oh, fine. Most of the time we were on the beach," she said and was silent nearly half a minute. "You should see the way they dress out there. Mother would die. You remember what a stickler she was for the proper scholastic appearance: long sweaters and long skirts. She would just have died." The cab stopped then, in front of the museum. "We're here? Already?" She got out and walked a few steps toward the entrance. "I'm not joking now." She warned Leonard when he came up beside her, "One word of yours and I'm going right back to the apartment."

They purchased a token at the counter and went through the turnstile. "I won't say a word. Don't expect me to be too excited about the show, I was here a few weeks ago."

"Well, a little refresher won't hurt you. How do we do this, do we walk up?"

He took her arm and steered her toward the elevator. "No, we take the elevator up and get in a little car at the top and ride down," he said as the doors shut behind them.

"A car?" she asked, not believing him.

"You have your choice really of a car or roller skates; I usually take a car."

"Now that's just the sort of thing I was talking about. I've already decided to like the building and everything in it."

"Good." They stepped out at the top floor. The show, as it had been for over a month, was a collection of drawings and washes. Yvonne said she had come to see the building anyway. "What do you think of it?"

"I can't discuss architecture with you," she said. "You tear buildings down as fast as they build them. How come your boss moved from Chicago, anyway?"

"Doug? He was getting a lot of work from here anyway. They've got a funny ruling about sunlight on the sidewalk and he thought he could lick it. Do you know where I was when I got the announcement of your and David's marriage?"

"Do I want to?"

"It was the morning I applied for my job. I'd stuffed it in my pocket when I left the house and I opened it at his office. I was so shocked I forgot to be nervous."

"Good. I was pretty shocked myself by that time."

"How is David?"

Yvonne moved in close to a drawing. "I don't know. Fine."

"You can be a little more enthusiastic than that, can't you?"

Yvonne passed her gloved hand over the glass of the drawing and stared intently into the frame. "Damn."

"What?"

"My hair's a mess."

"You want my comb?"

"No. Not here. I guess it doesn't make any difference." She moved away from the drawing and into the next area. "How enthusiastic is any woman after five years of marriage and a frigid train ride?"

"What's he doing by now?"

"I don't know. Come up and see us. He'll tell you."

"—after your whirlwind courtship." It wasn't a question exactly, but a means of keeping the subject in the conversation.

Yvonne laughed, remembering. "It was more whirlwind than courtship. What can I tell you? What's anyone like? One thing he's like—he steals ashtrays. He's going to get caught at it sometime in some hotel and embarrass me to death."

"Ashtrays?"

"Sure. All over the house: Americana of San Juan, Joe's Pub, Fisherman's Wharf. You'd die. We don't have an ashtray of our own in the whole house."

Leonard took her to see the auditorium, from the balcony. They left the museum by the side door. He had told her while they were in the area she should go by the Metropolitan Museum as well, so they walked slowly down Fifth Avenue. They got lost looking for the collection he had wanted her to see and wound up in the smoking room, a small barren room with an awkward marble fountain resembling a birdbath rising from the center of the floor. The walls were hung with old hunting tapestries: the display cases in the room, in transition, were half filled with Delft tiles and half with faded prints of balloons and early dirigibles. Leonard and Yvonne sat on a stiff-hided leather sofa under the tall windows. Yvonne crossed her legs and looked gloomily around the room. "I probably wrote you about Anthony, didn't I? I must have." Leonard was looking through into the next room where three high school students, girls, were chatting, bundled up for the street, holding books. They stood in a private circle in the center of the room. Through the doorway behind them the huge gates made them seem very small and their voices were lost somewhere in the corridors and rooms.

"Anthony? When?"

"Oh, God. I know I did. It must have been five years ago; when I was in school."

He loosened his coat and scarf and stretched his legs out in front of him, crossing his ankles. "Was Anthony the one who was the subject of about a five-page, totally incoherent, single-spaced, typewritten, stream of—"

"What makes you think so?"

"I remember thinking he sounded like a nut of some kind."

"Not really. You'd have liked him. He was just a nice guy."

"Where is he?"

"He retreated to Australia. His words: retreated to Australia."

"God."

Yvonne reached across him to drop the ashes of her cigarette a few feet from the ashtray. "You sounded very serious about him, I remember," Leonard said.

"I was, I suppose. You got the feeling, though, that Anthony wasn't very serious about anything for any length of time."

"Hmm."

"God. He had the greatest sister. I used to pump her for information about him every time I saw her. You couldn't get a word out of him and she rattled on all the time. He had been the most promising poet—did I write you that? The most promising poet at Harvard or Yale or Princeton—"

"Or one of those."

"But he was so dumb. They devoted half of one issue of their magazine—you know those quarterlies they all have."

Leonard nodded. The girls had wandered off in three separate directions.

"And Christ, everyone reviewed it. They were all just insane for him. And he read somewhere, after that—you know, he was one of those people with enormous gaps in his background—you couldn't believe it. He could quote you volumes of Sappho, in *Greek*, my dear, and he didn't have the slightest idea who Picasso is, or any artist: he wouldn't have recognized an El Greco even if he got one for his birthday. And he knew but nothing about astronomy, I guess, so this came as a total shock—like a revelation—to him. He read somewhere that the sun, our sun, would burn out in about a billion years or two; you know, or whatever it's supposed to do—burn out or blow up. And he never wrote a word after that. Glenna told me he said he always thought anything that was written would simply always be around somewhere and if there was going to be an end to it all one day, he didn't see any point in bothering with it."

Several people had come into the room and wandered around for something to see; Leonard dropped his cigarette into the ashtray and watched the smoke climb almost unwaveringly straight up in the sunlight. "Glenna was his sister?" Yvonne nodded and moved, not restlessly, against the back of the sofa. "What did she think of this revelation?"

"I don't know. She thought he was great. But that's just the way he reasoned, see? So he left school and came out to California. Do you remember Dimmy Howard?"

"Dimmy? Sure. I haven't thought about him for years, though."

"Well, Anthony kinda looked like that. Tall and lanky like Dimmy; only they were a lot different in the face." Yvonne leaned forward to reach across him again and put her cigarette out against the sloped dish of the ashtray. She got up and wandered over to the fountain. "Have you noticed everyone who comes in here walks straight to that fountain and looks in?"

"No."

She looked into the shallow bowl and shrugged. "Water."

Leonard was still seated on the sofa. "What'd you expect, for crying out loud, crocodiles?"

"I don't know, I'm new here. I thought they must have been checking up on something."

They had not found the room he was looking for by five when the buzzer rang and the guards started herding everyone through the rooms. A crowd bottle-necked toward the entrance. "So why did he come to California?" Leonard asked as they walked toward the end of the room.

"Astronomy, of course. Mount Palomar. After he quit writing I guess he got interested in cosmology or something. For a while he was really passionate about it—all the while he was in California but I guess he lost interest. He was one of those types that's never interested in any one thing for any length of time. I think for about a month he was even interested in me. Glenna thought it was great. He apparently hadn't been much interested in people before."

Leonard laughed.

"Well, *you* know what I mean. *One* person. You would have liked him." They stepped out onto the front steps. "Do you know what I'd really like right now?"

"No. What?"

"A good strong alcoholic drink and some very hot Mexican food. Could you stand that? It's all that damn talk about California."

Leonard nodded. "Very well. It just happens that there is an incredible little place down on Second Avenue where you can get the best Mexican dishes this side of California; and they make a salty tequila drink that will absolutely burn the lacquer off your hair."

"You're joking."

"I only found it about a month ago." They stood at the curb trying to hail a cab. "It's just falling to the ground and it's a hole in the wall so you know it's the smartest place in town." It was nearly dark when they left the museum and in the long ride downtown, during rush hour, it became evening.

They had a margarita at the bar while waiting for a table and carried another into the dining room. Dinner was slow and pleasant; Yvonne raved, an effect perhaps of the second drink, about the food and swore permanent allegiance to the place.

Over coffee—the food had made her reflect again about school—Yvonne was saying, "And we all used to sit out on the beach at night. We weren't supposed to have a fire but everyone did and they never said anything to us. God, it was great. The nights there aren't really cold, but you need a sweater and the fire was wonderful. We used to build it way up—there's tons of old wood that washes up on the beach and we dragged it from everywhere. You could have seen it for miles out at sea, I imagine."

"And they didn't say anything about it?"

"They didn't really care. There must have been about twenty of us in the group. And, God, it was great. With the firelight lighting everyone's face around the circle and everyone looking so tanned and handsome. You should have seen us, we looked like some kind of Pepsi advertisement. My hair went all blond—by itself, I'll have you know, and I wore the sloppiest old sweatshirt and looked just dreadful, but I didn't care."

"I'll *bet* you looked dreadful."

Yvonne smiled and took up her purse, finding a cigarette. She leaned forward to light it from the candle and rested back, half sideways against the booth. "Of course I didn't, but if I had I wouldn't have cared." The waiter came forward and removed the things from the table, brushing the cloth with his hand. When he had gone Yvonne said, "Anthony and I used to wander off down the beach. You couldn't get lost because you could always see the fire and everyone running around it and dragging up more wood. We used to lie out on the beach, digging into the sand like a—like a—what's something that digs in the sand?"

"Little boys with shovels?"

Yvonne smiled. "No. Anyway it's warm on top—"

"And underneath it's cold and wet."

"How did you know?"

"It's like that everywhere, not just California."

"Is it? Hmm. Not cold, but cool, underneath. I even learned a few of the constellations. I told you he was studying astronomy."

"Anthony."

"Of course. They're easy, really. At first they're just a lot of stars all over, but once you start learning which constellation they belong to the whole sky divides itself up, like a quilt, in separate patterns and you can't look at it without seeing the Big Dipper and Orion and Andromeda . . ."

Leonard took her hand, which was above her head—she had been running her fingers across a simulated sky a few feet above them—and brought it back to the table. "Don't look now," he said, "but I think people were looking at you."

Yvonne looked but didn't see anyone. "Why, was I shouting?"

"No, but you were gesticulating like a lunatic."

"Well, I always do that, you know that." She withdrew her hand from his. "I'll be very still. Look, here is Orion—see, there are three stars, *big* ones *across*. That's the belt." She tapped them out across the tablecloth. "And here—perpendicular to the belt, three more, closer together—is his sword; smaller, of course. And here—" she drew a circle around the center star in the sword—"is the Great Nebula in Orion."

Leonard nodded, looking at the tablecloth. "The Great Nebula in Orion," he repeated.

"Which isn't a star at all," Yvonne said and leaned against the back of the booth again.

"Of course not."

"Do you know this?"

"No."

"Well, then pay attention, it's very interesting. You see, the Great Nebula is a lot of hydrogen or some kind of gas that's lit up by a couple of stars behind it somewhere. But see, this gas is condensing, getting compact, and after a few hundred years it's going to be so compact it'll start burning of its own accord, and then it'll be a star. And we could see that: it's sorta a big fuzzy spot at the center of the sword. A kind of pale green. And Anthony said there would be a star there someday."

"A star is born," Leonard said.

"Exactly. Are you making fun?"

"No. Do you want another drink?"

"No. I don't think so." She brushed her hand across the table as if erasing her diagram. "Anyway, you can't see it here. It just looks like another star: sometimes the sky's so hazy in Boston you can't even find the sword; though you can usually see the belt. I kept wishing you'd come out there; you would have loved it. I wrote you to come, didn't I?"

"Probably. In that letter that I didn't understand."

"I guess it *was* pretty garbled, but I wanted you to come anyway. I was pretty upset; Anthony had just announced his retreat to Australia."

"And then David came out there and you forgot about astronomy," Leonard said.

Yvonne looked at him for a long time. "Yes," she said, and started reaching around in the booth for her gloves. "He was stationed in San Diego. We had two dates, did you know that? And we were married the afternoon after the second date. I guess you could call that a whirlwind courtship."

"I guess."

"The announcement you opened in your boss's office was mailed the morning before we got married. Anthony went off to Australia and a week and a half later I was living in camp what-ever-it-is in San Diego." She stood up and ran her hands down her skirt to straighten it.

Leonard held her coat. He bent close to her and whispered, "We really should take the ashtray, don't you think?"

"Ashtray?"

"For David." She gave him a look that said she was not amused, and went to wait by the door as he paid the check. The waiter passed and smiled. She smiled back in a complimentary manner, then very broadly, and when her brother opened the door for her she whispered, "I might be just a very little touch high. I think I just flirted with the waiter. I intended to just be polite, but it got a little out of hand."

In the taxi, Leonard said, "How come you didn't go to Australia with the astronomer?"

"I wasn't invited. I told you he wasn't the type to be interested in anything for long. It's silly to talk about it." After a while she added, "I don't even know where he is by now. I was wondering a few months back and wrote a long letter to Glenna, but it's been five years and of course, she'd moved by now so it came back."

Leonard looked across the seat to his sister. She was staring out of the window onto the street. The street had dried considerably, though it had gotten progressively colder during the day. He reached across the seat and squeezed her hand. Yvonne looked over to him and said, "Whatever was that for?"

"Nothing. You're going to be able to visit often, aren't you?"

"I hope so. I intend to. Don't let me sleep in the morning, don't forget. We've got a lot of work to do tomorrow."

"I remember. Saks."

"Exactly."

The apartment was warm this time, after the cold evening. The light from the lamp was ocher and inviting. Leonard turned down the sofa and went into the bedroom to get blankets from the top of the closet. Yvonne changed into a nightgown and the robe and slippers. She said she was tired, probably from the train that morning and had a little headache, probably from drinking too much. Leonard made the bed in the living room for himself. Yvonne kissed him goodnight and went into the bedroom, closing the door.

Just after one in the morning, Leonard had changed into pajama bottoms and an old terry-cloth robe that had faded to about the color of watered burgundy and was seated in the chair under a pyramid of light from the floor lamp; he was holding a book, but not really reading it; she came back into the living room. Her face was red, she said she thought she might be getting a cold from the train ride; she was carrying his box of Kleenex from the bedroom and she blew her nose and asked him if it would be alright if she slept in that room instead of the bedroom, because the planetarium across the street was lighted at night and it haunted his bedroom and she had to get some sleep. She had her pillow with her, carrying it by one corner like a teddy bear, and she gave him the pillow off the sofa bed. He had nearly fallen asleep over the book anyway. He said goodnight and went into the other room, closing the door. The room faced south. The planetarium dome was lighted, a warm green; he had never noticed it before. He turned out the light in the room. It was a clear night, there were stars out, the winter constellations, dimly. He looked at them for a moment, he had not been aware of stars over the city before. He smiled, though of course Yvonne had been right. Once you knew the pattern of one of the constellations, even generally, it seemed to separate itself entirely from the rest of the sky.

Uptown in Snow

The noises of the office were coming back: the rapid staccato snapping of a dozen typewriters keyed in various stiff-pitched monotones; a dozen carriage return bells, now synchronized, now in quick succession, a dozen single notes from all sides of the room. The girls flitted about the room; to the filing cabinets, their heels clicking on the tile floors, to their desks, to the water cooler, in and out of the office, slamming doors and the metal drawers of cabinets; up to her desk that faced the room like an instructor's desk faces the class. The voices were there, sweetly: "Miss Matthews? The Standard account; do they have it in the conference room?" "Miss Matthews? Will you sign these for Mr. Billingly? Mr. Billingly is out of the office this morning." "Miss Matthews? Could you..." "Miss Matthews?" "Miss Matthews?"

"Yes? *Yes*?" As she said it she realized no one had spoken.

"What say, lady?" The cab driver looked half around.

"Nothing. I'm sorry. I was thinking out loud."

The car tires hissed against the wet pavement. The drizzle predictably had turned to snow, the season's first: a damp gray fluttering that obscured the distance and softened the edges of buildings along Park Avenue. It fell to the streets and the cab window as rain.

It had been exactly the same at the office. "Yes, yes?" she had called and as she said it she knew no one had spoken. The noises had stopped, the walking, typing. The girls smiled to her reassuringly. "I beg your pardon, Miss Matthews?" Tina with the nasal voice and concerned expression. They resumed slowly. Ines, a sudden blond three weeks ago, now gradually lightening daily toward platinum, was at her side. She felt the girl's hand on her arm, sensed the professional concern in her voice. "Is something wrong? Can I get you something, Miss Matthews?" Miss Matthews had heard herself say, "Nothing at all is wrong, Ines; what have you done to your hair? It looks like spun glass." Mr. Billingly had been understanding; end of a hard week, quite reasonable, of course, she could leave early. "Take a cab, Miss Matthews. Get some rest—have a nice weekend." Have a nice weekend.

The flakes had grown larger and more distinct and were beginning to stick to the sidewalk as she left the cab. She glanced up into the whirl of gray. It was the kind of snow that seemed to move sideways instead of downward; though the wind that directed it was hardly perceptible. The north side of the ornately scrolled iron fence across the front of the building would be white in a few minutes. On the cars parked along the street the snow was still melting, except for a pattern of the superstructure under the skin of the trunk. Miss Matthews had been rather like bright Ines, a secretary only twenty, wasn't it? Just out of college.

The hall was dark, it had been designed dark, with walnut paneling and small orange lights that glowed dimly behind frosted glass shields. Miss Matthews closed the door to her apartment behind her and stood just inside the room with her eyes shut to the perfect order. Yes, the noises were quite gone now. Only the very faint *sss* of cars outside and the refrigerator's low, very low murmur; the soft, continuous mechanical sound of the clock in the next room. She slid open the door of the hall closet and removed her hat, sat it on the shelf. The coat was damp, only barely, with scattered crystals of water in the hairs of the fabric. She made a motion to hang it up, but it fell noiselessly from her hand onto the floor. She stepped around it into the living room. The writing desk had been one of her extravagances when she furnished the apartment, eighteen years wasn't it? When she had just begun work. It had taken a year for her to pay for the desk; a Louis Quinze, very small, with three drawers and a delicate chair of the same design. On the desk was a green blotter to protect the rose and myrtle marqueterie of roses. It required special size sheets and covers but she had not been able to resist it then.

Miss Matthews sat lightly in the chair and opened the center drawer of the desk. From the square of stationery notes she drew one sheet and laid it on the blotter. In the fibers of the paper, against the green, the watermark Carter Tana-ak was visible upside down on the sheet. Through the window above the desk she could see the snow was driving down hard now, and the clouds had darkened. Probably it would be quite cold by dark.

She sat there motionless for a long time, looking out the window, her hand holding the pen, lightly, resting on the desk. Then very slowly it returned. Her hand clenched, she stood up abruptly, shouting, "Nothing, Tina, nothing! Go back to your work, please, and don't . . ." She reached behind her to the chair for support and felt herself falling backwards.

She lay on the soft carpet. The room was totally dark, night had come on. Miss Matthews sensed the overturned chair beside her. Yes, she remembered everything quite clearly. She had been going to write a note, but there had been no one's name, and no one who might be more than briefly concerned. Then the typing had begun around her, and the questions. Now everything was completely still again in the dark, except the faint sound of the clock in the next room and the cold inflection of the snow against the window.

Dear Mr. Goldberg

THE MAN BEHIND the desk lit a fresh cigarette and pushed his glasses back along the sharp bridge of his nose. "Naturally, we're interested in interviewing every possible candidate for the position we have in mind," he began. "It might prevent me repeating things you know about our company if you tell me, more or less, what the employment agency has already told you." The man behind the desk glanced casually at his secretary through the glass. The girl smiled slightly and turned away. "I have your resume but as the agency saw fit to call you 'Number 873,' for reasons regarding confidence I suppose, I think we can pencil your name across the top. Irvin Goldberg, is that correct?"

"That's right. I'm thirty-seven; I'm married and . . ."

"I believe we have all the rest."

"Fine. Then you want to know what I've been briefed on. Well, naturally everyone knows your products; everyone in the building industry. We've had occasion to use a number of your ceiling materials in offices. You may know that Standard . . ."

"That's the company you're with now." The man behind the desk underlined a word on the resume.

"That's correct. Standard recently bought a number of smaller office buildings, and they've done considerable rebuilding; complete modernization. So I am familiar with the product. Now as I understand it you're after someone with a strong sales promotion background."

"A creative sales promotion background," the man behind the desk emphasized. "You see, we have to have a man, as well as someone that fits well into our group; we have to have a man who can create new approaches; a creative fellow. Now I am familiar with your work at Standard and I think you've been doing very well there."

"We've had a lot of success. Things have been going rather well. We did come up with an unusual campaign that's been pulling very nicely. I . . ."

"It's because of that, that I am not too sure that you're the man we want," the man behind the desk said.

"I beg your pardon?"

"You've had success—a good deal of success, Mr. Goldberg, with one kind of campaign. I've seen all of your samples on it and, of course, they are good. But I have strong reservations about your ability to adapt to our way of thinking. Naturally, we couldn't run the same campaign as Standard has been doing for the past two years, and I haven't seen that you've had much experience along any other lines. Not, at least, since the campaign started."

"Well, we've been strongly interested; strongly interested in building a company, a corporate image. So we have stayed closely to the original format, you can understand the thing here, I'm sure. I wouldn't dream of trying to palm off the same campaign or an imitation of it on your company. I came up with the material Standard is doing, and I'm sure that I could develop just as effective an approach for you. I certainly wouldn't think that that campaign would be against my chance for sales promotion manager with your company."

"Just that the campaign has been kept so very close to the original concept; it's shown us variations on a theme, but not variations *of* theme, you see."

"But it was my original concept. If you like I could submit ideas to you; suggestions of what I would do in the position, but when I called your secretary she said that wasn't at all necessary."

The man behind the desk waved his hand. "No, we wouldn't have time for any of that. If all the applicants for the position submitted project campaigns, it would take us months to select our man. Frankly, I was hoping you could show us samples of work that we hadn't seen. Of course your work is good. It's damn good and we are certainly going to put your name high on our list."

"I wish I had something else, but again, it's been a very successful series. Our ratings have been consistently the highest in the industry."

"Yes, they certainly have. Standard has been doing outstanding work and you're responsible for it, I'm sure." The man behind the desk moved a few papers together and lined their edges along the side of the desk. "I have another man coming in shortly, Mr. Goldberg. We're trying to select a number of fine men that our president will choose from personally, and I'm confident he'll want to see you."

"I feel sure I could present a very interesting portfolio if you'd care to see some of the ideas I've had in mind. I don't see how you can tell much about me at all with such a brief interview."

"Well, I'm just screening, so to speak, separating the men from the boys; I'm very confident you'll be hearing from us shortly and then perhaps we will be asking for presentations."

Mr. Goldberg rose. "It's just that I feel the interview went badly, somehow. If . . ."

"No, no, no, Mr. Goldberg. It went very well, indeed. I'm sure you'll be hearing from us."

"I hope so," said Mr. Goldberg. "I think I'd enjoy working for your company; you seem to be a very progressive organization and I like that."

"A fine group to work for, it certainly is that. We do have a very excellent and capable staff." The man nodded. "Goodbye."

"Goodbye," Mr. Goldberg said. He walked through the room and nodded to the secretary.

"Good day," she said brightly. "We'll be in touch with you."

"I hope so. Goodbye, now, Miss McVicker," he said.

When she had closed the door to the outer office behind him, the secretary turned to look through the glass. The man behind the desk looked up and nodded. Miss McVicker took a fresh sheet of stationery from the drawer and inserted it into the typewriter with two carbons. She took a file from another drawer and looked briefly at the carbon of another letter, then began to type the form letter from memory.

Doors

It was late into the afternoon by the time I came to the last apartment on the list. I had been weaving in and out of a six-block area since early morning and would have called it a day had the Windsor Apartments not been on the way to the subway station. The building smelled faintly of disinfectant, but that was better than some I had visited that day. A woman straightened from mopping the marble-tile floor as I came in. "Is the manager of the building in?" I asked.

"You're talking to her, Mrs. Cora Bloom, Apartment One-A; are you single?"

"Yes," I said, "I'm just looking around the neighborhood now, I won't be able to move for a week or two."

"Well, I like somebody that gives notice; come on in, I'll show you what we have." Mrs. Bloom was a short bustling woman who puffed smoke like a train. She fluttered and lit in one spot then another with bumblebee preoccupation, looking as if she might burst out laughing at any moment. "This is the entranceway, we don't have an automatic door buzzer so you'll have to come downstairs to let your visitors in. People like a nice lounge." She made a happy sweeping gesture encompassing the dark stairway landing. The furniture was old but in fair shape and gleaming clean. "Christmas-time we move back the chair and put up a big tree; reaches almost to the ceiling. All the people help decorate it; we have a bit of fun." Mrs. Bloom paused with a deep gasp. "Come on up." She led the way, puffing. "We got a single and a two-room, separate living and bedroom; both furnished. That's all we have, one and two rooms. I guess you saw that in the paper." We passed the second floor landing. She stopped suddenly and turned: "You'll say this is the cleanest house on the block!" she burst out. "Everybody says it. Do all the cleaning myself."

"You don't say," I said between breaths for lack of something better.

"Do say; every bit. Used to do the sheets till Ben got sick and we started using the service."

We stopped a moment at the top of the stairs to catch our breath. "Not used to climbing are you? Do you a little good. Lift four times your own weight every time you go up one stair. Something like that. Room's down this way." She motioned down the dark hall. It was the kind of building that has the stairwell in the center and halls going off in three directions, so the corridors were not long and forbidding as most I'd seen.

The apartment was the same as most, only cleaner. Mrs. Bloom rubbed her arm across a mirror. "Sit down a bit and get the feel of the place. Can't tell if you like it till you're relaxed in it. Tell me about yourself. Going to school?"

I explained that I was just out and just in town. She frowned and looked relieved when I said I had had a job for some weeks. "I like it here," I said. "It's a far cry from the little town I came from."

"I don't think I know a soul that wasn't born and grew up in some jerkwater town." Mrs. Bloom lit a fresh cigarette from the old one, puffing vigorously: "Grow up in a small town, move to the city to make it rich and move back out to a small town–suburb. Never could see living like that." Her cigarette wagged when she spoke like a scolding finger. "Well, not in a long time have I thought about small towns. Used to think that would be the kind of life I'd have. I wouldn't have liked it much."

"I'd think you would. It must be a lot of work keeping up a house like this," I said, growing a little uncomfortable in the stiff chair.

"Oh, it's not as bad as I try to make it sound. I haven't been at it so long that the new's worn off. My husband, Ben, he did most all the work, except washing the linen till a year ago when he had his stroke. So if I didn't do it now, he'd have to and he can't be working. It's all in taking care of him in a way."

"Was it very serious, your husband's stroke?" I asked.

"It was odd a bit." She looked like she would laugh, then changed. "I married late in life and he married early you might say. He was still young so it was unusual. But it wasn't too serious except for leaving him so weak." The light from the window was fading a dull orange and passed to near-darkness but she didn't turn on the lamp. I've seen a number of men weakened by strokes; their hands, sometimes their bodies crippled. It's not a pleasant thing, even if it only leaves them older looking, and tired. I didn't care for Mrs. Bloom's casual attitude about it.

We finished with the apartment and the one-room on the second floor. Rooms with closet-kitchens and baths a few doors down the hall, as most apartments I'd seen that day. "I'd like for you to stop by and see Ben, if you will.

I have to ask what he'd like for dinner anyway," she said as we were leaving the last apartment, then added: "Ben always likes to know when people come to look at the rooms. Those who answer the ad in the paper. We run it there every day, just the same whether we're full or empty. It was his idea."

I don't enjoy visiting sickbeds, especially a stranger's. There are those who do, I suppose, but I'm not among them. "I've been around a lot today," I said, "and it's been so hot, I'm really anxious to get back home."

"Oh, it's not out of our way," she said cheerily. "Ben has his room on this floor. We moved him up here to be away from all the noise when he was so sick." She guided me around the hall and toward the other side of the building. "Then he liked it so well, even since he's better now he still spends most of his time up here. It's quieter for him." The halls were now quite dark, but they held the heat of the day. Very small orange bulbs glowed behind shell-shaped glass shields along the hallway, giving no light. They were hung like magic little electric heaters along the wall. The door at the end of the hall was ajar and light striped out across the floor. "Now see? The door's open. I never bother him unless he has the door open." Mrs. Bloom tapped lightly: "I've brought someone to see you, Ben." She turned to me. "What did you say your name was?" she asked, pushing the door open. But her words were lost; I couldn't help but stare at her husband. Mrs. Bloom, as I said, was a robust, slightly ludicrous woman of around sixty. Her husband was thin, but looked quite normally healthy. He had dark hair and deep-set eyes that blinked slowly and seemed to nail you where you stood. He was very young. I'm sure he was not older than twenty-seven, though I'm a bad judge of age; he was possibly younger. "I'm glad to meet you; how do you like our house?" Ben asked, walking across the carpet with a hand outstretched. He wore a deep wine–colored robe and sandal shoes that brushed the floor.

"How do you do, Mr. Bloom," I said, taking his hand. "You have a very nice place." But he had turned away. Mrs. Bloom kissed his forehead and they talked quietly for a moment, I suppose about dinner. I heard her say, "And you're sure you won't come down?" and "Well, as you like it."

Quietly the door across the hall opened and a girl, perhaps a model, for I seemed to recognize her from somewhere, stepped out into the hall. She pulled her door shut and turned, looking into the room. She didn't look toward me, but Mr. Bloom glanced up at the sound and for a moment their gaze held and both registered just the slightest trace of a smile; then the girl moved quietly down the hall. "Anything you say is alright with me, dear," Ben said, turning again to his wife, who was gathering up glasses from the bed table.

"Very well then, easy to please, that's what I like about you," she said. "I won't be long. Would you like me to come up and rub your back later?"

"If you feel like it."

She turned and smiled to me. "Easiest to please in the world," she said. "We'll run along now and not tire you."

"It was nice meeting you, Mr. Bloom," I said, but he had turned to the window, looking out toward the street.

We were quiet going down to the entranceway. The bucket and mop were standing in the hall where she had left them. The house was very dark now as night had come and no one had turned on the lights. I thanked Mrs. Bloom there in the dark doorway and turned to go but she caught my sleeve. For a long time we were turned facing each other and she was quiet; I could hardly see her expression in the dark. When she did speak, it was not the gay voice, but tired. "I just didn't want you to go away thinking I was blind. Or stupid. You see? I'm nobody's fool; but what could I do? You understand?"

She turned back into the house and was gone.

SECTION 5
POEMS

Fig. 6. Lanford Wilson, Ozark, Missouri, 1952; photographer unknown; Lanford Wilson Collection, Special Collections and Rare Books, University of Missouri Libraries, Lanford Wilson Estate.

OUTSIDE TULSA

Outside Tulsa,
By an abandoned well
Is a horse
Run away from a carousel;

Her daughter is near
Somewhere, Big Sur
With wild eyes
And a broken rocker.

MOUNTAINS

Among the hills recently
above Bluefield
(quiet town of low
farms, high forests of blue fir)
there are caves, the hills
are porous with them, but
when you say "Are you
going to the cave?" there's no doubt
but which cave you mean.
"Don't touch them"—they've been
saying that for 100 years.
Near the entrance of Matter
Cave a tall arm of stalagmite
reaches up from the sloping floor
to nearly touch, nearly touch
a matching stalactite; only
inches apart. For nearly a
century generations have watched
them grow together.
And one day, of course,
they will, perhaps fifty
years hence, maybe shorter,
maybe 200 years.
But will the people still
be watching—or will
no eye be open to see?
No ear hears the perfect
key of "E," nor marvels
at the tall slender column.
And perhaps the flow
that devises these things
shatters prisons as well.
Shape the stalactite

serve the stalagmite like
a length of glass pipe.
To quiet the cave this troubling
away when they both be
shattered on the floor of
the cave; to begin again
from nothing.

ORANGE GROVE

The atmosphere within the grove
Cannot be inhaled;
All the air that's thin enough to breathe seems to be impaled
Above the arches of the trees.

So wait until the spring;
In late March when a wind
Lifts off the ocean:

Climb the hills above the grove,
Though the view is clouded and impaired,
And stand in the first winds
That bend up from the valley.
Breathe the fragrance of the orange rains.

FLOWER BOX

Connie's made a window box
      Planned in each detail
Planted just the flower to bloom
      Without fail
Twelve and one half inches high,
      Match the kitchen wall
Christ has made the flowers grow
      Ten feet tall

MARIGOLD

What's that thing that smells so awful
That tall orange thing?
Grandma laughed because I had really
Yelled when I picked off the spent flower
And now I was spitting on my hands,
Trying to wipe off the smell.

You don't like that?
That's a marigold
Maybe it's a smell for old people
It smells like something
You'd have in the kitchen
That works real hard
And gets the job done right.

As I think back, she often related
Good qualities to hard work. But
In that almost fanciful way we talked
Only to each other.

That night at dinner I said,
Tell mom and sissy what you
Said a marigold smells like.

She narrowed her eyes, giving me a look,
A warning not to admit how silly we talked
When we were alone.
I said it smelled like a marigold.

That came back to me this autumn morning,
As I was deadheading the garden.
I was five then and am exactly her age now.
She was right, of course

Maybe it is a fragrance only for old people,
An astringent fragrance, like no other flower
I like it too
It smells like a marigold.

OAKWOOD GOTHIC

There is a house on Harper's Hill;
Oakwood Gothic sentinel of the
Finley Valley.
Years ago
For generations beyond memory
It stood the owners' fortress from
All the world but time.

People tell when the house first
fell deserted, children overran it;
tore at its siding,
pulled its arched doorways.
Still it stood unyielding though they
carried off its ornamentations,
stoned its windows, bent its iron
fence to the grass.

Lovers drove once up the sharp-angled
drive to park in cedar shade;
stayed to see the stars more closely,
so bright on a moonless night they
etched elm leaves across the windowshields,
years ago; before weather split the
columns, weight the roof,
rutted the orange drive
until it vanished under orchard grass
and seas of goldenrod raising pollen
spindrift to the wind.

Now people look toward the hill
to wonder at time—give a quiet shudder
and turn to the valley to leave the house
alone, unused, unvisited, an
awkward curiosity quietly overlooking
the Finley Valley.
A patient sentinel of the years
keeping tally of time.

[WELL, THERE SHE IS, AFTER ALL]

Well, there she is, after all;
On her island just like in movies;
Like on half the postcards in
Times Square.

Lord! but she looks high and proud;
She really is something to see:
All big and strong and green
And brave and bronze
And lonely.

CATHEDRAL OF ST. PAUL

On a high
Lilac and green
Overlooking great;
Vaster home holds
Yawning serenity,
Houses whispering silence
(Corinthian darkness,
vaulted light)
breathes enormous;
lives God.

THE STREET ARTIST

On a street blocked
at Columbus and Amsterdam
where the broken, pocked
tenements are marked for razing

A dark child working all day
has diligently covered the pavement
with designs:
drawn enormous squares, x's and
ellipse for a tree, a hexagon;

Long, winding herringbones,
lopsided houses with a thousand
windows
and fantastic childish hieroglyphics
in ochre clay and pointed arrows
of blue-white plaster.

VILLAGE WALKING RHYME

Bend from Barrow
    Back through Banks
Trees in yellow
    Files and ranks.

To Macdougal
    Through the square
Dancing people
    Everywhere.

Cross from Thompson
    Home in view,
Toss through autumn
    Back to you!

Off you go through
    Christopher
Turn about to
    Where you were,
Curl through Patchin,
    St. Luke's Place,
Running children
    form a race.

St. Luke's Place to
    Waverly,
Home again come
    Back to me!

ON A DAY OF CRISIS

On a day of crisis last spring
I paused outside St. Peter's Church
And saw the sanctuary burning.

The fires were not fires
But reflections:
Statues usually in darkness were banked
With flaming votive jars
Spreading unsteady flames over stone and walls.
Even the great-beamed ceiling
Oscillated with heart;
Every feature of the church revealed.

Threading the island's maze of streets
The faithful and fearing had found
Their way here to light a candle
And pray for peace.
They had known the direction all along:
That here like the fearful minotaur
At the center of the labyrinth
God slept.

[FIFTH AVENUE WAS QUIET]

Fifth Avenue was quiet
Uptown, downtown, the village
Was quiet
Times Square was dark and quiet
Where people went they whispered
Or did not speak;
They worried; they wondered
About the future and they felt
Displaced. They felt uncertain,
And they could feel no more.
Sadness takes longer
Sorrow does; you cannot
miss something so immediately.

So they gathered on the street
And were quiet
In front of newspaper kiosks
And around loudspeakers
And television sets set out on
    the street.

And listened but would never understand.
For a moment they spoke to anyone
To strangers on the street
For confirmation for to question,
To wonder, to worry, then they were quiet.
Everyone was quiet that afternoon.

And the following day was rainy.
And the day after that was
    the beginning of the
    cold.
And the day after that
They were sad; there was sorrow,

And they felt the loss then
And they were silent again that
Afternoon.

WINTER

Silent silhouettes once swept
The skies
Of gray,
But now they
Have wept away their leaves
And stand with sleeveless limbs

In utter desolation.
The winding wind
Still whistles life's medley;
Spring's only a month away.

SO THE SKY

So the sky was that color a sky
Should always be in spring
And the trees in the park were taking
The last bit of sunshine
They would require to leaf.

Beside each other we lay on our backs
Our hands folded behind our necks

Looking at the sky
Or more nearly at the moon
In daylight a smoky evanescent negative
You might expect on that moment
Would disappear forever.

LULLABY

Turn now,
sleep.
Smile now, even in the
darkness; our arms locked
closely together,
moving down through dulcet
dreams to
lull.
And maybe in the morning
you won't
leave.

LULLABY (2)

Now
if we both
lie breathlessly
still
perhaps
a million years
will pass and
never
notice us.

[IF YOURS CANNOT BE]

If yours cannot be
the lips I kiss;
when I think of
you my soul, my mind,
is held in the fragile
palms of children,
and whistled to the
winds, like the
gray-white down of
a dandelion.

I SAW ALL THE WORKERS IN THE FIELD AT NOON

I

The train rammed through the tunnel;
Commuters crammed close together, with
Hardly a space left to stand.
The green eel sped swiftly; steel
Wheels sparked on steel; screeched
Through the twisting tunnel.

An old woman sat by a window,
Reading a tiny black book of scripture
She held in her thin black hands.
Her lips barely moved at times.
Then she closed the book as if
In contemplation.

When she looked back, and turned the yellowed
Page, I saw a tear draw a wet stripe down
Her wrinkled face, and a trembling
Hand hastened to blot it.
And I wondered if Job's pain or
Some private reflection had touched her.

II

I stood in the stillness of an
Autumn night. The stars gleamed so
Brightly in the moonless sky, light
Shadows scratched the darkened street.
Quietly I stood in the crisp cellophane
Of the fallen amber leaves.

A happy whistling broke across
The air—faintly as the smell
Of burning leaves far-off.

With the sound of his footsteps
Through the night,

I could see a young lad
Stepping briskly on the path.
His dark skin blended with the night,
And as he passed I saw his smiling face,
    famed in the square of
Pegasus.

III

I saw all the workers in the field at noon;
Their black bodies bare and bent in grace
Laced a glare of reflected light. The
Blinding heat of a hefty soul, hot lava
Of a restless race, cooled in a silent
Obsidian.

Slowly moving down the rows they worked
With patient quietness. Then lowly, at first,
I heard them softly singing; their bodies
Swaying in sun-logged undulation to the
Spirit-rising ringing as the song, as if from
Nowhere, filled the fields.

Their chorus swelled until the whole
Field seemed to sway; no row remained
Unbent as the unrestrained crescendo
Echoed back from hills untilled with
Truth to twist like Vincent's cypress
Toward the sun.

WHY WHEN I LOVE YOU

Tall tall with immense arms wide shoulders;
women wheeling when Collins walked through town,
walked by as women held their breath, swallowed.

Came from Chadwick to live near the valley
alone a year, build a rough-logged house
six miles from town where coldwater spring
undercuts limestone, with diagonal birches
"X"ing white on black cedar.

Always smiled never spoke.
Walked silent through town;
Block ending shadows in the evenings
Circling from his step, thrown from streetlamps
Across buildings.

People in town looked after Collins
as he walked
and said he needed, was looking for
a woman when he left; when he left to find one,
knew he had to give the tenderness that they saw
and would find the loveliest girl.

Always will protect
and guard
and keep and give.
Left the house he made in the birch for a month.
Left crops curling on rockledge hills around the spring, after a year of alone
for a month and came back married.

Collins strong with pure and laughing blue eyes
streaked sun. Dancing clear blue eyes smiling
from gentle

to blaze blue
with a palpable warmth that draws
outstretched hands as breathing embers.

Collins found his oncelove girl,
returned home with her in August,
younger than a child;
thin white, white hair falling past her shoulders.
from the moon, daughter of no one,
from no family.

And by the spring he brought her
To be his wife in love:

For once love is
And gentle,
And this once was.

Girl with the softest skin, violet staring eyes.
August with white hot moons.
August through brambles running, dancing against
roughbarked oak. And enchanted some said
for she sang when sounds of untamed
floated through the evenings. Running insane
through the hot day; standing in cobalt night
calling to darkbirds.

She could not speak
but made whining sounds and childish giggling;
never looking toward Collins.
Heard were words of love from the man;
tenderest warmth of earth
spoken through her babbling,
endless babbling in meaningless childvoice.

Rabid. Insane. And then through the winter

lying on the bed in shadows both day and darkness
seldom turning, feeling with her palm
the child growing inside her she wept tears
cold as snow.

Collins sitting by the quilts of her bed
Speaking lowly, touching her forehead,
"But I love you."
The girl screaming suddenly. Everyone near
Heard her each evening.

Finally, when Collins came to the neighbor's farm
next and when with almost her own wild eyes,
with tears, with burning hands
calling for help;
calling to the neighbor and his excited wife.
And they ran these three through
fields.
To the house frozen in cobalt night.

White hair streaked red,
blood trail to the spring
over broken splintering ice.
Dragged her from the shallow water
alive in labor chilled dying in weakness fevered,
murmuring and never once knowing.

Screaming weakly as an injured frightened
animal with each recurring pain and
with each recurring pain weakening
while Collins with closed eyes
whispering, "Why when I love you?"

And to the farmer's wife huddle over the girl:
"Care for her, Goddamn the child.

no one no one no one
but her. Care for my wife."

And the girl never knowing when the end;
with Collins: why when I adore you?

And Collins while they told him
never speaking.
Walked to the barn to embrace the scythe,
both hands gripped strongly around its handle.
Gripped the white-knuckled
while he died.
And only the child lived.

A boy so fair
so strong with pure white hair
and laughing blue eyes streaked sun.

Dancing clear blue eyes smiling from
gentle
to blaze blue
with a palpable warmth that
draws outstretched hands
as breathing embers.

NOTES ON A POEM FOR BILL

It is not enough that we have danced
like imbeciles through the winter streets,
(not quite touching hands)
skating on the puddle ice-rinks, laughing.

Though in early spring we see the monastery,
wander through its dormant mazes
puzzling at Barbara's clumsy castle,
Anthony's tinted windows; and
from a hill's vantage examine
the gray harp intricacies of a bridge
and distant indications of the city:
it is not enough. The city is not enough.

Even when you hold to me your childhood,
turn it over as a globe that captures snowstorms,
and we share the pain of seeing sterile
tenements built now on the open hillsides
where you played, and you indicate the woods
where you received your first kiss;
Even with all this it will not do.

When later we walk by the East River's
thawing bank, inspecting the fine
new bridges primed in orange
that will rise to replace the old, the outworn;
and we press into a sheltered stairway
by a park because we can no longer bear the
nearness without remembering: it is beautiful,
it will live with me forever,
but it is not enough.

When the warm bed at my hotel,
covered perhaps by a mended sheet

(printed over along its seam with the
names of three hotels, former owners)
to the continual amazing pleasure
that our bodies lie so perfectly together,
that we turn and breathe as one,
that the feeling of you firmly against me
completes my composition;
—at the height of pleasure I am not alone,
not alone, but am rejoicing in the very
presence of you! It is wonderful past
all I should ask but it is not enough.

Not enough that you come to me
(frightened as you always are, unsure,
cautious, with embarrassed rushing gentleness,
with hazel and green and warm eyes always
questioning) and as I smooth your soft
and softly freckled shoulders,
give yourself completely.

It is enough and right only for the
first carefully quarried stone
laid in the foundation say of a monument,
the amazing superstructure
on which a skyscraper will hang, the tall and
ornate poles on which a gateway (perhaps)
will swing,
right for the pilasters that will
support the weight of a mammoth,
stretching, spanning bridge:
it is right and perfect for that,
and as that it surpasses everything.

NOEL

I've just received from home
as I have every year since I left,
a package resembling a pastry shop
of cookies and Christmas cake and sweets
and a jar of walnut meats.
Think white cookies cut like trees
frosted in green, flat red bells
and a candy cane. There's a new
one this year, a round cookie that
won't taste as good as the ones
I remember.

Yes, I remember cookie time;
and gleaning the woods for walnuts.
Measuring raisins and level cups
of flour.
"Don't heap it up, that's a cup
and a half. Cut off the top
with a knife. Don't pack
it down! Here, I'll do it. You can crack
more walnuts, you can't get too
many walnuts."

And a banana cake that for a week
I'll eat with coffee in the morning,
while the coffee gets cold and look
down from my window to New York's streets.

All from a town, little town, in Iowa.
baked in an oven falling down,
it has a door-hinge too tight
that sings, "We-ouch" when you open it.

Most of the bells came intact,

and the sugar sprinkled trees.
The cookie-man is a bit of a wreck,
with his orange-mouth gone
and a broken neck, and both legs
I found at the bottom of the package.
He's the one I piece together,
reconstruct like a jigsaw puzzle
of a little town in Iowa.

And sit and stare at his raisin
eyes, and raisin buttons and
orange-mouth gone.
And just now, I can't make out
the cracks that mend his legs and neck.
Just now, when everything around me
is so still; I can hear the snowflakes
against the windowsill, but
I don't see it snowing.

[THE GREAT-HEARTED DEAN]

The great-hearted Dean
With the greatest of zeal
Has suggested I repeat
"Great" a great deal.

The suggestion at first
To a great extent
Seemed the greatly grating
Kind of comment.
But then, all great writers,
Though their style varies
Have much greater than
One-word vocabularies.

*

So this splendid boy's
Splendid observation
Might be a splendid aid
To my occupation.

Just possibly the splendidest.

A LOVE STORY ABOUT THE NEXT BEST THING

Write about us, Lance
Oh, please yes write about us
one day. A poem or a story
write a love story about us one day please

bewildering lips and shapeless;
frail, narrow hips and shoulders
pleading, primping sparrows
simpering sparrows

A love story, and we run away.

with a milkman
(laughter)
well, or the postman or a truck driver
or we make some cowboy or farmer happy
and we live

way away somewhere with him.

Empty arms, of course, hugging
the imaginary hero
spreading kisses on the imaginary lover

But make it real and truthful.
Oh, yes, now do, oh, please do.
and you must say how he fell
in
love with us, in spite of himself,
and left his wife.
YES, YES, HE MUST LEAVE HIS WIFE!
No, that's very important.
That's very important.
We're better than they are, you know it.

We are, we're as good as a woman, you know it.
We are, we're the next best thing.
You can't deny it.

A marvelous open-mouthed smile now
a dreamy
(can't you just see how I must look
but I'm in a GOWN, see, and on stage, see
and in JEWELS see, and in colored spotlights
and men MEN are cheering, and pulling at
my furs) Oh, yes please. One day.

And don't make it sad, make it truthful.
Make it happy, because everything you
read like that isn't true, it's always
so awfully sad and maudlin and terrible

vapid smile now, slight
from the unfunny shapeless mouth,
the thin shoulders hunch, the eyes
(lined blue) bat twice. Imploringly.

It should be happy you know. And beautiful.
Oh, please do. One day. I've just got
to see something like that in print.
Wouldn't that show them? Please Lance.

Fig. 7. Lanford Wilson and Marshall Mason, Circle Repertory, Broadway and 83rd Street, New York City, November 3, 1973; photographer, James D. Gossage.

AFTERWORD
BY MARSHALL W. MASON

In his plays, Lanford Wilson celebrated the spirit of America more eloquently than anyone of his generation. Frank Rich, chief theatre critic of *The New York Times*, described him as a writer "who can truly make America sing." Lanford's special gift in describing the times in which he lived had several components: complicated, deeply rooted and driven characters; groundbreaking innovations in dramatic structure and style; and, perhaps most of all, his ability to write dialogue that was at once everyday speech, tailored uniquely to a character's voice, and at the same time expressed with a lyricism that elevated the ordinary into the sublime. Of course, his goal was not to write with exquisite technique, but to expose the truths overlooked in the lives we lived.

It should be obvious that no one since Athena has been born with full-fledged talent; rather, skills are developed over a period of growth, learned from both human trials and artistic errors. This selection of early exercises in prose and poetry gives us an opportunity to dig beneath mere biographical data to see how a young man grew in both aptitude and proficiency. All the stories in this collection predate Lanford's epiphany of self-discovery that he was meant to be a playwright. This occurred in 1961 when he had been taking an adult education course in creative writing at the University of Chicago. Some of these stories can be identified as assignments from that class. After submitting several of them and receiving his teacher's critiques, his assignment was to write a short play. Lanford wrote only a few lines of dialogue before he exclaimed out loud: "This is who I am. I'm a playwright."

He delighted in recounting that moment of self-discovery, and nowhere is it more joyfully recalled than in his play *Angels Fall*, in which the young tennis player Zappy relates the revelation of destiny he experienced the first time he hit a tennis ball:

> "That's magic. That's magic, that's magic . . . that magic that happens and you know who you are . . . like when I found out I was a tennis player . . . no joke. I went to church and lit a candle. . . . But that was it. I hit that first ball and I said, 'This is me. This is what I do. What I do is tennis.' And once you know, then there's no way out. You've been showed something. Even if it's just tennis, you can't turn around and say you wasn't showed that . . . Anybody had asked me what I did, right there I'd have said, 'I play tennis.' Didn't know love from lob, didn't matter. That's what I am. 'Cause once you know what you are, the rest is just work."

Throughout his life Lanford remained steadfastly loyal to his identity. Hollywood offered little appeal for him. He only half jokingly referred to the lures of the film industry, with its promises of wealth and fame, as temptations of the Devil. He was convinced writing for movies choked off the talent of promising playwrights like Clifford Odets. He would not give in to enticement. Although he wrote a couple of television scripts (an original screenplay ironically entitled *Tennessee Williams's The Migrants* and a drama called *Taxi* for Hallmark), he remained stubbornly, proudly a man of the theatre. His tombstone in Sag Harbor, New York, reads simply:

LANFORD WILSON
PLAYWRIGHT

But as this volume reveals, that is not the whole picture. He began writing stories when he went to San Diego to live with his father after high school. Finding his new home environment challenging, he sought out like-minded people who appreciated his sensitivity and humor. He took up with a family of artistic bohemians, encouraged by the poet LoVerne Brown and her creative children, Tony, Jonni, and Tim, who lived in a beach house, virtually on the sand, in Ocean Beach, California (memorialized in Lanford's lovely one-act play *The Sand Castle*). After his traumatic expulsion from his father's household (recounted in the autobiographical play *Lemon Sky*), Lanford fled to Chicago, where he earned a living as a commercial artist and enrolled in an evening class for creative writing to explore and develop his potential at working with words. Some of the stories you'll find here explore his early encounters with city life and the broadening experiences they provided in his transition into adulthood.

Afterword / 243

Following his years in Chicago, Lanford took off for New York with a costume designer he had met at the Art Institute's Goodman Theatre named Michael Warren Powell. Living on the Upper West Side of Manhattan, Lanford continued to work on his prose, sending several stories out, doubtfully but hopefully, to magazines like *The New Yorker* and *Saturday Evening Post*. All were rejected. But he was not discouraged because he had already identified himself as a playwright, so he was aware that prose was not his forte.

He came to the capital of American theatre to pursue his destiny. His earliest plays (unpublished, but I have read them) are as unpolished as some of these early stories, with embarrassing titles like *This Dreamer Cometh* and derivative images like *The Bottle Harp*. But he turned an important corner with his first play, *Home Free!*, quickly followed by *So Long at the Fair*, which became his first produced play at the Caffe Cino in June, 1962. (He had given the script of *Home Free!* to Gian Carlo Menotti for his consideration at the Spoleto Festival, but Menotti lost it on his flight to Italy; until Lanford learned that, *Home Free!* was unavailable for production, so it became his second play presented at the Cino.)

Once he started writing plays that could be produced, he desisted from writing prose completely, returning to it only many years later, when he spent a portion of an unproductive summer writing a teenage mystery, which he abandoned, despite my encouragement, as soon as he got an idea for a new play. Among our many conversations over the years, Lanford mentioned a few of the stories he had written that he felt showed some promise. I remember his description of "Fish Kite," and he may have even let me read it. But most of these stories were new to me when the archivists at the University of Missouri unearthed them and let me see them. As I read some of them, I could recall snatches of conversation in which Lanford may have mentioned images like the carving in "The Polar Bear," and of course, some of them, like "Fuzz on Orion's Sword," became refined in dramatic form, as in *The Great Nebula in Orion*.

All these stories were written between the ages of eighteen to twenty-five and paint a fascinating portrait of a young artist struggling to make sense of the world around him and his place in it. They reveal a paradox of uncertainty and rock-solid conviction that are the hallmarks of Lanford's lifelong quest for the truth in his writing. If some of the stories seem crude or clumsy, they are the fossilized footprints of a young artist seeking his path. Some of them transcend his limitations, suggesting a substantial understanding of human nature beyond his years.

Lanford never showed me any of his poetry, so these were a revelation. I was deeply moved by most of them. It seems to me he had a clear path to expressing himself in poetry that was previously unknown to me. Unlike the stories, the poems seem to me mature and complete. I suspect they were written over the entire span of his life; several I feel certain refer to experiences following his success as a playwright. But like Shakespeare's "sugared sonnets," they seem to be deeply personal and reflective, not written for public inspection. I found them breathtaking, and I am deeply grateful to the editors for making them available.

EDITORIAL NOTE

The stories, sketches, and poetry published in this volume may be found in the Lanford Wilson Collection at the University of Missouri Libraries' Special Collections and Rare Books division in Box 9 of Series Three—Works and Manuscripts, Sub-Series One—Prose and Poetry. The folders discussed in this note include file folders (FF) 17–18, which include all the poetry in the collection, and FF 19–55, which include all the short stories. These notes will follow the organization of the work in this volume. Unless noted, all the stories and poetry are undated.

The latest, most complete version of the stories and poems were used, based upon the address marked on each manuscript. All corrections made by Wilson were incorporated. Any additional edits were made for consistency and to standardize spelling. Correspondence relating to the stories and interviews with Marshall W. Mason, Wilson's longtime director, made it possible to provide some chronological organization of the stories and poems. Most of the correspondence is from other writers to Wilson; there is very little correspondence from Wilson to others in the collection.

The entire collection consists of 53 linear feet of manuscripts and approximately 100 books. The vast majority of the collection consists of manuscripts in various genres but especially plays. In addition to his works, there is also a sizeable number of plays sent to Wilson by his colleagues and friends, and files of reviews and promotional clippings for productions of Wilson's plays. Correspondence received by and sent by Wilson from the early 1960s until his death in 2011 also form part of this collection, as do photographs of both a professional and personal nature. Finally, the collection contains family materials from Wilson's childhood and records of his personal interests such as gardening and art collecting.

There are a total of thirty-six folders containing about thirty stories; of these, eighteen were included in this volume. Many of the folders contain unfinished stories or different versions or copies of a story, though there are several completed, though immature, stories which were not included in the collection presented here. These include "Hedge," "How I Spent My Summer Vacation," "If You Like It," "I'll Be Honest with You," "The Pepper Tree," "Persimmon," "Why When I Love You," and "The Wisteria Candidate."

Some of the stories were typed on regular office paper, others are carbon copies that have handwritten corrections, still others were typed on what seems to be yellow composition paper from Wilson's college in San Diego, and finally others were typed on the back of letterhead from Walter I. Conroy & Associates, the advertising agency where Wilson worked in Chicago while he went to school part-time. Quite often it was possible to tell where and when the stories were written or revised on the basis of the various Chicago and New York addresses. Otherwise the stories are undated, and it was a matter of conjecture after reading different versions of the stories to determine which seemed to be the most finished version that Wilson had intended for publication.

SECTION 1: Six Stories

"A Section of Orange"

This story is found in file folder 44. There is one manuscript, typed double-spaced, with no address, and corrected in black ink. This was the text used here.

"Goodbye Sparta"

FF 30. There are two versions of the story. The first is on thin yellow paper, typed edge to edge, single-spaced, in red ink. The second version is a carbon of the first. Neither manuscript has a New York address, and this seems to be a much earlier story, written and completed in college, as suggested by the paper used for the first version. This was the version used here.

"Miss Misty"

FF 36. There is one version, typed single-spaced, edge to edge, for a total of five pages. There are a few corrections in ink, with a few words struck out. There is no address on the manuscript. This was the text used here.

"The Beautiful Children"

FF 19. There are eight versions of the story in various states of legibility. The first is typed double-spaced, on yellowed paper that is crumbling, totals seven pages, and was made on an older typewriter, with smaller type. It is clearly the earliest version, probably written in San Diego. The second version is typed double-spaced, and is noted as being the second version (the word "Second" was written in pencil and then erased). It has no corrections marked on it. It is typed on the back of Walter I. Conroy & Associates letterhead (with a Chicago address), but the manuscript itself has an address of 230 West 76th Street, New York 23, New York, typed in the upper left corner. It is nine pages long, with a narrower left margin. The third version is typed double-spaced, and is noted as being the third version ("3rd" written in pencil, then erased). It incorporates some of the changes to the first version that appeared in the second version, and is also typed on the back of Walter I. Conroy & Associates letterhead, with a 230 West 76th Street, New York 23, New York, Apartment 96-1 address. It is ten pages long, with a slightly wider margin than the second version and many small corrections in pencil. It is missing page seven.

The fourth version is a single page, front and back, and dated 7/29/62, the time Wilson was moving from Chicago to New York. The fifth version is typed double-spaced, no address listed, with word count handwritten in pencil at the top (2,720 words), which suggests it was being prepared to be submitted for publication. It is lightly corrected in pencil, with many typed strike-outs, totals nine pages, and is on lightly yellowed paper. The sixth version is a carbon copy of the second version. The seventh version is a carbon copy of the third version, with the words "missing page 7" written in pencil and then erased (page seven is included in this version).

The eighth version is typed double-spaced, with the address of 230 West 76th Street, New York 23, New York, Apartment 96-1, and typed on the back of Walter I. Conroy & Associates letterhead. A burn hole in the manuscript (probably from a cigarette) appears through the entire copy. It has a few corrections, both in ink and pencil, which incorporate all the changes from previous versions, and changes the number of grandchildren from seven to nine. It has larger type than the first version, on newer paper that is less crumbling. It has a wide 1½ inch margin on the left and is thirteen pages long. This is the final version of the manuscript in the folder, and is the text used here.

"The Polar Bear"

FF 39. There are three versions, with the final one complete. The file folder begins with a single page with the words "He just got out of reform school" in ink. The first version is four pages long, typed double-spaced, no address, with the title and corrections in pencil. The second version is single-spaced with heavy corrections in pencil and many strikeouts. It is typed on the back of Walter I. Conroy letterhead, with no address. It is fifteen pages long, with handwritten sections at the end. The final version is double-spaced, typed on the back of Walter I. Conroy letterhead, with Wilson's name at the top but no address. There are thirty-one pages with many small corrections in pencil and pen. This was the text used here.

"The Canary (A Fairy Tale)"

FF 20. The first version is typed double-spaced, on the back of Walter I. Conroy letterhead, with a final address of 230 West 76th Street, New York 23, New York, Apartment 96-1. It is missing the first page and is eight pages long. The second version is typed double-spaced on yellowed onion skin paper, same address, with light corrections, and is eight pages long. The third version is typed double-spaced, on yellowed onion skin, same address, and incorporates the corrections in the second version, with red ink asterisks at certain points. This is the final version, eight pages, which was used here.

SECTION 2: Travels to and from the City

"The Train to Washington"

FF 46. There are three versions. The first is typed single-spaced on yellowed paper, no address, and is eight pages long. There is a second complete, mostly clean version with the address of 230 West 76th Street, New York 23, New York, and just a few corrections. At thirteen pages long, it is the longest and most complete version, and it was the one used here. There is also a carbon of this version, twelve pages long (missing one page), which was corrected and edited, but the corrections are illegible in places. Most of the corrections that are legible dealt with misspellings and were included here.

"The Water Commissioner"

FF 53. There are three versions. The first version begins on legal-sized paper, typed, with no address and multiple corrections, and is continued on letterhead from the Loews Americana Hotel (now the Sheraton New York Times Square Hotel), on Seventh Avenue between 52nd and 53rd Streets in New York. This version is eleven pages long. The second version has an address of 230 West 76th Street, New York 23, New York, and is seventeen pages long. The third version has the same address, is corrected in blue ink, and is the most complete. This version, typed double-spaced, is nineteen pages long. This is the text used here.

"Fish Kite"

FF 28. The first three pages in the file are a selection from the beginning of the story. There is only one full version of the story here, twenty-four pages, typed single-spaced, heavily marked up in red and black ink, with many parts struck out, and typed on the back of Walter I. Conroy letterhead. This was the text used here.

SECTION 3: Sketches of Town Life

"The Rimers of Eldritch"

There are four folders containing material for this story, FF 40–43. FF 40, which is dated 1963, contains the first draft and a carbon copy, both undated. The typed original is marked up with black ink, and is four pages long. There is no address. This is the text used here. FF 41 contains handwritten notes—essentially character studies—and the beginning of a third draft, but no final version. There is an elaborate diagram of the plot with characters like Sheepman, Driver, Miner, and Eva, and the diagram even suggests that Driver Junior is raped, rather than Eva. There is no date, except that suggested in the first folder. FF 42 contains a typed sketch for the character of Skelly, to begin another version of the story. There is also an aborted attempt at another version with just a paragraph of typed text. FF 43, titled "Riming Lynn," contains a note which dates the manuscript May 13, 1963, and seems to be the second version of "Rimers," though it was never completed. It is typed double-spaced, with no address. On the back of the typescript there are versions of a poem, "The Street Artist."

"Green Grow the Rushes"

There are two folders, 23 and 24, which contain versions of this story. In FF 23, there is a version titled "Cling to the Valley." This version is typed double-spaced, with notes by Professor John Theobald, and no address, but clearly this was a version written at San Diego State University. There is a second typed version in this folder—a "copy," as noted in pencil on pink paper—with the title "Green Grow the Rushes" in pencil. FF 24 contains a single version, also titled "Cling to the Valley" with "Green Grow the Rushes" penciled in. It is typed double-spaced, with the address of 5316 S. Spaulding, Chicago 32, Illinois, and a word count of 3,250. There are a few corrections in ink. This is the text used here. There is no version of the story with a New York address.

"Chalk Eye"

FF 22. There is only one copy of the entire story in the folder, typed single-spaced, four pages stapled together. There are also six unstapled single pages which are incomplete and don't seem to be related to the completed version, with the exception of the first single page: (1) the ending of the story with a word count noted (2,380); (2) the ending of the story typed in red ink with penciled corrections; (3) a few paragraphs from the story; (4) the beginning of the story, with a note that it is the "3rd or so writing" of the story and that it's an "installment, the ol' American way"; (5) a description of the wall in the story; and (6) a single paragraph of the story. The text used here is the stapled version with the ending from (1).

"Drift"

FF 27. There is only one version, with an address of 230 West 76th Street, New York 23, New York, Apartment 96-1, and a note: "Filler (Short Short Story) Approx. 590 words." A note in pencil indicates it was being sent "To Redbook." Three pages long, typed double-spaced on the back of Walter I. Conroy letterhead.

SECTION 4: Sketches of City Life

"Mama"

FF 35. A single version, typed double-spaced, with a total of three pages. There is no address, and it is typed edge to edge.

"Fuzz on Orion's Sword"

FF 29. There is one complete version, typed double-spaced on onion skin paper, with an address of 230 West 76th Street, New York 23, New York, and a total of twenty-eight pages. This was the text used here. The folder also contains many incomplete versions, some of which seem to be copies, some on legal paper, that are only a few pages or more, with some of the pages handwritten.

"Uptown in Snow"

There are two folders containing versions of this story, 51 and 52. FF 51, which is titled "Uptown in the Snow, Baby," contains three different versions. The first is typed single-spaced, no address, with one small correction in red ink. The second version has the address of 673 Broadway, New York, New York, and is very similar to the first, incorporating the ink correction. This is the text used here. The third version (original and carbon copy) is unfinished, with the address of 309 Third Avenue, New York 10, New York. FF 52 contains one complete version of the story, typed single-spaced, no address, with corrections in pencil. This seems to be an earlier version of the story. There are a few single pages which seem to be carbons as well.

"Dear Mr. Goldberg"

FF 25. There is a single copy of the story, typed double-spaced, with the address of 9 Walnut Road, Glen Ellyn, Illinois. There are corrections at the end, in red pencil, which were incorporated into the text used here.

"Doors"

FF 26. Four versions of the story are typed double-spaced, with the address of 9 Walnut Road, Glen Ellyn, Illinois, at the top. A fifth version has a New York address, 230 West 76th Street, New York 23, New York, Apartment 96-1, with a word count of 1,585. This was the text used here. The first version is five pages, the second version three pages, and the third version four pages, with the fourth page torn. The fourth version is five pages and has corrections not incorporated in the fifth version, which is six pages long. This version was not used because it did not seem to be the version that Wilson sent out to publishers.

SECTION 5: Poems

The poems are contained in two folders, 17 and 18. FF 17 contains forty-four poems, of which there are ninety pages of different versions. FF 18, titled "New York Sketch Book," contains fourteen poems, with twenty-two pages of slightly different versions. The twenty-three poems selected for this collection are from both folders, drawing on the ones that had New York addresses and were prepared to send out to magazines.